Between Ourselves

AN INTRODUCTION TO
INTERPERSONAL COMMUNICATION

Second Edition

GRAEME BURTON

RICHARD DIMBLEBY

ARNOLD

A member of the Hodder Headline Group
LONDON • NEW YORK • SYDNEY • AUCKLAND

First published in Great Britain 1988
Second edition published 1995 by
Arnold, a member of the Hodder Headline Group,
338 Euston Road, London NW1 3BH
175 Fifth Avenue, New York, NY 10010

Reprinted 1996

Distributed exclusively in the USA by
St Martin's Press, Inc.
175 Fifth Avenue, New York, NY 10010

British Library Cataloguing in Publication Data
A catalogue record for this book is available from the British Library

Library of Congress Cataloging-in-Publication Data
A catalog record for this book is available from the Library of Congress

ISBN 0 340 60585 5

Typeset in 10/12½ Sabon by
Textype Typesetters, Cambridge
Printed and bound in Great Britain by
J W Arrowsmith Ltd, Bristol

Between Ourselves

Contents

Preface to Second Edition

In this second edition of *Between Ourselves* we have expanded and updated some areas of the first edition but have tried to preserve the integrity of the whole work. We have given greater acknowledgement to cultural issues and cultural experience. We have also provided a focus for, and a summary of, the various topics through the use of key questions punctuating the text.

The introduction of skills sections is intended to bring out the practical implications of theory. They also emphasize our belief in the importance of the act of communication, and in the possibilities of doing something practical with ideas.

The glossary and reading lists have been updated; we have also responded to requests to make the index more detailed. Each chapter has been revised with additional sections and new case situations.

In this edition, as in the original, we seek to steer a course between academic research texts and popular self-help books, and to reflect some of the insights of both by making complex ideas accessible. Research into human communication has expanded and diversified in the past two decades: as authors and teachers we still find the study and practice of communication endlessly fascinating.

This book draws together insights from a range of academic disciplines including anthropology, cultural studies, linguistics, media studies, psychology, social psychology, sociology, and of course communication studies. We aim to synthesize these into a coherent and readable treatment of key aspects of communication between people.

In common with other students of communication, we too have come to the view 'that expert professional communicators are those who have come to appreciate their lack of expertise' (Peter Trudgill in the Preface to *Intercultural Communication*, by Ron Scollon and Suzanne Wong Scollon, Blackwell 1995).

Finally, we want this revised text to remain accessible and thought provoking, to avoid transient intellectual fashions, and to contribute to a comprehensive understanding of various acts of human communication.

Graeme Burton   January 1995
Richard Dimbleby

Introduction

This book is about communication between people, whether they are in pairs or in groups.

We hope that what we have written will help explain how and why this communication is carried on, as well as help encourage more effective communication practice.

We believe that understanding what happens when we interact with others is of value in itself, but can also be useful in giving us more control of our own communication.

So this book is also about understanding what influences and governs interaction between people, and about how such understanding may lead to more constructive and sympathetic control of that interaction.

We believe that there are identifiable communication skills which, in the area that this book covers, would be described as social and perceptual. These skills can be recognized, understood, and absorbed with benefit to our working and social relationships.

This book is very much about people, not least because communication is such a fundamental human activity.

Although we do make reference to the evidence of research, you will not find that this book catalogues research in great detail. What we have tried to do, where it is appropriate, is to bring together the evidence and significance of relevant research and of communication practice. This is related to the topics identified in each chapter. We hope that readers will find this a book in which ideas are explained thoroughly and are seen to make sense in their own experience.

We have written for a range of students on various academic and conventional courses where interpersonal and group communication is an object of study and of practice. We also believe that other people, not least teachers, will find this a useful point of reference for their work and for their interests. So we hope that all you readers will indeed find that this book contains something of value to you, both in your work and perhaps for yourselves.

TO YOU, THE READER

You may well be involved with a communication course at college or at school, but whoever you are we hope that you will find this work accessible and relevant. We would like you to use it in understanding what happens when we communicate at work and in leisure. You should find explanation and example which reveals this, and which positively helps students in their studies. Understanding people and their communications is not straightforward in many ways. Yet, as we learn to read and to write, so do we learn to produce verbal and non-verbal communication for others, and to understand what they produce for us. It is a fascinating process, full of ambiguities and problems of meaning. We hope tht you enjoy trying to unravel it, and that we have given you some help.

Please be clear that this is a book for courses, not specifically a course book. There is nothing to stop you working through it from beginning to end if you want to. But we have organized our work so that you can take what you want from it. So far as teachers are concerned we see this book as supporting their role in promoting active learning. So for students what you have is, we hope, a straightforward and structured piece of writing which gives you a base from which to work. Here is a point of reference, here is a means of checking what you may have missed or understood imperfectly. You will find ideas about human communication brought together from a variety of sources apart from ourselves, with references and cross-references given. Most of all we hope you will find that we have made these ideas clear through examples which relate to authentic experience.

COMMUNICATION STUDY, COMMUNICATION BEHAVIOUR

The study of communication has three main strands at the moment.

These may be described as the process approach, the semiotic approach, and the cultural study approach. They are not mutually exclusive. They may be described briefly as follows. The process approach involves a holistic view looking at everything that is part of a given communication situation: it tries to describe all these variables and their contribution to the communication. The semiotic approach is more specifically concerned with the production and meaning of signs and with the structuring of the interaction. The cultural approach is concerned with the creation of distinctive culture through communication, and with how that culture may be maintained and transmitted through communication.

There is much more that may be said about these approaches. But this should at least make clear what we mean when we say that it is the process and semiotic approaches which are particularly represented in this book.

In talking briefly about study and theory, it is worth remembering that there is a reciprocal relationship between this and behaviour. That is to say, one might agree that interaction, communication and behaviour have a great deal in common, even if they are not strictly synonymous.

It is also worth remembering that our theory must come out of observation of behaviour, and is only verifiable through such observation or through making enquiries which themselves require communication to take place. Whether one is trying to describe characteristics of groups or the mental processes behind any communication, we need to look at communication itself in order to see if we are correct in what we suppose. This means, happily, that theory and practice need to be seen as equally important and as complementary to one another.

This study of communication and concern with actual behaviour is also underpinned by the fact that one is looking for what is significant, and that what is significant is usually that which is repeated. So it is that a great deal of communication study returns to a key concept of **convention**. Conventions show themselves through repeated behaviour (or content and treatment of material). It is worth bearing in mind, then, that much of what is in this book is, in effect, about patterns – patterns of behaviour that seem significant because they *are* patterned, and perhaps because they are frequent. Think about this when you are reading our work and when you are using it to make sense of what you see people doing as they communicate. Look for the patterns. Question what we say. And always be prepared to ask the most important question of all, with reference to what you read or what you observe – SO WHAT?

We have also written this book on the premise that all communication is about **meaning**. That is to say, about how meanings are constructed in the mind, about the exchange of meanings through verbal and non-verbal communication in particular. You will see that we begin by looking at communication within the person, where meanings are made, where we make sense of a world which for all of us is, most importantly, about people.

ASSUMPTION UNDERLYING THIS BOOK

In what we have said so far in this Introduction we have already given you some assumptions on which the book is written. Here are a few more.

The book is based on the assumption that readers are interested in understanding how and why communication takes place, and in developing communication skills. A further premise is that the study of communication should be directed towards helping these interests.

We also think that such study can be approached through a three-part notion of **description, interpretation and practice**. That is to say, we may describe what happens when communication takes place, we may then try to make sense of what we have described. This understanding can then, with practice, lead to more effective and more appropriate communication with others.

Perhaps the most important assumption that we make is that readers do have a basic level of knowledge and understanding as represented in our previous book *More Than Words: an introduction to communication studies*. Reading of the three relevant chapters would be helpful, though not essential. There is some overlap of topics. But we do not, for example, reproduce very basic communication models. And we do assume understanding of terms such as 'perception'.

HOW THIS BOOK IS ORGANIZED

It starts with examination of the Self, of the individual as communicator. Then we move to ideas about how we interact with others, and develop these points into an examination of communication in groups. So we move from a point within the Self to ideas about the Self relating to others.

Before we look at groups in particular, we deal with the theories of Self Presentation and of Transactional Analysis (after Goffman and Berne respectively), because these offer some stimulating ideas about motivation and regulation of interaction.

The last chapter is a general one about theory which draws together what has gone before and puts it in an overall framework.

At the back of the book, you will find a glossary of main terms, and a section referring to further reading and to some relevant learning/activity materials.

Finally, you will find an index. Don't forget to use this (and the table of contents), to find your way around the work quickly. Books for study are there to be used, not necessarily to be read from cover to cover. It's your book, so make it work for you.

To this end, we have also tried to make each chapter clear in structure as well as in style. Notice that there is a review/summary at the end of each chapter. It will be a simplification of course, but it should also answer the question, what were the main points that I was meant to get out of that chapter?

Within the chapters, look out for the key statements and main concepts which appear in **bold**. We want to help you learn by sorting out some of the material for you. This is why we have provided at least some case situations/stories which incorporate concepts in a live context in order to make their application and meaning more clear.

This is what we hope that we have done. If you want to comment on this piece of communication then feel free to give us some feedback via the publisher of this book.

Acknowledgements

We should like to thank many friends, colleagues and students who have in various ways made this book possible. In particular we wish to acknowledge: Terry Williams for his drawings; Mick Garland for a photo on p. 202; friends, family and students for appearing in the photos; Lesley Riddle our Editor at Edward Arnold for her continued support, encouragement and patience; and more generations of students than we care to admit for their challenging docility and for showing us what we needed to write.

Special thanks from GB to Judy and from RD to Gill, Nick and Caroline for their personal support and forbearance at our daily practising of interpersonal (mis)communication and our preoccupation with researching, book buying (and reading) and then for leaving us in peace at the word processor.

We and the publishers would like to thank those listed below for their permission to reproduce copyright material:

Addison-Wesley for Fig. 6.4, after Bales 1950; Blackwell Publishers for the extract from Scollon, *Intercultural Communication* by Ronald Scollon and Suzanne Wong Scollon; Faber & Faber for the lines from 'The Love Song of J. Alfred Prufrock' by T.S. Eliot; the House of Ulay for the advertisement Illustration D; National Press Books for Fig. 1.4, the Luft model for the Johari window; Piatkus Books for the extract from *He says, she says* by Lillian Glass; Prentice Hall for Fig. 1.2, the Barker model of intrapersonal communication; the Spastics Society for the advertisement Fig. 3.4 and John Wiley & Sons for Fig. 2.1, the March and Simon model of perception.

Every effort has been made to trace all copyright holders: our apologies to those in cases where this has not proved possible.

Illustrations

A *The Ideal Self – we are not always seen as we would like to be seen*

1

Intrapersonal Communication

Each of us entertains a notion of our own separateness from others and relies on the essential privacy of our own consciousness.

Bannister and Fransella, 1980

1 WHAT IS INTRAPERSONAL COMMUNICATION?

1.1 Introduction

This chapter is much concerned with **the Self that is at the beginning and end of all communication**. We will deal separately with the Self, but one should also acknowledge the artificiality of such an exercise. The process of communication is really one whole thing. All our acts of communication and our experiences have a bearing on one another. And we ourselves must be part of all this. So what we are going to do is to examine parts of the communication process separately, in order to describe them and to explain how they work together.

Similarly, this book is a whole thing, but you have to work your way through it, and connect one part with another in order to make sense of it as a whole. We hope that we have helped you to do this by describing separate concepts and by explaining their significance for the whole communication process.

What we have to say about the Self and Intrapersonal Communication does have a bearing on everything that follows. All the communication activities and processes that are described in subsequent chapters must relate back to those described in this chapter. So it would seem to make sense to start with who we are, how we come to be the kind of people we are, and why this matters in terms of making sense of communication.

1.2 Elements and Activities

Let's start by saying simply that Intrapersonal Communication (IRPC) is defined as **communication within the self, and of the self to the self.**

So we would say that thinking about this paragraph and making notes on this paragraph would both count as examples of IRPC, as we may abbreviate it from now on.

The main elements in IRPC can be described as follows:

• There is the **core of self** which can be divided into a number of different elements, the most important of which are: how we see ourselves, how we value ourselves, and our personality.

• There are the **needs (motivations)** which drive that Self to generate communication, to interpret communication and to change the way it presents itself in different sorts of interactions with different people. The Self and its personality are not static and unchanging but rather active and dynamic.

• There are internal activities by which we make sense of the world, which is called **cognition.** We develop internal cognitive maps which we can then apply to various situations when we are trying to interpret and make sense of what is happening. We call on these past experiences and the ideas, values and concepts we have made a part of ourselves to interpret other people's communication activities and to generate our own acts of communication.

• There is the internal activity of **monitoring the reactions of others to our communication.** The Self is continuously interacting with the outside environment including other people. We are constantly obtaining and checking feedback from others, that is, information that tells us about the effects of our actions on other people.

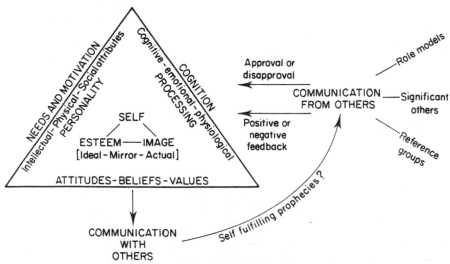

Fig 1.1 *A model for intrapersonal communication*

In Fig 1.1 we have tried to illustrate this model of the Self and the intrapersonal communication processes that take place when we are alone and when we interact with others.

1.3 Encoding and Decoding

The self is in a constant state of activity giving and receiving messages, that is, trying to express our own meanings to others and interpreting what others are consciously or unconsciously doing around us. These active elements of encoding and decoding are crucial to IRPC.

Encoding is about the composition of the communicative signs within the brain, and then their external expression (through speech for example).

Decoding would be about the physical acceptance of external signals (through hearing for example) and then understanding (or the construction of meaning from those signals).

In this way all communication involves intrapersonal processes. Whatever the Self is, with its various characteristics and needs, it must work through the intrapersonal processes of encoding and decoding if there is to be any contact with others.

1.4 IRPC Activities

There are those which are entirely internalized, and those which have external manifestations. The following examples are by no means exhaustive, but they should make sense of what we are talking about in real terms.

Internal activities are those thought processes for which we have labels such as reflection, evaluation, problem solving. Communication is within the Self and addressed to the Self. Any time you sit and think about what you want to do tomorrow, or come to a decision about buying a pair of shoes, or think about an argument that you have had with someone, you are engaged in intrapersonal communication.

Externalized examples may involve talk, but could just as easily require some other form of communication. We all talk to ourselves in private, especially when emotionally aroused or dealing with a tricky physical task. Cars get repaired to the accompaniment of – *now maybe if I tried to . . .*

If we haven't got someone else to bounce ideas and problems off then we are just as likely to talk to ourselves about them. Again, we may write – keeping a diary is an intensely intrapersonal activity. Or we may draw a plan of a room to see if we can change its layout. In this case, too, the communication is from ourself and to ourself.

If you try to extend this list of examples for yourself, you will realize that we do indulge in a great deal of IRPC activity.

What is Intrapersonal communication?

Use the model in Fig. 1.1 to analyse your own intrapersonal communication processes during a conversation with (1) your mother or partner about why you cannot have dinner with her/him next Satuday, and (2) with your work colleague asking her/him to come on holiday with you.

Analyse your intrapersonal communication processes whilst you are deciding whether to stay in and do some work tonight or go out with friends.

---

2   SELF DRIVES

2.1 Needs and Motivation

Communication, whether intrapersonal or interpersonal, must be motivated by something. There are reasons why we choose to initiate thought processes, or interaction with others.

One kind of motivation is discussed in section 4, where we offer some ideas about how we use communication to maintain and evaluate our ideas about our Self. We are motivated to keep on checking as to whether or not our view of what we are like actually seems to hold true in the light of the ways that others communicate with us. We check their reactions, or feedback.

This kind of motivation can itself be subsumed in one category of **need** – personal needs (Dimbleby and Burton, 1992). The notion of needs as the driving force behind human activities is well established. Maslow's (1984) hierarchy of needs is often quoted. He proposes that such needs have to be aroused and unsatisfied for them to motivate behaviour (including communication). These needs are described as physiological needs, safety needs, social needs, esteem needs (i.e. the need to achieve a sense of worth, perhaps from others' communication to us), and self-actualization needs (i.e. needs to achieve fulfilment and potential). Such needs, as they become less important to physical survival, also become more sophisticated and more important to the psychological well-being of the individual.

Schultz (1966), on the other hand, suggests a rather more simple set of three needs. Two of these fit other comparable categories, that is, the need to control and the need for affection. But he also proposes a need for inclusion, which is defined as a need to be recognized as an individual by others.

From all this it can be seen that there is general agreement that certain needs are geared to satisfying a sense of the Self, to defining that Self with relation to others, to producing a sense of esteem and worth for that Self. From this motivation, communication follows.

In particular, and with relation to our need for self-esteem (see below for definitions and further discussion), it may be argued that **we are motivated to** construct a Self that is attractive to others. Yet again, we would argue that such a Self only becomes apparent when it communicates. This motivation would take account of both personal and social needs. That is to say, if we want to get on with others, if we want to form relationships, if we want to think well of ourselves, then we want to present ourselves in such a way that we will be liked. There is a separate chapter in which Goffman's views on Self-Presentation are discussed with relation to communication. But even now it must be apparent that communication is a crucial bridge betwen ourselves and others. **We can only be known through our communication.** Within the bounds and the values of our culture, we learn what is attractive to others, what will allow us to join groups. We learn that to be a certain kind of person who behaves in certain kinds of ways will bring success and satisfaction in social relationships.

So these various motivation, mainly described as needs, initiate the formation of a certain kind of Self. They also stimulate that Self to initiate external action – communication.

KEY QUESTIONS

Self drives
Think back to the most recent face to face or telephone conversation you initiated. Describe the needs/motivation that led you to start.

Describe yourself in terms of your clothes, hair, facial appearance/make up and posture and analyse how far they are used by you to define your concept of self for yourself and others.

3   ELEMENTS OF THE SELF

3.1 Self-Image or Self-Concept?

One problem in dealing with Self is that different writers will attach different terms to the word to describe the same thing. For example, Turner (1982) refers to self-image as a part of a self-concept. The concept he suggests is relatively firm. The image shifts from situation to situation and draws from the concept. The one may differ considerably from the other. This bears a close relationship to the debate about personality – do we have a fixed core personality (a 'true' Self)? Or is our personality a flexible notion, with certain features predominating at certain times? There is an increasing body of evidence for the latter view. We will use the term self-image from here on, and regard self-concept as a synonymous term.

The nature of Self also reflects the society and culture in which a person has grown up. If we accept the model of Maslow's hierarchy of needs (see page 4), then a society, or a section of a society, where physiological and safety needs are still a major preoccupation the concept of Self may be less developed and group social needs may be more significant. Maslow's highest need in the hierarchy is the product of a Western, industrial, individualistic culture where 'self actualization', being able to fulfil your own needs and wants, physical and emotional, and to achieve a sense of freedom is the ultimate motivator.

In a culture where social cohesion and mutal co-operation or equality of treatment for all are the highest values, the ultimate need of the Self may be inner peace and harmony through the service of others and the subduing of your own personal needs and wants.

3.2 Public and Private Self

This idea of **shift in the emphasis of self-image** is illustrated by the fact that it is common for people to display a different Self in public and private situations. Some people also believe that they have a private Self within them that is at variance with the one which is commonly displayed to others, even to friends.

Gahagan (1984), in referring to self-awareness also touches on the public and private self. She identifies various forms of self-awareness, including awareness of private physical and psychological events; awareness of ourselves as public objects and characters. In the first case we are aware of internal pain or aware of a state of guilt. Pain messages are transmitted along the nervous system. Guilt notions are rationalized through the nervous systems of the brain. In the second case we may find ourselves watching our own performances. Many people become self-aware when they have to stand literally on a public stage. They monitor their performance – that is, what is being revealed of themselves to others in this public situation. There is usually a difference between the public Self and communicative performance which happens when we collect some prize with due gravity and gratitude, and that private intrapersonal communication when we are on our own and give vent to our feelings of joy and satisfaction.

So the Self has its public and private dimensions. We may communicate with ourselves about our Self even in a public situation. But in a private situation this communication with the self may be externalized – talking to ourself about what we have done. And we will feel that the Self that operates in private is rather different from the one that is represented in public. The cultural conventions about intrapersonal communication in public are powerful. Put simply, people who talk to themselves in public are considered to be eccentric. They are performing a private activity and revealing a private Self in a public place.

3.3 Self-Image

In general, self-image is about how we see ourselves. It is about ways in which we categorize ourselves. The way we categorize ourselves also depends on how we believe that we are categorized by others. To this extent the self-image, however private a construct, must be in a dynamic relationship with the outside world. The link with the outside world is communication. Many people see the Self in terms of role and personality traits for the most part. Dominant roles are, not surprisingly, those of occupation or family relationship. In terms of personality, there is some evidence that items such as confidence, intelligence and social worth predominate in many people's views of themselves. You could try for yourself offering a group of people cards with statements on them covering possible areas of personality, and see which ones are most frequently chosen. The only problem is that someone may choose a statement about, for example, their capacity for leadership because they feel that they ought to choose it because of the value that our culture appears to place on this quality. They may not feel privately that leadership is an important trait in themselves at all. We will have more to say about personality in section 3.7.

■ Three Kinds of Attribute

One pretty well agreed set of categories to describe self-image comprises those identified as **physical, intellectual and social attributes**. The **physical image** that we have of ourselves is demonstrated through sufferers from anorexia nervosa. Among other conditions, these people believe that they are fat even when they are not. They have an obsession and have acquired a distorted self-image. They cannot recognize themselves objectively and suffer from low self-esteem (see section 3.4). The result is that their communication with others reflects this lack of personal and social confidence. There is a direct connection between self-image and communication style. Physical self-image also relates to other definitions of self-image (see rest of this section). For example, it is notorious that many of us will reveal, when describing ourselves, a tendency to exaggerate height (evidence of the ideal image). Obviously any optimistic views of our physical selves will also reflect on our communication behaviour, for better or for worse. If we see ourselves as being devastatingly attractive to the opposite sex then we may behave as if we really are (see self-fulfilling prophecies section 6.1, below)!

Intellectual attributes of self-image are to do with problem solving, reasoning, analysis, logical thinking. These may be related directly to a description of intellectual skills, such as the ability to correlate pieces of information and to draw conclusions. Such attributes become valued and recognized through education to a fair extent. Your reading of this text is part of this educative process. How you approach the text is partly predicted by your existing view of your intellectual Self. Putting it colloquially, if you don't see yourself as being very clever then you may well approach reading books like this with a bad attitude – which isn't justified if only you reappraise yourself and realize that, like everyone else, you do have the capacity for reading and understanding if you are prepared to give it a try.

Emotional attributes of Self may, with reference to Turner's argument about concept and image, be easily seen as relatively fleeting. Without even defining particular emotions, some people see themselves (and are seen by others) as being 'emotional'. That is to say, they have a propensity for making emotional responses to situations, especially those involving tension and conflict. Such responses may range from rage to fear to misery. Again, one has to emphasize that the frequency and quality of such responses is often misjudged. Others who fear rage may, for example, judge other persons to have an 'angry Self' even if they have only seen them lose their temper a couple of times. People who have panicked once or twice in a crisis may feel that they always panic. In many ways the emotional Self is the one which it is most easy to misjudge. What we have just said also indicates how **it is easy to confuse temporary Self conditions with more permanent ones**. It is possible that individuals will tend to certain kinds of emotional behaviour. But there are other behaviours which are particular to particular circumstances. In essence we are saying that when judging ourselves, or when others judge us, it is important not to assume permanent characteristics of Self from a temporary condition.

With all these three sets of attributes which may be said to compose the Self, it is important to remember that they work together. Barker (1984) talks about the *need to maintain a unified conceptual system*. We are more than the sum of our parts. We communicate at any given time out of the whole of our Self. Views of the Self which emphasize a few attributes and ignore the rest are, in truth, stereotypes. We may stereotype ourselves as much as others may stereotype us. This is why there is a strong argument for developing self-awareness through Communication or other studies, so that we become more objective, and obtain a more complete picture of ourselves.

■ Ideal and Realistic Image

Another common way of describing self-image is through the pairing of ideal and realistic self-image. These two coexist within the consciousness. It is argued that many of our actions, including communication, are motivated by a desire to bring the one closer to the other. Both may be themselves described in terms of the attributes already referred to. Ideally we would like to be one kind of person. In fact, we know realistically that we are another. How objective we are about our realistic image is open to question. Probably no one is entirely truthful with themselves.

It is possible for people to see themselves as dull and incompetent because they are ineffective at managing social relationships. But in fact they may be extremely competent at a range of tasks from model building to dress making. These people have fallen into the traps of generalization and of undervaluing themselves. A realistic appraisal of the Self would distinguish attributes, might well raise self-esteem, and could lead to a more positive attitude towards dealing with those areas in which such a person could improve performance.

■ Looking-Glass Self

One common definition of Self is described through a phrase of Cooley (1902)

– the *looking-glass Self*. That is, we see ourselves reflected in how others see us. Communication is crucial here, because we only 'know' how others see us through their verbal and non-verbal communication. This may be direct feedback as in a conversation. It may be indirect comment, as when we overhear others talking about us. Obviously this version of Self underlines the importance of feedback and of perception. To construct a looking-glass Self, we must have evidence to work on, and we must process that evidence. Such processing is an act of intrapersonal communication, and is the subject of section 5, below.

■ Self as Seen by Others

A variation of this description of Self was proposed by Mead (1934) when he pointed out that people do have a view of themselves constructed from the view that they believe others have of them. This view is achieved by putting ourselves in the position of that other person – the Self as seen by others. Interestingly, this kind of mental act identifies with the social skill of empathy, where we are also said to view the world as viewed by another person as well as to experience their feelings and attitudes. This ability to stand outside the Self and at least attempt to see it as others see it is clearly an attempt to be objective. Of course, in describing the *Self as seen* we are making assumptions about the person who is perceiving us. Those assumptions are only as good as our perception of them. Nevertheless, we will continue to communicate on the basis of those assumptions.

■ Self and Role

Finally there is a description of the Self in terms of roles (referred to in the introductory paragraph). We develop these sets of attitudes, values and behaviours that orientate us towards others, as we grow up. Some roles are **ascribed**, that is given us by others – e.g. we will all be daughter or son. Others are **achieved**, that is earned and learnt – e.g. work roles such as counter assistant. It is also true that some aspects of achieved roles are also ascribed by others. So, if one was appointed assistant manager at work, then one would have achieved this role knowing what was expected of someone in that role. One would also behave within the role according to qualities that others also ascribe to it (their expectations).

The roles that, from one view, add up to our self-image may be categorized in terms of family relationships, religion, political affiliations, age, sex and occupation. We will communicate out of the role which dominates in a given situation. We see ourselves as having that role, as having qualities attached to that role, as behaving in ways appropriate to those qualities and to that role in general. This role performance is likely to have characteristic verbal and non-verbal communication. Someone who sees the role of Sister as being characterized by loyalty may defend a sibling fiercely in some argument. On the other hand, that same person as Supervisor, may not defend one of the work team who has got into an argument with a colleague.

A number of books, for example Coates (1991), Glass (1992) and Tannen (1991), have analysed Self and role in interpersonal communication by focusing on gender differences. The use of language and non-verbal behaviour patterns is contrasted between men and women.

Lillian Glass was used as an adviser to Dustin Hoffman as he prepared for his role in the film *Tootsie*, in which he plays the part of a male actor Michael Dorsey who adopts a female persona as Dorothy Michaels and becomes a famous 'actress'. Glass in her book *He says, she says* contrasts the acting required to convey masculine and feminine Selves:

> In the scene where Dustin (as Michael) is in his agent's office, he is abrupt in his physical movements and vocal tones. His movements are angular, broad and away from his body, while his legs are spread apart when he sits down. In essence it takes up more room. His speech is faster, more clipped and staccato, and even more nasal, since he barely opens his mouth or his lips when he speaks. He uses hardly any facial animation, even though his most openly expressed emotions appear to be anger and hostility as a result of his frustration at being unable to get work as a 'male' actor.
>
> In contrast, recall the scene in the Russian tea room when Hoffman, as Dorothy, first enters to meet 'her' agent. Her gestures are more delicate, smaller and directed towards her body. When she speaks she puts her hand on her upper chest, smiles more and uses more facial animation, which makes her appear more receptive and acquiescent. She uses a soft, breathier voice with upward inflection at the end as she declares: 'I will have a Dubonnet on the rocks with a twist'. This upward inflection makes her statement sound as though she is asking a question. It is an all too common female communication pattern which may give the illusion that the woman is tentative, weak, unsure of herself or even a helpless victim.

Clearly, Dustin Hoffman as actor in a role was 'programmed' by Lillian Glass to express these culturally expected male and female 'personalities', perhaps in a rather exaggerated way. You might like to watch a factual TV programme such as news or documentary with the sound turned off to observe the non-verbal expressions used by men and women.

KEY QUESTIONS

Many people become self-aware when they have to stand literally on a public stage (p. 6). Describe the feeling of self-awareness when you have to stand up in front of others to give a talk.

We have suggested that our self-image comprises physical, intellectual and social attributes. Describe yourself using those three categories first as you believe your boss or teacher sees you, and second as you believe a friend sees you.

3.4 Self-Esteem

This important aspect of self-image qualifies one's view of the various kinds of Self already described. It defines how we value ourselves, how we rate ourselves, what we think of ourselves. If we have high self-esteem then we think well of ourselves. Such esteem necessarily depends on a value system which is also part of the Self. That value system is learnt through communiction with others as well as through observing others. We learn what other people think is desirable or not, attractive or not, worthwhile or not, important or not, and so on. It is possible for the individual to come to value behaviours or personality traits that most other people do not. But **on the whole what we esteem represents a fair measure of agreement with what other people esteem**, within our own culture. We take up attitudes towards our Self which approve or disapprove of various aspects of our self-image. Self-perception and attitudes towards Self operate, it is supposed, in much the same way that we perceive others, and form attitudes towards them. More of this follows in later sections and in chapter two. But for example, one fundamental criterion is a scale of liking or disliking which we have of ourselves. Those with low self-esteem do not like themselves very much.

There follows the question of what it is that is liked or disliked. To a fair degree this is defined in terms of **perceived competence**. We see ourselves as being more or less competent in terms of motor skills, social skills, intellectual skills. For example, students may have low self-esteem in respect of their sporting abilities, esteem themselves highly in terms of getting on with other people, but see themselves as only averagely capable in their academic work.

■ What Self-Esteem Depends On
Self-esteem also depends on self-image to the extent that one may approve or disapprove of one's attributes (as one believes they are). People who have been brought up to believe in the virtue of self-control may despise themselves for a perceived attribute of becoming emotional in times of stress and crisis. Other people may see themselves as being both clever and good-looking, and will

esteem themselves highly for these attributes. In short, the positive or negative qualities of the self-image will bear a relationship to the degree of self-esteem that we have. The degree of esteem will relate to our use of communication. Without wishing too much to turn on a single example, one might assume a contrast of self-esteem is shown in two kinds of request approach, one of which runs – *Have you got a left-handed thimble in stock* and the one that runs – *I don't suppose by any chance you've, um, got something like, um, a left-handed thimble?*

Self-esteem also depends on the approval of others. This approval will be communicated non-verbally in particular. If you were to greet a couple of friends in a restaurant and then receive strong non-verbal signs that your presence was not welcome, two things might follow. One could be that you deduce a message about not interrupting a precious moment. The other might be that you then feel incompetent for not perceiving their relationship and for offering inappropriate behaviour. Low self-esteem follows. It may not last for long if you have a strong and positive self-image. But still you will have felt this way as a result of the disapproval offered by others early in your life. This early response offered by others will have contributed to the construction of the various kinds of self-image. Even the ideal image will have been constructed at least partly out of the responses of parents and others to the young person's behaviour. Coopersmith (1967) found that there was a positive correlation between high self-esteem in teenage boys and the degree of affection and approval shown towards them by the parents when they were younger. Boys whose parents were authoritarian, offered less approval, showed less recognition of the worth of their sons, were distinctively lower in self-esteem.

Because **most people would prefer to think well of themselves rather than not** (see also personal needs), they will also seek the approval of others. In effect they will adjust the kind of Self which is presented so that it fits social values or the norms of a particular group. This may mean adjustment of physical, emotional, intellecutal or personality attributes. This selective adjustment of self-image happens internally in the first place, because self-image is an internal construct. But again it must be manifested externally for it to be known. Such self-presentation means communication. The most common example of this adjustment seeking approval is when people dress up and adopt certain behaviours which they think will make them attractive to others. If they receive feedback which confirms the success of this behaviour then not only will their esteem have been strengthened but also their awareness of their attributes will have been confirmed. In the first place it could be that being kind to others is something of an experiment in the child. But when it receives approval for kind acts this will firm up kindness as an attribute. Kindness will rate high in self-esteem.

Such approval and feelings of self-esteem are a strong motivating force. High self-esteem brings satisfaction which may be described in other terms, but which still depends on that esteem to a large extent. *'In large measure the "pursuit of happiness" is the pursuit of self esteem'* (Patton and Griffin, 1981).

It is beyond the scope of this book to discuss what might be called 'disturbed self concepts' and to get into the realms of psychotherapy. However, Carl Rogers' book *On becoming a person: a therapist's view of psychotherapy* (1990) provides some very stimulating explorations of self-concept and self-esteem. Carl Rogers is credited with being the originator of 'client centred' therapy and approaches his clients' problems by seeking to develop with them a positive self-concept. In order to be self-confident communicators, do we need to like ourselves?

Carl Rogers suggests one way of looking at self-esteem which makes it clear that it is not a form of arrogance or superiority:

> We have established the fact that in successful psychotherapy negative attitudes toward the self decrease and positive attitudes increase. We have measured the gradual increase in self acceptance and have studied the correlated increase in the acceptance of others. But as I examine these statements and compare them with our more recent cases, I feel they fall far short of the truth. The client not only accepts himself – a phrase which may carry the connotation of a grudging and reluctant acceptance of the inevitable – he actually comes to *like* himself. This is not a bragging self-assertive liking; it is rather a quiet pleasure in being one's self. (Rogers, 1990)

■ When Self-Esteem Varies

Self-esteem is a variable factor. That is to say, it varies in general and in particular cases, and it varies on some assumed scale. So one may talk of **a general level** of self-esteem for an individual, but also of **particular levels** in particular circumstances. We have all come across that person who seems in general to have weak self-esteem, to be reticent and withdrawn. Put that same person in a canoe and it turns out that they have a gold badge and can tell everyone else a thing or two about handling the canoe. Their confidence blossoms.

Equally it is the case that self-esteem is not an item which simply appears or disappears. **We have a notion of degrees of self-esteem.** The problem for an observer is how to define the scale used. It is an interanl construct, like self-esteem itself. But we can only use communication to recognize and evaluate it. Psychologists must produce a form of words and then ask people if that phrase corresponds to something in their consciousness. So while it may be agreed that there are various levels of self-esteem, it is difficult to measure these. There is no clear agreement about using descriptive terms as scales of measurement, though notions of high and low are fairly well defined. Thus the work of people like Rosenberg (1965) does show a correlation between his subjects' estimate of themselves and the estimates of others of those subjects. And there was agreement about terms of reference in that, for example, subjects with low self-esteem were seen as being easily discouraged and either avoided social situations or remained detached from them.

■ *Self-Esteem and Communication*

To develop this point about behaviour and to conclude this section on self-esteem it would be useful to come back to its representation through communication. **High and low self-esteem is represented through communication style** as much as through particular phrases. It takes a collection of characteristics to add up to this style.

People with high self-esteem tend to talk firmly, with a relative lack of hesitation, and through a wide and flexible vocabulary. Their talk contains phrases which acknowledge others and their views – *I take your point*. They may use phrasing which admits responsibility and misjudgement – *I'm sorry, I shouldn't have said that*. Their non-verbal communication is open and assured, and capable of giving strokes to others without being condescending. They are concerned for others and show other social skills such as empathy. So they are not self-regarding and their view of Self is firm enough that they can accept failure and criticism.

Those with low self-esteem communicate in contrast to the above. They are defensive about their Self, and this is shown in extremes in slack body posture, protective gestures and lack of animation in expression. In short, they do not appear confident, and are reluctant to take risks in social encounters. They are defensive in their approach to social interaction, may talk about themselves with persistent deprecation, and about others in terms of envy. Their very speech patterns may be hesitant and/or heavily larded with the phrasal habits of their peer group, from which they desire approval. Tics such as *like* and *you know* are probably the most recognizable examples of these. Not surprisingly, such people tend to have a pessimistic view of their social skills and of the outcomes of activities in which they are involved.

KEY QUESTIONS

Self-esteem

Make a list of positive complimentary adjectives you would like other people to use to describe you.

Using the list of adjectives you have made in answer to the above task, adapt them to reflect how the same ideas of your self-esteem might be viewed by someone who you believe does not like you.

3.5 Self and the Media

In this section we want to take a brief look at **the relationship between the Media and people's notions of Self.** It is much proposed or assumed that the Media offer models for the construction of self-image as well as for interactive behaviour. Surprisingly, the evidence for such aspects of socialization is not so easy to come by.

This problem is bound up with Media effects, debates and research, in which much has been hypothesized about the influence of the Media on us, but relatively little has been demonstrated to be true, even under specific circumstances. Indeed in many ways research into the connection between Media and people has been very much concerned with the idea of effects above everything else, and even now with the idea that effects are about what the Media do to people. In fact there is plenty of evidence that people do things with the Media – take things from reading and viewing to satisfy internal needs. Equally, there is evidence that people can distingush fiction from reality and are well aware that the Media construct a world that is not life. This suggests that audiences do not so easily internalize qualities of Self or imitate forms of interaction. On the other hand, this need not stop us from making propositions even if they need effective testing. For example it may be proposed that people construct notions of an ideal Self for admired performers or characters in the Media. One can propose that the Media offer models for social behaviour – how to perform in romantic encounters, for example.

Some evidence does at least indirectly support the notion of connections between Media and interpersonal activity. For instance, we know that people in Britain spend an average of 4 hours a day watching television. It is also the case that Livingstone (1987) found that 60 per cent of viewers surveyed said that they became identified with the lives of soap characters. If one takes this on face value, it is possible to accept that this degree of identification could also lead to degrees of imitation or assimilation of examples of social behaviour. Duck (1993) also refers to Livingstone when he says that her work 'seems to suggest that viewers acquire a certain belief system associated with sex-roles'. The notion of role is bound up with role behaviour – so there may be a connection between the example of telelvision material and the way that men and women behave, including communicative behaviour.

In terms of one's sense of role or of internalization of self-image, it is also relevant to point to what the Media do not say. In a cultural context, if there is an absence of material that one can recognize, as an immigrant Bangladeshi or a Glasgow teenager, then a number of things may follow. Media could be dismissed as being irrelevant to one's sense of Self and of culture. One could turn more strongly to other cultural experiences, such as religious practice or activities based on a style of music. Or one could feel subconsciously resentful or damaged or cheated because one's sense of culture is being denied.

To sum up, it is assumed that the Media influence our beliefs and attitudes, that they therefore shape our sense of Self. It is assumed that we borrow from the Media in terms of how we communicate. It is assumed that the Media shape our sense of cultural identity. It is much less easy to be certain how this happens, to what degree and in what way.

3.6 Attitudes, Beliefs, and Values

These have necessarily been referred to already. But they should be dealt with separately, however briefly, as another distinct element of the Self. They are an important part of intrapersonal communication, serving as kinds of reference points when making judgements about the Self, and about information perceived as relevant to the Self.

We have attitudes towards our Self and attitudes towards others which are also part of that Self. (We also have attitudes towards other things such as types of behaviour or public issues.) With regard to people, **these attitudes are positions that we take up towards the person being dealt with,** and that we have before we start to deal with them. They have much to do with self-esteem because fundamentally attitudes are either favourable or unfavourable. They are based on a collection of beliefs – perhaps about ourselves. Once acquired they will affect communication because they create a negative or positive position towards the subject. Clearly it matters as to whether or not we feel negative or positive about ourselves.

Beliefs are not only about the Self. But some are, and this is important. **Beliefs may be defined in terms of what we think is true,** and how far we agree with a statement or an opinion. So we must have beliefs about our Self, what we believe its main features are. Indeed it may be said that to have a view of the Self is to have beliefs about the Self. As with attitudes our other beliefs are also part of the whole Self and will affect perception when interacting with others. Beliefs are more or less strongly held, and are more or less important to ourselves. Beliefs about the Self are strong and important for the obvious reason that a well formed and firm view of the Self brings a sense of security and certainty. People will confidently make statements about their qualities and abilities based on such beliefs, and are prepared to argue with others about this – *but you don't know me, I'm not like that really.* We even have beliefs about our ability to communicate. Such beliefs have external effects. Nothing succeeds like success. Positive beliefs produce positive behaviour which in turn reinforces this belief. The more we believe that we are good at communicating, the more likely we are indeed to be that good. Of course some people's beliefs are not geared to their abilities. If they believe their ideal image is much like their realistic one then they may 'fool' themselves into believing that they are great communicators. The correlation between belief and behaviour is referred to by Gahagan when she writes of the idea that *we try actively to get others to behave in ways which accord with our main beliefs about ourselves.*

Values **have to do with morality and ethics. They are ideas we have about what is good and bad, indeed about what is** *relatively* **good and bad.** Once more the idea that we have such values as part of our Self must be connected closely with self-esteem. As Myers and Myers (1992) put it, values are *'conceptions . . . of the relative worth you attribute to the things, people, and events of* *your lives*. And we have already defined self-esteem in terms of the degree of worth that we feel about ourselves. Clearly the terms are synonymous if not actually identical. **Values, like other concepts that we have described, are learnt.** We are not born with them. Once learnt they are quite persistent. We don't give them up easily. As part of a trinity with beliefs and attitudes, they are important in the intrapersonal processes because they offer standards by which we may weigh up experience, including communication from others. Equally, as good sceptical communication students we have to recognize that values are relative. What is valued in a person in one culture may not be so valued in another. What is valued at one time is not so valued at another time. Differences in values occur because of different needs and different environments, social and physical. For example, in Northern European and American cultures it is accepted as 'right' that old people should go to retirement homes or nursing homes. In many Southern European cultures this is seen as 'wrong'. In these cultures one could say that part of people's self-image includes a Self who will and should look after elderly relations until they die. There are historical and cultural reasons for such a difference. We make no moral judgement on such values. But clearly they are crucial to external and internal communication processes.

The concept of personality provides a way of us describing our own or other people's characteristics or personal traits. The psychotherapist Carl Rogers, whom we referred to above, came to the view that personality is a kind of mask which we adopt to deal with other people and to display the self-concept we have developed. From his experience as a therapist he believed that it was important that this expression of personality should reflect the concept we have of ourself. If we feel we are displaying a false view of ourselves we are likely to decrease our self-esteem because we feel rather a sham.

Our concept of ourself and of our personality may be a limiting factor in our communication with others. For example, if you have a concept of yourself which perceives yourself as introverted and shy, this will affect how you deal with other people.

Peter Hartley in his book *Interpersonal communication* (1993) usefully sums up his own view of personality and its influence on communication as follows:

> My own view of personality follows these developments (i.e. of recent psychological research) . . .
>
> • we do possess a range of personal character traits
> • these traits do influence how we behave and communicate
> • these traits are *only one* influence upon our behaviour
>
> Following this line of argument, I suggest that your personality influences your communication in two main ways:

- Predispositions: our personality characteristics predispose us to behave in certain ways.
- Limitations: our personality characteristics establish very broad limits for our communication.

One also has to be aware of how **contradictory messages about values may cause conflict in the developing self-image of the young person.** For example, a father may imbue his children with the idea that it is good to tell the truth. Then the children hear him lying to cover up the fact that he has forgotten an appointment (euphemistically called 'making excuses').

The concept of *Ideology* also relates to attitudes, beliefs and values. You will come across this concept in relation to the Media and Communication in particular, so we do not propose to spend much time on the topic here. But at least it is important to realize that the implications of ideology exist within the self-consciousness. These are, for example, that there are 'natural' social and power relationships in our society. It is communication which carries messages about what is 'natural'. We assimilate beliefs about the naturalness of the social position of women or about class from what the Media and people say to us from an early age. We process these beliefs intrapersonally, and they become part of the Self out of which we communicate to others.

3.7 Personality Traits

First it has to be said that the idea of personality is largely synonymous with that of self-image, and that to some extent we are dealing with it only because it is such a familiar term. Its precise meaning is arguable. Its most distinctive meaning seems to assume **a set of traits which are largely permanent and which are distinctive to the individual.** The traits or features of a given personality are assumed to be linked. The term attributes may reasonably be used to substitute for traits. With reference to the notion of a coherent personality Argyle and Trower (1979) dismiss it thus:

Many studies have shown that people are not as consistent in their behaviour as a personality theory would have us believe, but we go on believing in personality because it makes the world a more secure and predictable place.

One straightforward and useful notion that research into personality did throw up was that there are two key pairs of factors: dominance and submission, friendliness and hostility. These are accepted as traits which most people have in some degree, and traits which we like to assess in others before and during interaction with them. Having said this, **there is still no effective distinction between use of the words, *traits* and *attributes*.** Terms used to describe traits can be categorized within the **three kinds of attribute – physical, social and intellectual.** What we can say, as with attributes, is that what are described as personality traits will hinder or aid communication. For example, the person who is open-minded will be a good listener and will tolerate views and arguments which do not fit with his or her view of the world. The opposite would be true of someone who is dogmatic. The communication style of this latter person would be opinionated and assertive. Their speech might include phrases such as – *any fool can see that* . . . Yet again the Self affects interpersonal communication. And the intrapersonal processes are likely to involve degrees of self-justification given this type of personality. This kind of person will rationalize errors of judgement internally as being, for example, based on false information from others, rather than actually being misjudgements.

3.8 The Emotional Self

Our map of ourselves includes an area for emotion. **We attribute emotions to ourselves.** Those who use the term personality would identify certain emotions as traits in the personality. We are fond of referring to ourselves and others as, for example, good natured or passionate. But once more, the idea that there are fixed and dominant traits within individuals vanishes the more closely one looks at it. People simply do not behave this way. We think they do. They may think they do. But if one examines their behaviour over a range of situations it usually becomes evident that they do not, for example, represent passion or strong feelings the whole time. Whether one is talking about perception of the Self or of others, it seems that there is a distorting factor by which the perceiver fastens on some behaviour, ascribes meaning to it, and sees the behaviour as frequent and dominant when in fact it is not.

Obviously there is an emotional element to the Self, it is represented strongly through non-verbal communiction. We cry in sorrow, laugh in pleasure, and shout in rage. In many ways our words for emotion seem to define the behaviour as much as the state of Self. Research into emotion finds it difficult to pin down. The most acceptable description of the intrapersonal state simply identifies a **state of arousal.** Which way that arousal will express itself is less certain – as we often say, laughter is next door to tears. Research by Schachter (1964) tends to confirm his theory that there is firstly a state of generalized physiological arousal in the person which then has to be labelled and directed. Cognitive labelling follows. The effect of Schachter's research was to prove that once aroused his subjects' emotion could be labelled as euphoria or anger, depending on how he manipulated the social interaction of the situation. Essentially this is a cognitive approach to explaining emotions, in which emotions are attributed rather than being a distinctive physiological experience.

People do not have consistent descriptions of their internal states when feeling emotional. They describe emotion largely in terms of external signs – which brings us back to communication. In this case the medium and the message are thoroughly mingled.

Research by Ekman (1982) who showed photographs of expressions to subjects in a wide range of cultures did confirm a considerable degree of agreement in reading the emotions of anger, fear, surprise, disgust, sadness and happiness. This is in accord with a study carried out by Shwartz and Schaver (1984) in which, when asked to describe their own experiences, people agreed pretty well on the meaning of sadness, joy and anger, fear and love. But again, the expression/meanings are externalized. In fact **there is some evidence that external signs feed back to internal states.** You might try this simply by making a rule that you will smile as much as seems socially sensible for a given morning. See if you actually feel happier by the end of the morning than at the beginning. Your feelings might have to do with the expression (though of course some good things might happen to you as well, to make you smile).

It is clear that emotion is an important element of the Self, but that its origin and nature is not clearly understood. What is most clear is that emotions are recognized through communication and that once recognized by either the producer of the emotion or by the receiver, judgements about the state of that Self are confirmed or adjusted. Emotional states and predispositions are believed to be part of the Self, even though there is no evidence that they are to any consistent degree.

3.9 The Self as Free Agent

One dominant view of the self held by many in our culture at least, is that we are free agents. We have the power to make decisions, to change our lives. Strictly speaking this is not so much an element of Self as a specific belief. But in that we are trying to describe that range of components of Self which are generated through intrapersonal communication and which affect interpersonal communication, then it is important enough to merit separate mention.

We are aware of something which we call our Self. **We see ourselves as decision makers. We see the Self as cause, and our actions as effect.** '*We accept a partial responsibility for the consequences of our actions*' (Bannister and Agnew, 1977). We also recognize that in part others and external events may also influence our actions. But we may also influence them.

This belief in the individual Self and in responsibility is a version of the belief that we determine our own destiny. It strengthens a view of the Self which believes that we have the power to influence what happens to us perhaps through influencing others. We attribute to ourselves qualities and competence that will tend to support this view. For example, people like to see themselves as being able to work things out and as being decisive. Conversely, people show distress and anxiety when actually denied control over their lives (and when presumably their view of themselves and their esteem suffers). For example, in a study by Schultz (1976) of old people in a home, it was shown that those who were denied the right to arrange their own visiting times and decided their visitors had a lower level of morale and health than those who were allowed to do this. So it appears that we believe in a certain kind of Self, we attribute certain qualities of Self, and we become distressed if that belief or that attribution is contradicted.

3.10 Self as Moral Person

The notion of responsibility extends to a moral sphere. **We also have a view of ourselves as a normal person making moral decisions.** This sense of morality (related to the values described above) has particular reference to social behaviour. Much social behaviour is of course communicative. In this case Gergen and Gergen (1986) refer to the notion of **social accountability** and describe the ideas of Shotter (1984). Shotter suggests that we are engaged in **social accounting** when we use non-verbal and verbal communication to convince others that we are 'normal'. We would contend that this normality has a moral dimension. We will adopt behaviours and make utterances that are seen as 'right and proper' by those to whom we are rendering accounts. If we make such an account and receive approving feedback then our sense of self as moral person with moral responsibility is strengthened. We have exercised that responsibility and have had it confirmed.

For example, someone who clips their neighbour's car when backing out of their driveway, even without causing damage, will see themselves as morally responsible. They will go through an apology – for no material reason – but because they see themselves as being socially accountable.

KEY QUESTIONS

Write down about ten beliefs and values which are important to you. Comment on how you think they affect how you deal with other people.

Do you see yourself as a 'free agent', and if so how does this affect your life?

4   MAINTENANCE AND EVALUATION OF SELF

4.1 Influential Factors

These are described by Argyle (1973) as **the reactions of others, comparisons made with others, roles played, idenitifications made with others.** (See also reference to 'significant others' made below.) So it may be seen that **it is other people who are most influential in respect of the building, changing or maintaing of the self-image.**

Reactions or feedback from others have most effect if the other person is seen to have status and expertise. So people will listen to therapists or counsellors because they are regarded as knowing what they are talking about. Anything that they say about a person's behaviour or inferred attitudes, for example, will be respected and may well cause adjustment of the self-image.

Comparisons are likely to be made with groups or sets of others as much as with individuals. But those who are the object of comparison are realistically chosen. Children compare themselves with members of their class, not with those who are two grades higher. Evidence suggests that people tend to grade themselves up rather than down. So if members of the second team play with the first team and do well they revise their self-esteem upwards. If they play with the third team and perform poorly they are more likely to put it down to an off day than to revise their personal rating downwards.

It appers that **taking on new occupational or social roles affects self-image,** though obviously there will be a simultaneous effect from the reactions of others to these roles played. People who are promoted to a new post at work adopt a self-image appropriate to that role, seeing themselves as newly competent or as having qualities that they did not have before. If they behave in a way appropriate to this self-image then of course their new view of, say, their leadership qualities will be endorsed. Clifford and Clifford (1967) refer to an increase in positive self-rating among boys on an Outward Bound course – because in effect they had 'proved' themselves. This is what leaflets for such activity courses mean when they say that the experience of such a course will be 'character building'.

Identification with models is concerned with the **ideal image** as much as the realistic self-image. Obvious examples are parents, teachers and stars. Young people for the most part infer attributes of that model person from their behaviour, whether in life or in fiction. They then build those qualities into an ideal image which becomes an object of aspiration; one on which they would model their own behaviour and one whose attributes they would like to develop in their realistic self-image. Again, we have a situation in which **the process of identification (and of attribution) depends on communication.** Indeed, given the fact that self-image must be made known only through communication, one could argue that people aspire to certain kinds of communication behaviour and habits of the model. They want to be seen to be acting like the model because the actions suggest the internalized iamge. The assumption is that a form of behaviour signifies a specific content of of character.

The last two parts of this section have been mainly concerned with building the self-image out of which we communicate. They can be read with reference back to the previous section on Self Drives.

4.2 Maintaining and Changing (Developing) Self-Image

There is a tension in ourselves between stability and change. It is more secure to seek to endorse and stabilize an established image of the Self. On the other hand, one needs to change and develop self-image to be able to cope with new situations. And there is even an element in the ideology of our culture which values growth and progress (however one defines these terms). Staying the same and changing are both desirable things to do, but they contradict one another, hence the tension.

With regard to stability we may operate **self-maintenance strategies** (see Gergen and Gergen, 1986). Bascially, these strategies operate a kind of bias inclining towards the ideal Self or at least screening information which does not fit the realistic Self. **Biased attention** involves us preferring to notice feedback from others which confirms our view of ourselves. **Biased interpretation** involves us making sense of information that is obtained in ways that suit ourselves. **Selective affiliation and presentation** involves us in seeking friends and contacts who are likely to confirm our self-image, and in presenting ourselves in such a way that we are likely to get feedback which also confirms our self-image. A clear implication of these three self-maintenance strategies is that intrapersonal communication must operate selectively in order to deal with external information selectively. There is evidence that this is indeed the case. One experiment indicated that people process information more quickly if it fits with the terms of reference for their self-image. Other research (Sentis and Markus, 1979) also indicates that people better remember information that is consistent with their self-image.

A variation on this theme of bias is seen in another tendency, which is to form a lower opinion of those who indicate that they do not share our view of ourselves. This is **discrediting the source**. So if one's Supervisor at work writes a poor progress report, then one's inclination is to say that he/she is a poor judge of character and performance anyway!

The ultimate device for maintaining Self is simply to ignore any evidence that does not fit what we want to believe. This is an extreme example of selective attention. At worst this represents a pathological condition in which the person denies having heard what the other has said, or asserts that they did not say (or non-verbalize) what in fact they did say. Such a person may live in a world of their own, a world of delusion.

In summary, it may be that those who live a well-defined life style, meeting with a selective and well-defined set of people, are in some measure engaged in protecting their self-image and may have low self-esteem anyway. A wide range of social engagement and new experiences mean that we must take some risks with our self-image. But those with firm self-esteem and fairly stable view of the Self will feel able to cope with this, and be prepared to make adjustments as they learn more about themselves from others.

■ *Change and Self-Image*

If one is to change or develop one's self-image and to take the risks that this involves, then one must have a good reason for doing so. In which case you might want to refer back to the section on motivation. However, we can give you **two good reasons** here. One is **to win the approval of others**; the other is **to cope with changes forced upon us.**

It is in fact difficult to draw a line between the ideas of building and of development if one believes that people develop throughout their lives. We have made a tacit assumption that change and development occur after building, after a period when the self-image has stabilized. In which case examples from our two reasons would be, first, an occasion when we make a new group of friends, or perhaps meet someone who becomes special to us. We might then wish to change our behaviour to please them. Unless we are capable of keeping up a deceit, this change in the way we act and talk will be accompanied by a change in the way we see ourselves, presuming that the other(s) give us positive feedback for doing this. In the **second** instance, one could think of changing jobs, or getting maried. Either of these important changes in our life position means that we have to learn to get on with new people. Again, we would have to adjust our behaviour and our self-image. The fact that such a change does mean something is summed up in phrases people might use such as '*I just can't see myself working in that place*' – or – '*I'm not ready to marry him, I can't imagine myself as a wife*'. In both cases the speakers have recognized that they would have to change their orientation towards others and change their self-image.

Sometimes we volunteer for such changes, sometimes they are forced upon us (being made redundant from our job). But one can be positive about it and argue that **the more change is risked, attempted and successfully negotiated, the more adaptable and open to change we become.** Patton and Griffin (1981) refer to this when they say:

> There can be no guarantee of continued self-esteem as we attempt changes. We must risk our self-esteem with each attempt to improve it. Our doubts about our self-worth can be dissipated only by putting them to the test of self-exposure and feedback.

The process of making changes to the Self absolutely depends on use of communication. If one accepts Radley's hypothesis of a **three-part change** (1974), then this may be seen to be true. In the first part the person has to be able to visualize what the changed Self will be like – a piece of storytelling. Then we may start to act out the new role experimentally – particularly to communicate the way we feel as this changed Self. Finally at stage three we may have so far practised this role with success that we really have either changed our Self, or have at least added new dimensions to it which can be called up for that role.

4.3 Communication from Others

It has already been made clear that **what we are and what we think we are depends as much on communication from others as on our own communication skills and style.** This part of this section adds a few more points explaining how received communication operates on our ability to construct, maintain and evaluate Self.

The research of Videbeck (1960) among others provides support for the view that not only is the self-image learned through communication, but that also '*the evaluative reactions of others play a significant part in the learning process*'. There are oft-quoted examples of experiments where a female has been the recipient of communication which treats her as if she has attractive qualities. The effect of this has been to influence the female so that she behaves as if she is indeed attractive, and may be assumed to have enhanced self-esteem. (You might like to try the same experiment with males!)

Myers and Myers (1992) define communication from others in terms of **confirming and disconfirming responses.** Further, they suggest that confirming responses can be described in five ways: (1) acknowledging what is heard, (2) agreeing with what is said, (3) being supportive, (4) offering and seeking clarification of what has been said, and (5) expressing positive feelings. Disconfirming responses are these seven: (1) ignoring what has been said, (2) interrupting, (3) saying something irrelevant, (4) going off at a tangent, (5) being impersonal or generalizing, (6) not replying coherently or comprehensibly and (7) offering non-verbal communication (NVC) which contradicts what is said. This useful set of examples mentions specific types of verbal and non-verbal behaviour which may be interpreted positively or negatively as feedback, in terms of self-image and self-esteem.

At the same time as accepting the importance of communication from others, one has to remember the point previously made – that **communication from others only affects our self-image as far as we may 'allow' it to.** Eiser (1986) refers to the idea that people *seek consensual validation for their attitudes and beliefs*. In other words, **we may seek out communication from others that tends to fit our self image.** This does not mean that people seek only praise. Someone with low self-esteem may actually seek critical comment from others because this confirms their low opinion of themselves.

Our ability to accept or reject statements relating to our Self in particular depends on our previously built image. If we cannot accept critical statements, then we will tend to privilege maintenance at all costs. If we are more resilient, then we can accept such remarks, deal with them, and contemplate change in our behaviour and image.

Communication from others concerning our Self is often not intentional, and not put in explicit verbal terms. What people think of us is usually expressed in non-verbal terms (including paralinguistic features). It may be expressed through absence of communicative behaviour. Recognition by others of the Self that we present is very important to us as confirmation. Lack of recognition can be interpreted as rejection – *what have I done wrong? You didn't talk to me today. I've passed you twice and you haven't even blinked!* The point to be made here is that the most apparently trivial smiles and greetings can act as confirmation and recognition. Indeed this kind of communication with its tenuously implied messages is identified specially as **phatic communication** (see glossary).

So other people are important in an communicative sense to holding on to and even developing our understanding of who we are.

4.4 These Other People

People whose utterances matter specially to us may be categorized in three ways. What we are saying here is that it isn't only what is said that affects our self-image, but also **who** is saying it.

Hayes (1984) talks of **significant others**. These are people such as best friends, parents, respected team leaders, whose judgements we respect, who have status, who have some particular relationship with us.

Then there are **reference groups**. In this case it is the group norms and values (see Chapter 6) and group communication which matters, rather than individuals. The family lets you know what it thinks of your behaviour; the gang lets you know whether you 'fit'; the club offers approval or disapproval – by admitting you or not in the first place.

Finally, there are the **role models**, who may also be significant others. These are people whom we don't just respect or listen to, but those on whom we may wish to model ourselves. These models may fall within the categories of role described above. So, for a girl, one particular person may be seen as a role model for being female, while of another person that girl may say – *I hope I'll be as nice as him when I grow old.* Of course role models don't just remain an external influence. At some point they become internalized, and that model for image and behaviour can be called up through intrapersonal communication.

4.5 Self-Perception and Self-Attribution

The process by which the Self is maintained or changed also depends on how we view and evaluate what we believe to be our Self. One view of this process proposes that it is much the same as interpersonal perception (see Chapter 2). This approach suggests that our own bevhaviour is as important as the behaviour of others. In other words, **we watch ourselves and make inferences from this observation** (Bem, 1967). In effect we say, if I do that then I must be this or that kind of person. There is no effective difference between this idea and that of self-attribution, where the principle of trying to explain observed behaviour by attributing characteristics to ourselves is quite comparable.

4.6 Cognitive Dissonance

Lastly in this section we refer to a well established theory (Festinger, 1957) which can explain how we deal with the Self throughout our lives, and which indeed could just as well be seen as a basic drive for the Self. The simple principle of the theory proposes that if **we find any of our attitudes, beliefs and values are inconsistent with our experience, or if they seem to contradict one another, then we feel so uncomfortable that we have to do something about it.**

Since we have already suggested that these same three elements are at least a part of the Self, it follows that to change any of them is to change the Self. The theory is attractive not least because our society and its moral positions are so often manifestly contradictory that individuals must adjust in some way to accommodate these contradictons. For example, the virtues of being employed and the rewards this brings are incorporated within the self-image of many people, especially males. So what do individuals feel if they do not, on the other hand, actually believe that the job they do is important or attractive? They feel that somehow it ought to be – but it isn't. At the least they will feel unhappy. But then they may assuage this unhappiness by adjusting their self-image to that of a person whose efforts are justified because he is doing it for his family.

It can be argued that experience of this dissonance creates alternative models of behaviour with regard to what happens to our self-image. But people's experiences are so diverse that one cannot easily predict whether a person will respond to dissonance by 'holding on to what they have got' or by making a change in themselves.

The internal communication processes through which this change may occur are the subject of the next section.

KEY QUESTIONS

We have suggested that taking on a new occupational or social role affects self-image. Describe examples of these changes that have happened to you, or in someone you have observed, or if necessary imagine what they might include.

'Significant others', 'reference groups', and 'role models' may have a particular effect on our self-image. Give two examples from each of these categories that you believe have affected your self-image, and say how they have affected it.

5 INTRAPERSONAL PROCESSING

What we are going to deal with in this section are the key elements which make up active processing of communication within the Self. We will be coming back to these and adding points in the next chapter. So although you should find it useful to refer to Chapter 2, you should also remember that we made a general description of intrapersonal communication at the beginning of this chapter.

As a kind of opening excuse it also needs to be said that no one is very sure of what goes on inside our heads, though there are many ideas around. For instance, no one is perfectly sure of how we remember things or of how we make guesses.

On a basic level it may be agreed that through these intrapersonal processes we must take in information, shift it to various parts of the brain which have various functions, do something with that information to make sense of it, perhaps store the information, and perhaps act on it. In which case we may also formulate messages for action. What sounds so simple is immensely complex.

What we want to deal with now is some kind of map of intrapersonal activity which identifies the main landmarks.

It could be argued that there are five main elements in the process, all of which overlap to some extent. These are **decoding or cognition, integration, memory, schemata or perceptual sets, and encoding.**

5.1 Decoding

Decoding is that part of the process through which information (communication) is taken in to the brain and made sense of. The signs of communication have to be recognized and interpreted.

Cognition is another term which you will come across which means very much the same thing as decoding. Literally it refers to 'knowing'. But to know something one has to recognize it, and to recognize it one has to make sense of it. Hence the difficulty in truly separating the parts of the process.

■ *Three Kinds of Processing*

Barker (1984) refers to three kinds of processing in his model for intrapersonal communication (see Fig. 1.2). **Physiological processing** is concerned with messages about our body. In this case one is aware of continual feedback about things like outside temperature, or pain from the table edge on which one has just bruised oneself – a kind of body monitoring. **Emotional processing**, which is also relatively subconscious and instinctive, is concerned with internal feedback about our emotional state (refer back to what we have already said about the attribution of emotions). **Cognitive processing** covers everything else, including the handling of information that comes in the form of messages from other people. But don't forget that messages handled in this way can also be

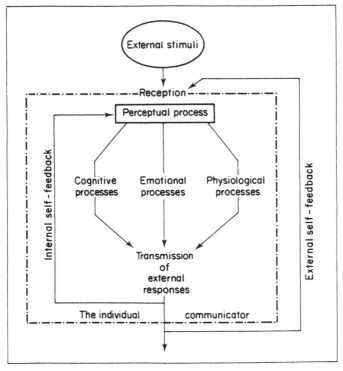

Intrapersonal Communication

Fig 1.2 *Barker's model for intrapersonal communication (Barker, 1984)*

generated intrapersonally. If you are making notes from this book, for example, then you are the initiator, the marker, and the receiver of the communication that is your notes. You are communicating with yourself. Barker describes this processing as the '*storage, retrieval, sorting and assimilation of information*'. Which leads on to the next point.

5.2 Integration

Integration refers to that part of the process through which the information identified is put together to make sense of it. One piece of information has to be related to another, comparisons have to be made, categorizing takes place, analogies are made, distinctions are drawn. In the end, a decision is made about what piece of information fits with what. For example, if one were trying to make a sweater or a wooden storage box and things were going badly, one would have to decide what this failure meant in terms of one's view of the Self. It could be integrated with notions of physical co-ordination, or with the ability to visualize, or with the ability to plan and organize activities. Further integration of all three would probably take place so that conclusions could be drawn not only about the Self but also about what to do next.

5.3 Memory

Memory is the storehouse of intrapersonal communication. In it are kept all the referential parts of the process. It is not just a store of facts and events. It is a brain function which keeps attitudes, previous judgements, beliefs. Though the operation of memory is not truly understood it seems that it is not really like a set of boxes in which we put things, but more like a set of messages moving around one tiny part of the brain, waiting to be tapped into the main message system. When we try to think about who we are, then some of these messages are collected together and organized into a pattern called Self-Image.

Because memory is also about competence and performance – i.e. how to do things and what to do – it really is fundamental to our existence, let alone communication. The experience of those who suffer from types of loss of memory (aphasia) is tragically instructive in this respect. We have all read about those people who are found wandering, having forgotten everything about identity, usually after some trauma. But even more sad is the case of the person who had lost parts of his or her long-term memory. In particular they had 'forgotten' about the death of a loved one. So every time they were made aware of the death of this loved person they suffered anew the grief that went with this knowledge.

Memory involves both the ability to store information and also to recall it. Both these subsidiary processes are selective. We have already indicated that there are things that we learn about ourselves and may choose to store, and others that we may not. This is allied to the idea of **selective attention**. Equally there is every evidence that we do store a lot of material without being aware of it. To an extent, the memory is more like a camera and a tape-recorder than we realize. It takes many things in. Whether or not we choose to take these things out is another matter. One experiment (Anderson and Williams, 1985) asked one group of people to make a conscious effort to remember and recall positive thoughts and feelings. Another group had to remember positive actions and achievements, and consciously keep on calling them back again. A third group was the control group and was given a basically meaningless task. When all three groups were later given a standard test to rate self-esteem, the two active groups came out with markedly higher esteem ratings than the control group. The one that was asked to keep recalling private thoughts and feelings came out best. In this sense there can be a clear relationship between the active use of memory and our view of ourselves. Intrapersonal communication is a private inward activity, but it seems it can be a very positive one. The two key groups in this case were in effect asked to involve themselves in a certain kind of IRPC, and it improved their view of themselves.

■ Three Types of Memory

As far as memory is understood it seems that there are three types of memory: **sensory storage, short-term memory, and long-term memory.** In the first case, information is held only for a moment – fleeting impression. This is why you see movies as moving – you hold the picture information for a fraction of a second, by which time the next image is coming in, and you assume that the sequences of still images must be moving. In the second case information is held for a few seconds so that it can be identified, labelled and associated with other information. Only the third example is really a proper 'holding store' in which information is kept.

Of course long-term memory is only as valuable as the use we are able to make of it, and this depends on our ability to retrieve informtion. When we recognize a person or an experience, this is a kind of retrieval-recognition. But to really use memory we have to recall fully the information and its relationship to other information. It is of little use to recognize someone in the street if we cannot remember their name, where we last met them, and so on.

We remember what has been communicated to us, what we have communicated, and how to communicate. Remembering how to communicate is not just about the function of producing speech, for example. It is also about how we make sense of communication. We remember meanings and how we construct meanings. We remember actions as well as objects.

5.4 Schemata and Perceptual Sets

These two terms are effectively interchangeable. What they describe are **structures of thinking, ways of organizing information.** Through these sets certain pieces of information are interrelated – playing word-association games is some evidence of this. In terms of the idea of roles we might say that each role has its own sets. We perceive ourselves in terms of these sets. Our image of ourself at work and in the work role relies on one set, and our evaluation of that image will be measured against that set and the expectations that it creates.

These perceptual sets may be described as cognitive structures. In principle they would seem to be the same thing as those structures identified as **self-schemata** (Markus, 1977). Eiser (1986) in referring to Markus's ideas describes these schemata as '*cognitive structures embodying networks of meaning associated with particular attributes, that together coalesce to form the self-concept*'. People might, for example have one schemata for organizing masculine or feminine traits.

So in effect what happens in the intrapersonal process is that information being dealt with is assigned and organized according to these cognitive structures. They are pre-programmed plans for making sense of experience which are built up, it is assumed, through learning.

5.5 Encoding

This is the final organizing part of the process, in which meaning has been assembled, and perhaps symbols have been arranged prior to some communicative act such as speech. Where interpersonal communication is concerned, the term is also taken to include the composition of the speech utterance itself – putting the words together audibly.

In this case we are concentrating on the prior mental activity in which that 'putting together' must already have taken place. It is perfectly possible to 'hear' words in the head or to 'see' pictures in the mind. For us to believe that we are so hearing and seeing we must have encoded the communication. We have done this intrapersonally, within ourselves.

> Describe from memory a supermarket, or other type of shop, which you know well. Analyse why some areas of the shop are more clearly recalled than others.

---

6   THE SELF TO OTHERS

In this section we want to say a few things about how the Self matters when we are communicating to others. So this is not a section about interpersonal communication, but it is about the Self in interpersonal communication.

6.1 Self-Fulfilling Prophecies

Or, **what you want is what you get**. We can say this because what we want affects how we communicate and how we communicate affects others. If we affect them the 'right' way then we get what we want. A crude little formula, but consider seriously the fact that our self-image really does influence our communication behaviour. We have already referred to the way in which our general self-esteem may cause us to use a set of body-language cues from which others infer that our state of mind is depressed or miserable. And if one behaves as if one is miserable then people will deal with one accordingly. Some people have a version of negative self-image which actually desires rejection and alienation – this confirms their negative self-image. One could almost say that they feel good about feeling bad. More likely you will come across the version of the negative Self in which someone simply feels sorry for themself and wants others to feel sorry for them. It is relatively easy to put on a performance which other people respond to with comfort and words of cheer. This is what we have been waiting for – a boost to our self-image. Someone else does the work of raising our self-esteem.

This is a self-fulfilling prophecy: **what we are affects how we communicate, and how we communicate affects what we are.** This is the principle on which all cheapjack psychological 'success courses' operate. This is why you hear phrases like 'think positive, be positive'. All you learn through such courses is that the principle of feedback works. If one is pleasant to people then they usually respond pleasantly, which feels OK – and so one has the courage to be even more pleasant another time – and so it is not really so hard to get on with people. Only don't try too hard, because where sincere effort is rewarded, plain deceit is found out.

Langer and Dweck (1973) refer to a **circle of success or failure** which is another version of the self-fulfilling prophecy (see Fig. 1.3). Basically their argument is that someone is likely to be a success in dealing with others if they

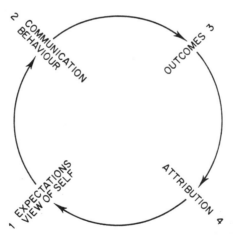

1 . Believes in ability to manage the interaction successfully

2 . Communicates in accordance with this belief

3 . Sees the outcome of the interaction as successful

4 . Attributes success to self and ability to manage interaction

Fig 1.3 *A model of the self-fulfilling prophecy*

believe that they are the kind of person who is likely to be a success. The converse is true. In more detail, there are said to be four stages in the circle. Firstly, the person has **expectations** of their success in, say, persuading someone to go out with them. Then that person uses **behaviour** that should fulfil those expectations – i.e. they will communicate in ways that they believe will make them attractive and will persuade the other person. Then, having either succeeded or failed to get the person to go out with them they take a **view of the outcome**. This means deciding whether or not they succeeded in what they set out to do. Finally there is **attribution**. Here, a lot depends on one's self-image. Someone with a positive self-image will certainly have this reinforced if they succeed in getting what they want. But even if they don't, it is entirely possible that this person will attribute failure to some fluke of circumstance rather than to themselves. They will still be able to approach another encounter optimistically. And nothing succeeds like success, or even partial success.

6.2 Saliency

This term refers to the idea that in a given situation some element or feature becomes more important than others, becomes more apparent. It refers to Self in two ways.

In the **first** general case it is observed that the Self and our awareness of this become more important in some situations than others. These kinds of situation are those where there is an audience and those where there is an element of assessment involved. These situations lead to greater awareness of Self – a state in which we are active intrapersonally as well as interpersonally, and are monitoring both our external behaviour and our internal states. For example, this is likely to happen if we have to stand up and make a speech at a wedding celebration, or if we are being sensitive to the kind of Self that we are presenting to others.

In the **second** case one is dealing with particular features of the Self. Here, it may be noticed that the salient features of Self depend on situation. This kind of saliency may well be tied in with role. So, if someone is looking after children in a summer camp, then that person may adopt some kind of parental role. In which case it is possible to suggest that there will be salient features of Self displayed, perhaps a controlled demeanour coupled with directive behaviour.

6.3 Self-Presentation

The reference to audience above should be related to presentation of Self. That is to say, the notion of audience applies to many situations other than those where a collection of people exist as audience for communication from one other person. In the wider sense there are many situations in which a single person is audience for a performance from one other person. When doctors deal with a patient they are in effect playing to an audience. They bring out certain features of Self through a selected kind of communication behaviour. Intrapersonal communication had played a part in bringing out that Self, and continues to be involved in the process of monitoring Self and receiving feedback from the patient.

At this point we would like to refer you forward to Chapter 4 on presentation of Self which you will see picks up the remarks made in this last paragraph. Another example perhaps of why you need to read the whole book to get the whole picture!

7   THE PERSON AND PERSONAL DEVELOPMENT

This last section of this chapter is concerned with idea that understanding of the Self and intrapersonal communication may be of benefit to the individual. This benefit is not easily measured, but may be described in terms of having a sense of one's personal worth in most if not all situations. It is about being honest with oneself, without having to wear the heart on the sleeve. It is about having an adaptable Self which can adjust to one's own needs and to the needs of others. It is about being able to grow or develop that Self so that, without being smug, one is able to say – *I knew myself pretty well and I know where there is room for improvement.* It is about understanding how one's Self relates to others and can be adapted to making those relationships happy and satisfying. This is easiest if indeed one does feel good about oneself.

7.1 Self-Knowledge and Self-Control

In the first place there is a premise that – as for Communication Studies generally – **self-knowledge brings the possibility of self-control.** This is not control of Self in a repressive or defensive sense. Nor is it control in the sense of learning how to control oneself in order to control others. It is a control which leads to the benefits described in the first paragraph. It is a control which stops one, for example, thinking badly of oneself when there are achievements and qualities which, if recognized, should create satisfaction. It is a control which stops one unleashing blame on others, when the concept of blame may even be irrelevant. It is a **control which allows rather than denies because it makes possible an increase of self-esteem and an expansion of self-image.**

This view of knowledge and control is akin to **consciousness raising.** The more one is conscious of what is happening in one's life and how it happens, the more there is at least the possibility of deciding what happens. One does not have the option of using communication in any positive ways unless one is conscious of how it works.

7.2 Self-Deception and Self-Concealment

One of the things that we need to know is that **we are not always honest with ourselves about ourselves.** More often we are not honest about ourselves with others. Deceiving or concealing the Self is unproductive. It is also likely to create tension. People who are labelled 'poseurs' are trying to conceal something from others by giving off false cues. But the fact that they are recognized as poseurs suggests that such concealment is difficult. It creates tension all round. Trying to pretend creates tension in oneself, and makes others tense because they know that they are not dealing with the real YOU.

In proposing that one should recognize and avoid self-deception and self-concealment, we are not arguing for a kind of pretentious baring of the soul. Sometimes we tell lies to protect others' feelings. Sometimes we should not be perfectly honest about ourselves if it is going to embarrass someone dreadfully. Sometimes, temporarily, we need to conceal ourselves from others – perhaps in times of grief. This might be self-protection. The point is that most of us could probably be rather more honest than we are for some of the time. In being honest a lot depends on the way one goes about it. Putting it rather simply, if you have a friend who is a real exhibitionist and even makes a fool of themselves, it is one thing to say – *Cut it out. You're a real pain in the neck!* It is another thing to say – *I wish you'd stop doing that. It makes me feel uncomfortable.* **Honesty has to take account of circumstances and people, and of the way in which one communicates.**

When we deceive ourselves we are denying knowledge of ourselves, and this is silly because one cannot run one's life on false information. We need to know what we are capable of in order to be able to plan ahead, to anticipate how we will cope with situations. It is also true that people are capable of a great deal more than they give themselves credit for. This is precisely because we do have the capacity for growth and change. The Self is not fixed. We may practise avoidance techniques because we feel that we cannot cope with certain social situations. But if we stop deceiving ourselves it may be possible to pin down *why* we avoid such situations. We may be able to reach a state where we can say – *I've nothing much to lose really, if I'm honest with myself.* In this case it becomes only a small risk to engage in this situation and see how one gets on. If nothing too terrible happens then that is another small victory, and an expansion of the self-image.

To take one example – it is often difficult to say no to people. If some authority figure at work asks you to do something like running a personal errand for them which has nothing to do with your work, it can be hard to refuse. But then you might reflect on yourself and your avoidance of conflict. You might wish to change that part of your image which doesn't want to face up to the other person. You might decide to try asserting your belief in yourself for once and say – *no, I don't mind helping you out once, but I'm not paid to run errands, and I don't think that it is reasonable to ask me to do that.* In this case you might well find that your superior adjusts his or her view of you more positively. They might resort to blackmail and threats. But if these are not backed by real power they can be ignored. If this person does have the power to, for instance, dismiss you without justification, then at least your choice is clear – and you can still feel good about yourself for having taken a stand.

The worst kind of defensiveness, and a common variety, is that where people take a rigid view of what they are and are actually not willing to change their view of themselves. Kelley (1969) talks of hostility expressed by such people: attack is a form of defence. Examples of this behaviour are to be seen in teachers who try to 'put down' pupils to prove to themselves that they are clever. Such people are also often too inclined to play clever teacher to other people in their lives, apart from the pupils. Their self-image is fixed. Their social interaction is inflexible. It causes conflict. It attacks the self-esteem of others. This is maintenance of Self gone to extremes.

So, **to achieve self-knowledge we may have to overcome kinds of self-deception and defensiveness** techniques which we have built up to protect a rigid view of Self.

7.3 The Hidden Self and Self-Disclosure

Willingness to disclose information about one's **private Self** depends on a variety of factors apart from self-esteem. In the first place it depends on the values of one's cultural or subcultural group. If our culture discourages intimacy and conversation about one's personal feelings and private beliefs as a general rule, then this can be a real block to self-disclosure. Who the other person is matters a great deal. People of status don't like to reveal themselves to those without status. Men are less inclined to make disclosures than women (especially mothers) than to men.

Disclosure depends on trust, so we are more likely to talk frankly to those we trust. At the same time making disclosures invites trust and can bond relationships. If one's work or social situation is one of competitiveness then it is much harder to make disclosures than if it is not. Equally, and especially on the basis of work done by Rogers and others since the 1960s, it is recognized that **some degree of self-disclosure benefits relationships, leads to more self-esteem, and develops the stability of the self-image.** Self-disclosure may not be a skill, but in moderation it appears to be a practice which benefits the individual. It is in effect about the practice of communication.

In particular it has been noticed (Altmann, 1972) that self-disclosure encourages the building of a relationship. First, it is more likely to take place at the opening of a relationship than later on. Second, it seems to encourage reciprocal disclosure from the partner. It would seem that a degree of honesty is taken as a sign of trust and encourages more trust in its turn. As Myers and Myers put it:

a relationship develops only when you and the other person are willing to go through the mutual process of revealing yourself to each other. If you can't reveal yourself, then you can not be close. To be silent about yourself is to remain a stranger.

It is important to realize that self-disclosure cannot be used as a mere device to force the other person into a relationship. It is the kind of communication which works best a little at a time. It works when there is a degree of trust between the people concerned, when there are some non-verbal signs of approval which suggest that each person wants, experimentally, to try the first stages of a relationship. Telling someone your life story and your opinions within 10 minutes of meeting them is not going to start a beautiful relationship. You have to be sensitive to the other person's needs and feelings, to be empathic. And once more, even if only a little, you have to take risks. In fact most people, even if the relationship doesn't come to anything, will still respond to your trust with confidentiality.

■ The Johari Window

One way of illustrating the hidden self and of showing the capacity of change in the Self through disclosure is seen in **the Johari window** (Luft, 1969). First, it may be seen that the four panes of the 'window' (see Fig. 1.4) represent four

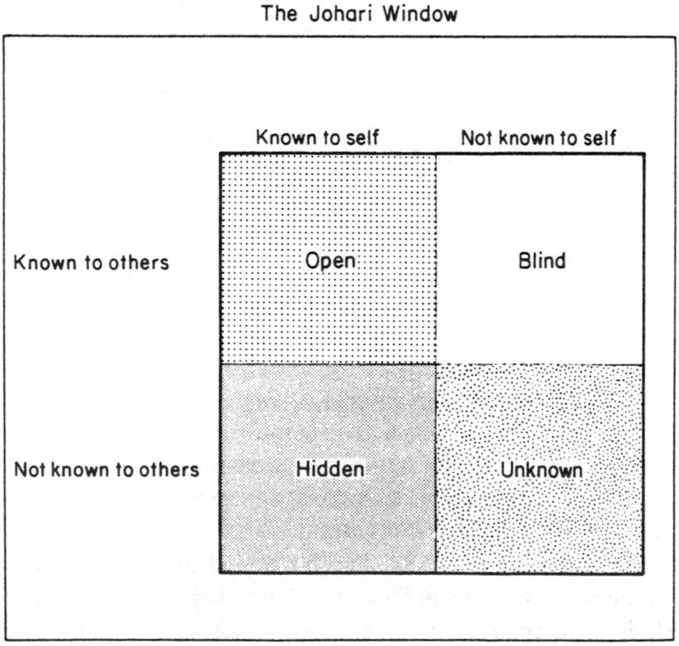

The Johari Window

	Known to self	Not known to self
Known to others	Open	Blind
Not known to others	Hidden	Unknown

Fig 1.4 *Luft's model of the Johari window (Luft, 1969)*

areas of the Self which are defined in terms of what the person does and does not know about themselves, and in terms of what others do or do not know about that person. The *Free Area* is the most public one, containing things which both you and others know about you – certainly things such as your name, your job, and facts like these. But the *Hidden Area* is one where you keep things from others which you don't want them to know – perhaps a fear of black beetles – and certainly your personal fantasies about things like the man or woman of your dreams! But the other two panes are areas where you don't know yourself. The *Blind Area* is one where, nevertheless, others do know things about you. They might see you as being very noisy or as using too strong a perfume – something like that which they don't tell you. And lastly there is the mystery area of the *Unknown*, known to no one, where the Self is buried in the subconscious and there are qualities waiting to be discovered.

One basic principle of the window is, change what is in one pane, and you change the rest. If you solicit feedback then you may find out things you didn't know about yourself from others, and shift them into the free area. If you give feedback to others then they will find out things about you, and again you will move information into the free area. In one sense, moving information about your Self into the free area means that you have more to share with others. Certainly to do this moving you have to communicate.

■ A Process of Self-Disclosure

A sequence of actions in a **process of self-disclosure** (which will affect the window), may be described as – **disclosures – feedback – self-esteem**. That is to say, if one reveals something about oneself then others will react to this information, usually with reciprocated trust. This trust, sometimes shown in the form of further disclosure from the others, makes one feel better about oneself, and so develops self-esteem.

In this process of self-disclosure, communication becomes the means through which sharing takes place and mutual trust is developed. It is the means through which we make ourselves known to others and they to us. Sharing brings personal growth, defined as a growth in our knowledge of ourselves and of others, a growth in the bonding of our relationships, and a growth in our sense of our own value. If communication can achieve this kind of growth then it is indeed worthwhile. We hope therefore that you will agree that this chapter has been concerned with very significant parts of our lives, that it has underlined that importance of understanding communication and of being able to use the understanding constructively and with respect for other people.

KEY QUESTION

The person and personal development
Look again at Fig. 1.4 the Johari window. Use this model to analyse a relationship between a person and her/his supervisor. What areas of the Self is the employee likely to disclose and what reveal?

8 SKILLS IN INTRAPERSONAL COMMUNICATION

At its simplest, and at the same time its most complex, the overarching intrapersonal skill is 'to know thyself'. Being able to recognize one's personal characteristics, strengths, weaknesses, and effects on other people and also to have a positive and accurate self-image can be described as intrapersonal skills.

Our ability to communicate with other people reflects our own ability at being able to be in touch with ourselves. We develop the skill of seeing ourself as both subject (I) and object (me), that is, we can both analyse our internal feelings and view them objectively in the way they are seen by others.

Intrapersonal communication skills are closely linked with interpersonal skills. Being able to express ourselves in words and in non-verbal behaviours to other people, and being able to recognize the effect we have on other people and to compare ourselves with others are all skills we can practise.

These general skills can be summarized in the following list of specific skills. Whilst for convenience here we have made them discrete skills, they all interrelate:

- Skill of being **self-aware** so that we can try to see ourself as others see us.
- Skill of **accurately knowing our own body image** so that we can recognize how others see us. We also learn to change this as we go through life.
- Skill of **developing a positive self-esteem** so that we value ourselves and generally approve of the sort of person we believe we are. Our self-esteem may be low if we feel that we fall short of a 'self-ideal' that we set ourself.
- Skill of **developing a personal range of social roles** so that we can relate to other people in a varity of situations.
- Skill of **recognizing what needs and motives we have** so that we can seek to meet our own needs through our own interaction with others.
- Skill of **being aware of other people's reactions to us** so that we can adapt our behaviour.
- Skill of **taking control of our own thoughts and actions** so that we can take personal responsibility for ourselves, our attitudes and beliefs.
- Skill of **self-disclosure both to ourself and in appropriate ways to others** so that we can build relationships on openness and mutual trust.

Intrapersonal communication is not confined to ourself. Internal processes of communication and the development of concept of self which we in turn present to others are products of our relationships with others. The nature of these relationships particularly in childhood is very important to the development of self.

REVIEW

You should have learnt the following things from this chapter:

1 What the term Intrapersonal Communication means in terms of its main elements and activities.

2 Self-Drives
How we are motivated by various needs, the main ones of which are physical, personal and social.

3 Self-Image
Is an internalized view that we have of our Self.

We have public and private Selves.

Our self-image is composed of physical, intellectual and social attributes.

We have both an ideal and a realistic self-image.

There is something called the looking-glass self – seeing ourselves reflected in the reactions of others.

Our Self is also partly something which we imagine others see in us.

Our Self contains ascribed and achieved roles.

Self-esteem, or how we value ourselves, is the most important aspect of self-image. A lot of our self-esteem depends on getting positive feedback from others.

It is suggested that in part we construct our ideas of Self from our Media experiences.

Our Self contains attitudes, beliefs and values which influence all our judgements.

We are all said to have certain personality traits which are described in much the same way as attributes. Different traits are brought forward in different situations.

We have something called an emotional Self which we construct from observation of our own behaviour.

Our Self includes a picture of our physical and social worlds.

Most of us see the Self as being the source of decisions and actions.

Most of us see the Self as having a moral dimension which affects how we view the world and how we deal with others.

4 Maintenance and Evaluation of Self
The four key factors in creating a sense of the Self are: reactions of others, comparisons made with others, roles played, and identifications made with others.

There is tension in us between a desire to maintain the Self in a stable state and a desire to change the Self. We operate various self-maintenance strategies in an attempt to hold on to our view of Self once created.

Communication from others is very important in confirming or disconfirming our view of Self.

The most important other people who offer us feedback related to the Self are described as significant others, reference groups, role models.

We attribute characteristics to our Self through a process of perception in the same way as we perceive others.

The effect of cognitive dissonance is to cause us to revalue or change self-image.

5 Intrapersonal Processing

There are five main elements in the process: decoding or cognition, integration, memory, perceptual sets or schemata, and encoding. IRPC involves us in making sense of information with reference to what we have known (memory) and to frameworks we have built up for making sense of experience (schemata).

6 Self to Others

Self-fulfilling prophecies are communication strategies through which we construct communication in order to get the response we want – to make our wishes come true.

Saliency refers to the fact that some features of the Self become more important in certain situations than at other times.

Self-presentation is about communicating a selective view of Self to others: described in Chapter 4.

7 The Person and Personal Development

Knowledge of what we are and how we come to be this, makes it possible for us to control our Self as it relates to others.

We may deceive ourselves and conceal ourselves from others because we lack self-esteem and are not prepared to take risks.

Self-disclosure, handled in the right way, enhances trust, improves relationships, and helps the individual grow in various ways.

There is a hidden Self which can be disclosed, described through the Johari window.

8 Intrapersonal Skills

These may be summarized in terms of being self-aware, being honest in self-disclosure, being positive in one's view of oneself and of applying these skills to one's own interpersonal behaviour.

CASE SITUATION

Know Thyself

> Read the extract below about an interchange between friends and answer the following questions:
>
> What is illustrated about Steve and Louise's relationship?
>
> How does Louise view herself?
>
> How does Steve view her?

Louise Thorne felt despondent as she stirred her coffee, and listened to the roar of the hot water filling yet another teapot at the counter of Meg's Caff. She was not a person much given to self-doubt, and not getting the job at Rayner's Shoes had actually surprised her. It wasn't the end of the world of course. She would apply for other jobs. But as Saturday jobs went it would have been quite well paid, and Louise had already made plans how to spend her money. She looked out of the window, feeling almost cross now, and hardly reacted to the grinning face with spiky ginger hair pressed against the pane on the street side.

'Hi,' said Steve, taking the opposite seat, 'mind if I share your cup?'

'Go buy your own, freckle face,' she said, almost automatically.

'This is not the girl we all know and love.' Her silence confirmed this.

'So, don't tell me, you didn't get it.'

'OK I won't tell you.'

'Hmm – I think you should. Hang on a minute. I'll get you one of Meg's special greasy doughnuts.' Which he did in less than a minute, and Louise was grateful to Steve even though she could feel every bite going straight to her waistline. She gave him a blow by blow account of the interview with the manageress.

'You know,' he said, poking at the sugar jar with his plastic stirrer, 'speaking as at least your third best friend, maybe you should think again about how you come across – you know, how they see you.'

'And what does that mean exactly!'

'It means that I don't see the point in giving you the what bad luck routine. I guess I'm trying to be helpful. You know, before I got my weekend job at the hardware store my brother did the same for me – asked me to take a good look at myself, if you see what I mean.'

'Hey, I don't want some heavy analysis.' Steve said nothing. 'Anyway, I thought I was pretty positive, and spoke up for myself.'

'You probably did. But maybe she thought you were just too pushy.'

'You won't sell shoes by standing around with a silly smile on your face.'

'No, but you don't back the customer against the wall and shove the shoes up their nose!' Steve stopped, looked embarrassed. The juke box had stopped and his last words had come out loud, which caused a couple of people to look round. 'What I mean is you're very determined. You always have to get your own way. Not that you're nasty with it, Lou, but you do like to organize people and push them into agreeing with you. Some people don't like it, even when they do end up agreeing with you.' Louise was looking slightly stunned. 'Don't get me wrong, I like you. You know that. But you really know how to cut up people who won't go along with you. You're lots of fun. But it sort of swamps some people. They don't get a chance to put over their ideas. Be honest, it is always you that runs our group sessions and that sort of thing.' For once Louise had not been able to get a word in edgeways. 'So what I'm trying to say is, if you act like that at an interview, you'll come over as too much.'

For once Louise was lost for words. Steve sat uncomfortably as she looked out of the window, then at him, then out of the window again. Her smile was a small one.

'It's funny, isn't it,' she said at last. 'I don't see myself like that at all. I mean, I know I'm no shrinking violet. It's difficult to be that when you're my height. But I always thought I was just positive. I thought I was just being helpful in the group work. Actually, I always felt I was a bit nervous, really, so I ought to – give something. I thought I was a reasonable sort of person. I'm not really that clever, you know, so I suppose I see myself as – a doer, not a thinker. And I do try to help people.' She sat back. 'Well, it's funny how wrong you can be about yourself.'

'I'm not saying you're wrong,' said Steve quietly. 'I'm only saying that other people don't see you quite the way you do.'

Suggested Reading

There are many books which are relevant in parts to the material of this chapter. We have chosen just six which you can read selectively. It is also true that these books cover more than one chapter of this work. So you will find that these six have a more general use.

Barker, L. (1984): *Communication*. New Jersey: Prentice-Hall (see Chapter 5).

Gergen, K. and Gergen, M. (1986): *Social psychology*. New York: Springer Verlag (see chapter 3).

Glass, L. (1992): *He says, she says – closing the communication gap between the sexes*. London: Piatkus.

Hartley, P. (1993): *Interpersonal communication*. London: Routledge (see chapter 6, Social identity).

Myers, G. and Myers, M. (1992): *The dynamics of human communication*. New York: McGraw-Hill (see chapters 3 and 4).

Rogers, C.R. (1990): *On becoming a person: a therapist's view of psychotherapy*. London: Constable (see chapter 1, This is me).

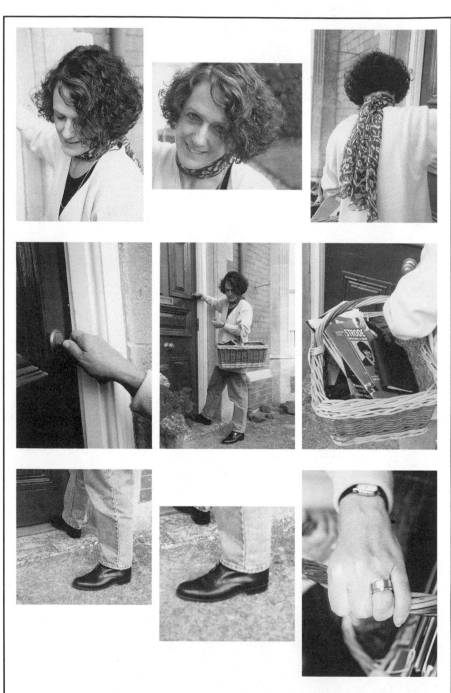

B Perception of Others – we are selective in what we observe and judge

2

Perception of Others

> It is impossible to interact with people and not try to make sense of their actions and to anticipate how they are likely to behave in the future.
>
> Richard D. Gross: *Psychology: the science of mind and behaviour* (1992).

1 INTRODUCTION

1.1 Perception as Communication

It is a truism to say that we perceive people as part of the communication process – a process within the process. But this **perception of other people is not,** begging a few questions, **a natural process.** The great weight of evidence shows that we learn to notice some things more than others about people, and that we learn to make sense of what we have learnt. So what follows is substantially a description of what we have learnt to do, why, and with what effect.

It should be clear that **perception involves internal and external communication activities.** Internal activities, in which information is categorized and meanings about the other person are deduced, are, strictly, intrapersonal communication. This has been dealt with in Chapter 1, but will be expanded upon in this chapter to the extent that it relates to how we understand other people. External activities are the behaviours of the two people involved in an interaction. Most of these behaviours are verbal and non-verbal communication. When we perceive someone, these are what we note when looking for meanings. The internal and the external communication co-exist as one in the whole communication process.

The quotation above draws attention to the importance of communication activities. We are indebted to the work of social psychologists referred to in this chapter. All the same, it is true that much of their work is concerned with cognitive processes, with evaluation and judgement. We will look at these elements, but would also wish to see them as part of the whole process of communication. Ultimately, it is the acts of communication which count. Meaning is in the communication. Medium and message are intertwined.

Perception cannot take place unless there is communication activity to assess. Research into how people perceive others also depends on observing the communication of perceiver and perceived, and on asking perceivers to communicate about their perceptions of others. So we would ask you to remember that behind what follows is always the reality of active communication – a dynamic interplay of verbal and non-verbal signals which is the only hard evidence that perception and communication is taking place.

It is also worth remembering, without devaluing language, that **non-verbal signals are pre-eminent in perception.** We are talking about judgements made about other people's attitudes, personality and emotional state. There is every evidence that non-verbal behaviour dominantly carries messages about these three items. It has been shown that people read this behaviour even while, say, they are listening to a reasoned explanation. They will believe what non-verbal behaviour 'tells them', however much the speaker may be trying to use words which run counter to this.

Perception is not only about communication that is happening, it is also about communication that is about to happen. This is so because **we make perceptual judgements in order to anticipate the behaviour (including communication) of others, and in order to plan our own communication in the conversation as it unfolds.**

Perception of other people is obviously different from our perception of objects or the natural world. In this chapter we shall explore ways of explaining how we perceive others as part of the process of interpersonal communication.

Before we embark on this we wish to emphasize that although perception of people is different from perception of things or animals, the personal mental and emotional processes are basically the same and consist of three principal stages:

- **Selection:** we select certain features or characteristics from all the possible ones for our attention.
- **Organization:** we seek to organize our sensory information into a meaningful whole.
- **Inference:** we form judgements based on previous experience, etc. which may for instance lead us to stereotypical or erroneous conclusions.

We shall explore these aspects of perception in the following sections.

The internal perception processes of 'selection . . . organization . . . inference . . . ' happen very fast unless we make deliberate efforts to control them. We can of course learn to handle our perception of others more consciously, but it is not easy:

> Try as we might to avoid hasty judgements, at first meetings we assess people by how they look. Body shape, facial features, hairstyle, dress and adornment all influence our impression and affect the way we react. By

influencing our assessment of personality and character, they may even affect the way we first interpret what the other person says and does.

We may find later, of course, that our first impressions were wrong – the apparently straight-laced matron might turn out to be a fun loving lady with liberal attitudes, or the seemingly radical young man with long hair may be a trainee lawyer with quite conservative views.

But we deceive ourselves if we think we can postpone our opinions about others until all possible information is in, and we presume too much if we expect others to disregard our appearance . . .

This extract from *Eye to eye: how people interact* edited by Peter Marsh stresses that we inevitably make quick assessments of appearance which lead to inferences about the Self within the appearance. It is a comprehensive, easy to read and well illustrated book that explores some of the ways we express ourselves and perceive other people. The point in the above extract that perception between people meeting is *two-way* is significant – the behaviour of the person you are looking at will change according to how she or he is reacting to you.

Those reactions and interactions and the meanings that are placed on them are also very much culturally determined.

As the stereotypes noted in the extract above show, phases that come to mind like 'straight-laced' with its Victorian corsetry resonances and 'young man with long hair' with its 1960s Beatles inspired swinging Britain resonances can determine how we view and categorize other people. There are cultural expectations that one can follow or flout, consciously or unconsciously. That is comparatively easy within the culture in which you have grown up and been 'socialized' where you know the expected codes of dress and appearance and non-verbal behaviour.

However, in intercultural meetings these first impressions can be very difficult for all involved. There are cultural differences of varying degrees in our behaviour patterns, and hence in our perceptual expectations, in personal appearance and personal expression as well as social customs such as:

• Body language: for example, southern Italians use what seem to British people rather large gestures to illustrate their speech; or comfortable distance in a conversation (what is called 'proxemics') varies between cultures so that what seems the natural distance for a Latin American person may feel very close and intrusive to a North American.
• Facial expression: for example, although smiling or eyebrow raising may be universally used signs they will be controlled in different ways according to what is considered appropriate. Stereotypically, the British male will maintain a 'stiff upper lip' so as not to show either extreme of happiness or sadness which perhaps reflects a cultural process that seeks to avoid extremes of emotion. The novelist, E. M. Forster, who challenged some of these stereotypes in the early part of the 20th century and explored cultural differences between

Britain and India and Italy quotes an Indian friend, who seemed to be showing an excess of emotion to British eyes, 'Is emotion like a sack of potatoes to be weighed out accordingly to need?'.

- Eye contact: for example, people from Arab or Latin American cultures will make and expect more direct eye contact than western Europeans which can lead to inferences that the other person is either insulting or stand offish.
- Contact: for example, touching is a powerful form of communication since it is used to express close personal affection, if the touching is considered too personal it can feel threatening or harassing. We tend to talk about some cultures being a more 'contact culture' than others – one researcher observed 180 touches on average between pairs of acquaintances spending an hour together in Puerto Rico and 110 in France, in Florida the average was less than 2 and in England it was nil.

With such differences, there is plenty of scope for misunderstanding when people from different cultures meet for the first time. Hence, there are training programmes for international visitors to learn what to expect to cope with what has been called 'culture shock' – a state of shock resulting from different behaviour patterns and languages.

1.2 Issues Raised

We wish to fasten on three issues before moving on to the main part of this chapter.

One is concerned with the dynamic nature of communication and interaction. The issue is about the difficulty of dealing with perception of people, when **people are not actually fixed objects for our evaluation.** When one considers the shifts in attitude and feelings that people may experience during a conversation, the wonder is that another person is able to perceive them with any accuracy at all. As we shall see, all of us certainly do make a lot of mistakes in evaluating others.

Another issue concerns the evaluation itself. It is assumed that we are looking at perception as it reflects on a view of another person. But in fact **whatever judgements we may make of someone else also say something about ourselves.** They may say something about our personality and predispositions. The fact that we judge someone else to be happy or sad may just be a reflection of our own mood.

The third issue concerns reality. We have already pointed out in Chapter 1 how physical and social reality are constructs in the mind, and are one element in a description of Self. The question is, what are we dealing with when we perceive others? It could be said that we are dealing with social reality, not simply a process of making judgements. People and our relationships with them are the main part of our social world. So **perception is fundamental to the construction of social reality.**

KEY QUESTIONS

Perception as communication

Make a list of some of the intrapersonal and interpersonal communication processes which are likely to occur when you meet someone for the first time.

Using the photographs on pages 46 and 188, from the appearance and expressions of those people in the photos describe their personality, attitudes, emotion and attributes as you perceive them. Then, if possible, compare your description with someone else's who had done the same task.

How would you use this section on perception to influence your behaviour when you meet someone for the first time whom you wish to impress?

2 WHY DO WE PERCEIVE OTHERS?

The question is not quite as naive as it seems. There are several answers to it. They emerge from the fact that perceiving other people is not a straightforward business of looking and understanding, nor is it a skill that one is born with. If one remembers that perception is about making judgements on the basis of sensory evidence about the other person, then it is the reasons why we feel the need to make these judgements which are significant. So here follows quite a list of reasons. . . .

2.1 To Remember Information

Perception is an active process. We remember experiences that we are actively engaged in, hence, the belief in learning by doing. But also (to anticipate section 4 of this chapter) it is clear that we organize the information which we trawl in. We organize it into units under headings as it were. And there is some evidence (Markus, 1977) that such organization does help us remember. So we are perceiving in order to make sure that we remember what the other person has said and has non-verbalized.

2.2 To Make Sense of the Other Person's Behaviour

It follows from the above that we are not only storing, but we are also categorizing. We are trying to deduce meaning from communication signs as to what the other person may be thinking and feeling. In particular, as will be explained in more detail later, we are trying to make sense of the other person in terms of their emotional state, their personality, and their attitudes towards us.

2.3 To Organize Social Understanding

Because we perceive many people in our lives, we build up a sense not only of individuals whom we are dealing with, but also of people in general. This is not to say that the sense we make of people, of their behaviour, is always accurate. But, as far as it goes, this is our understanding of social relationships and of social behaviour. It helps us deal with people if we believe that we do understand them in terms of their motivation, their orientation towards ourselves, their likely behaviour. This understanding through perception depends not just on individual cues that others give us about what they are like. It depends on the organizing power of perception. We understand one communication sign in the context of others. We understand one trait of personality in the context of others perceived. We put traits together to make sense of them. We organize these traits and our understanding of them around certain key elements perceived, such as the degree of friendliness or hostility which the other person appears to feel towards us. So, as the seminal work of Asch (1946) suggests, our interpretation of friendly cues depends on many other cues perceived. For example, it might be that a person is understood to be rather hostile towards us. In this case, a sign of friendliness will be perceived as hypocritical, and will actually deepen our sense of that person's untrustworthiness.

2.4 To Predict Other's Behaviour

We want to know what will happen next in any given interaction. We want to know how the other person may react to what we are going to say. Indeed there is some evidence that people perceive others with rather more interest in predicting their behaviour than in explaining why they are behaving the way they do. So there is a view which says that we perceive in order **to explain the behaviour of others**. But then one immediately asks, why do we want to explain the communicative actions of the other person? This leads us back to prediction and to the other answers that we are now giving.

2.5 To Plan Our Own Communication

If we believe that we understand the other person, and can predict how they will react to us, then it is possible to organize our own communication so that the interaction proceeds the way we want it to. It is very likely that we will want a conversation to proceed in a friendly manner. So we believe that we can aid that smooth progress through careful perception. To this extent a subsidiary reason for perception is indeed **to help effective communication**. But do notice that this follows from the ability to predict.

You may notice here that this planning and conduct of the interaction is also to do with **feedback**. We may indeed give feedback to the other person so that they will perceive us as we wish to be perceived, and so that the conversation will proceed satisfactorily for both people involved. It will be seen that perception is certainly not merely a 'watchful' activity in which one person pulls in information about the other person. It is part of communication as a dynamic activity. We are aware that others perceive us. There is, as it were, a dynamic exchange of perceptions in a conversation, where each person is continually monitoring the other and themselves, and continuously adjusting their communication according to social conventions and their own purposes.

2.6 To Maintain Our Self, Our Reality

It needs to be remembered that there is self-perception as well as perception of others. And others are part of that world of social reality which is in ourselves and in our heads. So by checking our understanding of other people we are also checking ourselves. We see ourselves in relation to others, so we have to check them to check ourselves.

2.7 To Reduce Anxiety

Putting it at its most basic, a world without structure is a world without meaning, and this is disturbing. Communication, in general, helps order the world. The physical sciences, for example, make sense of the physical world by labelling, relating, and explaining phenomena. We do the same thing when we perceive other people. We would be very anxious if we did not understand other people. It would be disturbing if their behaviour was apparently meaningless and unpredictable. This is why most of us find it unsettling to deal with people who are mentally disturbed, or drunk or drugged. We can't make sense of their behaviour. They make us anxious. Most of the time we can, through perception, allay anxiety by categorizing the communicative behaviour of others. We can assume reasons for their behaviour. We can guess how it may affect us. As Gahagan (1984) says, we want to believe that we can understand others. This creates a stable and predicable view of the world. The fact that our understanding often proves to be inaccurate is another matter.

2.8 To Satisfy Needs

The motivating force of needs and their satisfaction is behind all communication. Needs have been discussed already. In this case, one is concerned especially with human needs to relate to others and to be recognized by them. It is worth picking up the ideas of William Schultz (1958), with reference to interpersonal communication, and to his description of three types of need.

■ Schultz: Three Needs

The first is described as **inclusion**. This need refers to the idea of wanting to enter into relationships, of being interested in others. Clearly one cannot enter into a relationship without making some assessment of the other person so that one interacts with them appropriately. Perception becomes an essential activity if productive interaction is to take place.

The second need is to **control**. This is about being in control of oneself and being able to make decisions. It may lead to dominance in a relationship, or to leadership behaviour. But it does not have to be about 'bossiness'. It includes the idea of recognizing the other person's need to control. Unless perception takes place, such needs cannot be recognized, and balance in interaction or a relationship cannot be achieved. Both people have to represent their need and the fact that they are in control through communication.

Thirdly, there is the need for **affection**. This is particularly about dyadic relationships in which a pair of people want to love and be loved. Whether one is talking about friendship or caring or loving, these terms and the need behind them have no basis in reality unless communication takes place. Whatever the faults of our perceptions, whatever the limitations of words and of non-verbal behaviour as means of conveying needs and feelings, they are all we have got. We have to signal affection through eye and body contact, or through statements about our feelings towards the other person, or they will never know that we care. **Perception (and the communication associated with it) is the bridge between one person and another.**

KEY QUESTION

Why do we perceive others?
Select three of the purposes listed and give two examples of each to illustrate how it might work.

3   WHAT DO WE PERCEIVE?

In the first place one should remember that perceiving is itself described through a number of other terms. Those are, **making evaluations, passing judgements, attributing cause and responsibility, inferring personality traits.** More will be said about inference and attribution in the next section.

These statements begin to answer the key question. But first we need to acknowledge **the double nature of perception, that is, the sensory and cognitive elements.** Perception is about absorbing information through the senses on the one hand, whether the original stimulus is some verbal statement or a gesture from the other person. But then it is also about making sense of these stimuli. We tend to fuse these two activities, the interpersonal and intrapersonal, in our consciousness. When we fuse them, we tend to talk about someone's attitude towards us, as if this is as physically obvious as, say, the rude gesture that they are making. But it isn't. The gesture as signifier may be there for all to see. But the signified, the meaning, depends on how we choose to read the gesture. There is a lot that we may take for granted about perception that we should not.

So the first answer to the key question is that **we perceive verbal and non-verbal signs.**

The second answer is that we believe that **we perceive meanings in those signs.**

What follows is an elaboration of the second answer. These other answers are also best understood if one substitutes the word 'evaluate' for perceive. We are not seeing something that is given. We are weighing up qualities and motives in the other person which we think that we see, but which in effect have been constructed in our heads.

3.1 Personality, Attitude, Emotion

We perceive and evaluate these three key elements, which may be described as three dimensions of the other person.

■ Personality

Personality is usually referred to in terms of traits. These may themselves be described in opposing pairs such as generous–mean, dominant–submissive, and so on. Personality is inferred not only from behaviour, but also from physical characteristics, over which we have little or no control. So, females with full lips are thought to be warm-hearted and generous; tall people may be assumed to have more status or dominance. These assumptions are based on readings which are usually culture-specific. They are also affected by other characteristics and by the time over which perception takes place. So, given time, we may modify judgements. However, the importance of such judgements lies in the fact that we do not always have the time to make corrections (job interviews), and the fact that there is, nevertheless, evidence of a tendency for first impressions to stick to some degree. We will say more about this in the next three sections.

■ Attitude

Attitude is defined in terms of our orientation towards the other person, what we feel about them. Crucial dimensions of attitude are the hostile–friendly pairing, which has obvious significance in primitive survival situations, where one wishes to know if the other animal is for us or against us. Again, relevant non-verbal behaviour is often culture-specific, and may be represented through unconscious habits which we pick up in early years, for all kinds of reasons. For example, someone who stands relatively close to others and orientates his body directly towards them may do this because he comes from Middle Eastern cultures where, by convention, this is acceptable. In North Europe and

America this will be seen as aggressive and intimidating to a degree. It is the kind of behaviour that someone may even have learnt to adopt simply because it satisfies their power needs and has been found by them to help in winning arguments and generally getting what they want. This won't make such a stance any the more agreeable for those who have to deal with it, and this person will still be perceived as hostile or aggressive or pushy.

■ Emotion

Emotion is very difficult to describe, however sure we all think we are about what words such as sad–joyful, excited–depressed mean. It seems to be something like **a state of high or low arousal, in which we are positively or negatively orientated towards ourselves.** What evidence there is suggests that we define emotion in others by defining it in ourselves. That is to say, we perceive ourselves as offering certain non-verbal cues when we are experiencing an inward state that we have learnt to label jealousy or love. We assume that when others are offering the same cues these mean the same thing for them. This is not necessarily so. Once more, there is the same possibility of inferring emotional states in others from cues over which they have relatively little control. You may have heard someone described as a 'miserable looking devil'. What the speaker may mean is that the other person has been born with downward tucks at the side of the mouth. By the same token, someone may have strong eyebrows which meet in the middle and which are taken to signify ill temper. So, with respect to emotion, as with other elements that we evaluate, there is room for a deal of error.

3.2 Attributes

This term can be confusing in the ways that it is actually used by commentators. Since, strictly, it refers to anything which we attribute to the other person, it could be taken to refer to personality traits or any of the other items in the previous section. But there are also elements which the previous headings do not properly cover, such as cleverness–stupidity, or wealthy–poor, all of which are things we do perceive in others. Here, too, non-verbal cues can be crucial. Assumptions are made that a natural characteristic such as a high forehead signifies intelligence.

■ Abilities and Habits

The term attributes may be also taken to cover items such as **abilities or habits,** which we also like to infer from the appearance and behaviour of others. Habits are of course repetitious communication behaviours which become characteristic of the person perceived. They can be verbal – *sort of*, or non-verbal – *um, er*. Abilities might be exemplified by a judgement that a person is articulate or artistic. The former is clearly shown through communication activity. In the case of the latter, one might judge actions or might make inferences from the appearance of hands and their gestural use in conversation. Long slender hands used frequently may be taken to be artistic by at least some people.

3.3 Roles

We evaluate people's roles. We try to work out what kind of person we are dealing with in social terms. In effect, **we are trying to read items that have to do with class, status, occupation, family position, social grouping and the like.** Roles imply categories in themselves, and the perception is all about categorizing people. Role has attached to it not only the notion of some social slot and some social relationship with other people, but also the assumption of certain behaviours. Once we have categorized someone in this way and have made all these associations, we are in a good position to plan our interaction with them. Sometimes this planning may be rapid and nearly reflexive, sometimes there may be a degree of consciousness about it. To take one instance, it might be that a female at some social gathering initiates conversation with a male. But, as with all male–female encounters, both people want to know about the roles and social orientation. So the woman will notice communication behaviour which might, for example, cause her to assign the role of husband to the male. Obvious signs could be the wearing of a ring, or references to family life. Less obviously, she may attribute the role on the basis of apparent age combined with dress combined with a degree of restraint in body language. Once she has categorized the male role, she will feel able to organize her own communication accordingly, and indeed will feel happier about the whole interaction.

3.4 Social Reality

It also follows from the last paragraph that, in a broad sense, we are evaluating social reality when we perceive people. **Our collective perception of people adds up to making a map of social relationships, bound by beliefs about those relationships.** Certain individuals – family and friends – figure largely in our map of social reality. Communication with them, perception of them, is a way of checking and updating that map. The importance of this cannot be over-emphasized, because this internalized view of reality is the only reality we have. Perception and its associated communication activities do, as it were, mediate between this internal reality and whatever is going on externally.

3.5 Cause and Motive

When perceiving others we try to evaluate the true causes of their behaviour. If someone shows friendliness towards us not only do we have to perceive their communication as being friendly, but we then have to decide what this tells us about them. We may not take this behaviour at face value. We may not make the assumption, friendly face equals friendly attitude. If we do assume that we are looking at a friendly face, and that this stands for a friendly attitude within the person, then we are making an **internal attribution** of motive. But if we have other information which suggests that this person is being friendly because they have been told to be pleasant to us by a friend (perhaps because things have been going badly for us), then we will make an **external attribution**. We will assume that the cause of the communication is outside that person rather then inside. We may feel unable to attribute genuine friendliness to that other person.

This example effectively reminds one that the construction of meaning through communication depends on a great number of factors apart from the immediate signs of communication being offered. It depends on such factors as context and previous knowledge of the person whom one is dealing with.

3.6 The Unexpected – Predictability

There is evidence (Weiner, 1985) that **what we choose to perceive is often the unexpected** – and here again we then look for causes. So if we have just started a conversation with someone at a social gathering and they suddenly look round and walk away we will look for the cause of this unexpected behaviour. It may well be that we will perceive them as lacking in proper social orientation and social skills. In 'explaining' their behaviour we have accommodated it within our view of social reality. We have 'made sense of it'. We have made an attribution that does, as it were, restore the *status quo*. Eiser refers to this behaviour and quotes Heider (1958) – '*Attribution serves the attainment of a stable and consistent environment . . . and determines what we expect will occur and what we should do about it*'. This quotation also implies that what we look for in perception is predictability or lack of it. In this case, referring back to the last section, we are not only looking for explanations of what someone may be saying to us, but also for ideas about what they will say and do in the future. The person who walked away from us may be perceived as eccentric and unreliable, and we may feel that we cannot rely on what they will say or do in the future.

KEY QUESTION

What do we perceive?
Describe some of the verbal and non-verbal signs that are used to reveal our attitude to someone else.

4   PERCEIVING AND COMMUNICATING

4.1 Introduction

Having tried to sort out the purpose and the object of perception, now we will look at the process itself. Social interaction, communication, perception are *activities*. The question is, what activities are involved? If we isolate perception from our external communication activity, then it seems that the emphasis must be on reception, decoding and cognitive activities. At the same time, it needs to be remembered that this isolation is very artificial, a matter of intellectual convenience before we look at complete social interaction in the next chapter. So do bear in mind what we have already pointed out – that one reason for perceiving others is to adjust our communication. **Perception leads to external communication activity when we interact with others, as well as to the cognition behind these actions.** The analysis and description in this chapter is like dealing with the process in slow motion. In real life the interplay is very rapid, and the judgements that we make of the other person, and how to proceed with interaction, occur as rapidly as the verbal and non-verbal behaviours. It has been found that expression can shift up to five times a second, and all those shifts will be perceived and assessed, however much at a subconscious level. We make '*inferences about another person based on visible or audible behaviour*' (Argyle, 1973).

4.2 First Impressions

These are perceptions that occur at the beginning of an interaction. There is inconsistent evidence about the importance of these, in terms of fixing judgements about the other person. It is true that some people talk firmly about the importance of such impressions, and actually boast of their ability to perceive people accurately and quickly (though there is also every evidence that we are not good at doing this!). Some research throws up evidence of a 4-minute period in which judgements are made that are then hard to eradicate. Equally, it is true that extended interaction does allow first impressions to be modified.

But one also needs to bear in mind that in many situations there is not the opportunity to spend more than a short period of time perceiving the other person. For example, some job interviews last only 20 minutes, as may interviews for undergraduate places. So there can be important outcomes from first impressions. Berger (1974) says:

> We believe that the first few minutes of verbal and non-verbal communication between strangers may determine, at least under some conditions, whether persons will be attracted to each other, and by implication, whether the persons in the interaction will attempt to communicate at a future time.

There are many other examples of social and work situations in which we have to form judgements rapidly, from limited information. We are very prepared to do this, even if we don't know what that person's 'normal' behaviour is like. So a salesperson may be taken at 'face value' in a brief encounter, even though we don't really know how honest or capable they are.

Although we may all agree with the old adage, 'you don't judge a book by its cover', we do tend to judge other people by their appearance especially when we first meet them.

4.3 Symbolic Interaction

We communicate through signs and symbols. Perception, as part of communication in social interaction, depends on identification of signs and on the manufacture of meaning from a combination of signs so identified. Speech is a sequence of phonemes, gesture is a sequence of arm movements, and no more than that until sense is made of the elements (and indeed until the sequence itself is recognized). This is not the place to rehearse a semiotic approach to communication. But if we are talking about perception as a process, and a process in which the participants interact through an exchange of symbols, then it is also true that the meanings constructed through perception come indirectly. Directly we may apprehend the tightening of mouth muscles which we are going to label 'smile'. The cues given by the other person are part of the process. But the sense and meaning of these muscular changes happens indirectly through cognitive processes, once the message has been internalized. There is no truth or reality out there. It is manufactured in our heads. **People are joined by symbols and made real in their minds.**

4.4 Cognitive Process

We have already discussed cognition in the first chapter, with reference to intrapersonal communication. So it will be enough to say that clearly **perception involves a cognitive process in which data received from the other person are combined with data already held about the person or about communicative behaviour in general.** There must be a 'search' element when dealing with the data coming in, in order to find something already held in memory that can be related to that data. What is selected from the data coming in depends on factors such as *saliency*. How these data are organized in the mind may be in terms of structures labelled *schemata*. We will discuss both these terms in a later subsection, once we have looked at overall notions of what the process is about.

4.5 Data and Generalizations

From one point of view, perception is all about information handling. The data are dominantly about the behaviour of the other person (communication) and about the social and physical context (environment) in which the interaction takes place. From the data the perceiver makes inferences and predictions. In making these, the perceiver decides that the behaviour of the other person is produced either by external forces (context) or by internal forces (personality, emotion, attitude, attributes). For example, if you have invited friends around to your house, there might be a couple leaving and one of the two might say how much they had enjoyed themselves, thank you and smile. You might take in the words and non-verbal behaviour, and also take account of the fact that it is after all your party and your doorstep. But then as you rapidly reflected on the words and smiles (and checked that one was not prompting the other to say this!) you might compare this information with what you already knew about them. Then you might say to yourself, *OK from what I can see and hear, and from what I know, I perceive these people as being grateful and friendly – that's fine – I'll be friendly in return.* Data in, data out, and they in their turn will be perceiving you.

■ *Generalizations – Perceptual Sets*

In handling this information we make generalizations. **The generalizations are about what other types of information to attach the new data to, and about how these groups of data hang together.** Stereotyping is a kind of gross generalization in which we might see a man sitting in a cafe wearing paint-stained overalls, and immediately make assumptions about his occupation, class, interests, and so on. It is also the case that we appear to have a type of cognitive structure called **perceptual sets**. These sets are kinds of pre-formed patterns in the mind which incline us to handle information in certain ways. In the case of our man at the cafe, it would be the sets for clothes and for male which would be the reference points for dealing with the data that were there, and also for guessing at information that was not there. The guesses are assumptions. Sometimes they are right, sometimes wrong. It is very useful to be able to make generalizations – it is helpful to be able to predict. But it can also cause us to fall into all kinds of errors.

■ *Redundancy*

This guessing illustrates that principle of **redundancy**. Sometimes information is redundant (or we believe it is redundant). We can make guesses from the information that we do have. We can fill in gaps in our knowledge. This is the principle behind those aptitude tests that you may have taken years ago, where you had to fill in the missing numbers in a series, to see if you could perceive the numerical pattern. Unfortunately, people don't have the regularity of numbers. For example, parents may sometimes be guilty of saying things like, *I don't want to hear any more excuses about that broken window. It's clear what happened. You look as guilty as hell!* The unfortunate child might not have broken the window!

4.6 Distinctiveness, Consistency, Consensus

It has been suggested by Kelley in particular (1967, 1971) that when we are handling data **in perception we are actually looking for ways in which that person's behaviour does or does not stand out in some way.** In the first place what they say and do may be seen as either **distinctive** or not. If not, we may describe it as fitting a **consensus,** an agreement with the way that person or others usually behave in that situation.

Consistency can be judged in three ways – in terms of the consistency of someone's behaviour over a period of time; in terms of the consistency of their behaviour in similar situations; in terms of the consistency of their behaviour when compared with others in similar situations. So if someone says to you – *Oh, do shut up!* – you will have to decide if this is consistent with the way they usually talk, or consistent with the way they have responded before when, perhaps, you have tried to provoke them, or consistent with the way other people respond at times of provocation. McArthur (1972) suggests that if such an utterance is not very distinctive and is consistent in one of the three ways given above then you will put it down to an internal condition, and say to yourself, that person is just feeling irritable. But if that phrase was distinctive, then you might look for external causes, and might perceive that person as, perhaps, 'having problems'.

4.7 Validation of Perception

Myers and Myers (1992) refer more or less to the ideas of consistency and consensus when they define five ways in which we check data for validity (and by implication for meaning and action). Their list is useful and self-explanatory.

■ *Validation Type Method*
- Consensual   By checking with other people.
- Repetitive   By checking with yourself by repeating the observations.
- Multisensory   By checking with yourself by using other senses.
- Comparative   By checking your past experiences with similar but not necessarily identical perceptions.
- Experimental   By acting on the basis of your perceptual theories as if they were correct and checking the consequences of your actions by comparing them with what you guessed would happen.

4.8 Perception as Stimulus – Response (S–R)

A classic behavioural model to explain perception would see it as a way of responding to external stimuli. March and Simon's (1958) model (see Fig. 2.1) would regard the communicative behaviour of the person and the context as providing the stimuli. These stimuli are dealt with internally. Within the Self are internal states that have been learnt. In particular there is the content of the

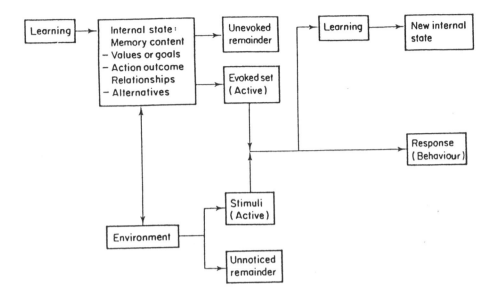

Fig 2.1 *March and Simon's model of perception in terms of behaviour (March and Simon, 1958)*

memory which includes values, relationships and remembered outcomes of previous interactions. This information in the memory is accessed through sets which are evoked when we try to deal with stimuli internally. Dealing with the stimuli, the new data, results in two things. Internally, we have learnt something from the encounter, so our internal states are changed, however infinitesimally, every time we talk to someone. Externally, we make a behavioural response – we reply to what that other person has said. Two other elements in this model are identified as what is unnoticed in the environment, and what is unevoked in the mind. These phases also relate to the idea of **selective attention**. With regard to the internal state, it does not appear that we evoke some sets as means of structuring information, and leave others dormant. With regard to the external stimuli one needs to question the word 'unnoticed'. We 'notice' everything within the scope of our senses. Whether or not it then gets filtered out through the process of perception is another matter. Clear evidence of this filtering is provided by the way in which one is capable of tuning in and out conversations overheard in some public place.

The problem with S–R theory is that it is rarely as predictive as it would like to be. The number of variables in a given situation, in the communication of the one who is perceived, and in the internal states of the perceiver, are so great that one cannot often be sure of response. Only in ritual situations and those involving redundancy, where there are powerful conventions, does one easily see S–R operating at all clearly. In the region familiar to the authors, the stimulis – *How're you doing, then?* will almost invariably meet with the response – *Not so bad, thanks. And you?*

4.9 Attribution

Attribution theory is well established with relation to perception and cognition. It is much based on the work of Heider, and **assumes that people are inclined to see their environment as predictable and controllable.** Predictability depends on identifying causes of events or behaviour. Some causes may be external to the other person, existing within the social and physical context. Some causes may be internal, lying within the person or people perceived. By reading people's behaviour we may be able to infer what it is in them that has caused that behaviour. And so one returns to the point that what is attributed may be described as personality traits, for example. Heider says:

> Attributions in terms of impersonal and personal causes, and with the latter, in terms of intent, are everyday occurrences that determine much of understanding of and reaction to our surroundings.

■ *Intentionality*

The problem of intentionality is a knotty one. We have already explained that, given the correct information, we may perceive someone's communication and actions as being caused by their environment. Someone who is under stress and snaps at us may be judged relatively favourably because of known conditions which are creating that stress. But it is not possible to make a glib distinction between internal and external attributions. We may just as easily say of someone who gives us a hard time at work – *I know he's been under a lot of strain lately, but all the same, there's no excuse for him being so irritable.* In other words we are attributing at least some blame internally. We are inferring that the person does have the trait of ill temper. There are also instances in which we will not know of external factors which have affected someone's behaviour. There will be non-verbal behaviours in particular that the other person will not be aware of, that will not be conscious and intentional. But if the behaviour is there to be perceived then we can and will still make attributions. The Self which is hidden from the speaker may not be hidden from others. So it could be that someone offers signs of displaced anxiety such as repetitive face touching or hair pulling which they are not aware of. The perceiver can still attribute anxiety to that person.

■ *Information and Discrimination*

Accurate perception and sound inferences depend on sound information and good discrimination. If we know people well and know a lot about their background, then we are more likely to make accurate judgements than if we don't.

If we check information about the other person (perhaps through reflective listening) and question the validity of what we perceive, then again we are more likely to make accurate inferences. **Rapid assumptions based on limited information are the least reliable acts of perception.** If you encourage someone to talk, and listen and watch them carefully, then you are more likely to get a better picture of their attitudes, beliefs, and emotions than if you do all the talking.

■ Deception

Attribution is also complicated by the fact that **people may wish you to perceive them in a certain way** (see Chapter 4 on Self-Presentation). For example, in public and social situations people may be quite good at keeping up their mask. They will wish to be perceived as cheerful, sociable and attractive. In other situations they may be different. Girl may perceive boy as humorous, considerate and cheerful when they go out together. Whether he is like this all the time is another matter.

■ Stable Attributes

Argyle and Trower (1979) refer to **stable attributes** and remind one that our inferences may be about stable, long-term characteristics of, say, belief or ability, but they could also be about temporary conditions. Again, unless one perceives the other person over a period of time, one has no way of knowing if one's inference about stable attributes is in fact correct. If we first meet someone who appears to be depressed, we have no means of knowing whether or not they are usually optimistic and cheerful. This provides yet another argument for reserving judgement as long as possible.

■ Influence of Self

Then there is the question of Self and the **influence of Self on attribution.** When we perceive others we are not some analytical machine. We are human, dealing with humans. **Our own moods, experiences, values may predispose us to make selective inferences about others.** Indeed, as we will explain in the last section of this chapter, we are too often inclined to assume that others think and feel as we do. The process of perception, the act of attribution, occurs in a complex interplay between participants in the interaction and their environment. For the other person being perceived, we are part of their social environment. How we behave affects them. If we were to perceive someone as being relatively unfriendly, it might be that our own communication behaviour is the real cause of theirs. The interviewer who bids the interviewee to enter with a curt *Come in* and a preoccupied frown (first impressions!), may cause that person to respond at least with restraint. Perhaps the interviewer will end up with notes reading – *Rather nervous. Not very friendly. Not likely to impress our clients if employed.* Apart from offering inappropriate communication, this interviewer has made false attributions on the basis of poor perception. To this extent, you get what you give.

■ Conclusion

Attribution theory tries to take a logical, structured approach to the making of inferences about other people. Put simply (see Fig. 2.1) it assumes that one sees behaviour as effect, and external conditions and internal states as causes. These causes are inferred with relation to the perceiver's own knowledge and experience, especially knowledge about the person perceived. What is perceived may depend on how distinctive or consistent the behaviour of the other person seems to be.

4.10 Schemata, Categories, Sets

There is general agreement that as we perceive people and make inferences there is, in the internalized part of the communication process, reference made to **cognitive structures which help organize understanding** (see Fig. 2.2). These structures are, it may be supposed, rather like collections of information placed under headings. They help organize the information which the other person is giving us through their communication. We can check that information against the collections, and so look for similarity or difference when making comparisons with previous communication. We can assign that information to one of these collections so that we have more to refer to next time. We can pull out information and combine it with what we are being told (assimilation).

The three terms of this subheading bear a close relationship to one another. We have already described perceptual sets as patterns which incline us to associate one piece of information with another and to use it in certain ways.

There is little effective difference between this and the idea of categories and categorizing. Tajfel and Fraser (1986) argue that having categories and being able to categorize is '*crucial to the general study of perception*'. There are many categories that we may hold in our heads, and even categories within categories. One example that is often discussed because it relates to stereotyping is the category of race. Within this are categories of various races and their attributes, as we have defined and stored them. **Categories also have social values attached to them.** In other words, it may be more desirable or attractive to be placed within one category rather than another. In terms of occupational categories, for instance, there is value attached to being a doctor which is not attached to being a boiler-room attendant. So discrimination between categories is not just based on, for example, physical differences, it is based on notions of worth as well.

■ Basic Perceptual Activities

Tajfel and Fraser (1986) describe **basic perceptual activities** which will serve as another useful account of process – the process of categorizing as part of the process of perception – itself part of the process of communication. These are:

• selecting for closer attention certain aspects of the environment

- identifying a stimulus, an object or an event for 'what it is'
- accentuating certain of its features so that it 'fits' in some important ways one category or another
- neglecting other features which are less important for the 'fit'
- recognizing a familiar object or event on the basis of partial information
- discriminating between objects, again on the basis of partial information, so that appropriate distinctions of category membership can be made between them.

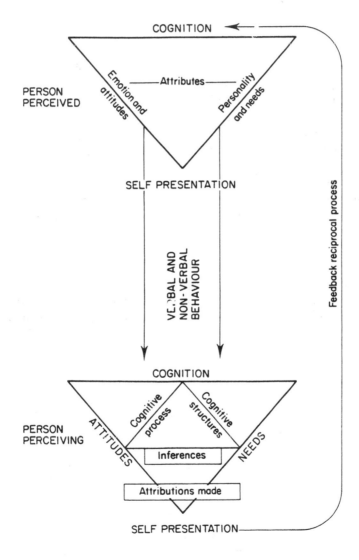

Fig 2.2 *A model for the process of perception*

It will be seen that some emphasis is placed on the fact that **categorizing necessarily means 'distorting' to some degree.** Categories are useful in one sense. But in another sense, their presence causes us to exaggerate or miss out some of the things that we perceive, just so that we can make the categories work. For example, someone may criticize some work that we have done. Their verbal and non-verbal phrasing indicates disagreement and disapproval. In fact their remarks are well founded. But they have criticized our work before, and that of other people we know. Because of this, we not only categorize them in terms of 'orientation' as being hostile, but also we may perceive them as being 'over critical'. If at the end of their analysis they mention some positive features and offer encouragement, we may ignore these comments because they do not fit the attribution made.

Two more points may be drawn from this. One is that perception is continuous, and that we do not wait until the end of an interaction before forming judgements. So categorising will happen early on. It cannot be stopped, only modified in the light of later information.

The other point has to do with negative assignment in categories. In the example given it may well be that because we have already had 'bad experiences' with this supervisor or tutor we are already prejudiced towards them. This will incline us to make negative assignments. A number of researchers including Tajfel (1969) have demonstrated the existence of negative predispositions which cause subjects for example to assign people wrongly to negatively valued racial groups.

■ Schemata

As we have said, the notion of a **schema** is fundamentally the same as the idea of categories. If there is any distinction to be made it is that a schema not only describes a collection of attributes, it also **describes the basis of relationship between those attributes.** It doesn't just assume a list with a heading. However, when you come across the terms in other books you should call them together in your mind. Gergen and Gergen (1986) describe a **schema** as *'cognitive organization of knowledge about a given person, object or stimulus'*. A schema includes in effect beliefs about what binds the attributes within it. Schemata actively help us select from and arrange the information that we are taking in about the other person. We will extend schemata when making inferences, often in terms of reaching a positive or negative evaluation of the other person. Because schemata aid prediction of behaviour there is, once more, a tendency to look for information which confirms our view of that person. If we concentrate on the idea of a schema being a kind of plan for making sense of the other person then there are some remarks we can add to those already made.

One is that there are schemata for people in general, and schemata for types of people, as well as schemata for specific people whom we know. The **schema is both a kind of proposition about people and a predisposition towards them.**

In the first case we can check the validity of our proposition – is *Becky as bouncy as ever today? – oh, yes, she's as cheerful as ever – there's the big smile and the loud good morning.* In the second case we want to confirm the proposition within our schema – *there's Becky – hmm, rather a wan smile – but she said good morning – oh well, she's probably quiet because it's the tenth time she's said it this morning – oh yes, she's as cheerful as ever.*

Gahagan (1984) refers to **schemata as implicit theories of personality.** She suggests that we all carry these theories in our heads and that evidence of them can be obtained from analysis of people's communication. She refers to an unusual piece of research in which Rosenberg and Jones (1972) analysed character descriptions written by the American novelist Theodore Dreiser in one of his books. They concluded that Dreiser was most concerned with whether or not people were male or female, conventional or unconventional. We might conclude that these pairs of factors would predominate in Dreiser's schemata. So Dreiser might have a set of behaviours seen as unconventional. He might also have a set of types of occupation which would be tied to the criteria of conventionality or unconventionality. The principle of having schemata operating within perception as communication takes place remains valid for dealing with real people as much as with fictional characters.

Whether one talks about schemata or categories, it seems possible that they may be tied to key concepts. We have to refer to these words on the page, but do remember, as competent communication students, that really it is only the idea behind the word which exists in our minds. The word itself is merely a sound-symbol that calls up the concept.

The classic experiment in terms of organization of perception around key concepts was conducted by Asch (1946) in which he found that the terms *warm* and *cold* appeared to be crucial when included in a list of personality traits used to describe people. These two words seemed to attract attention and to bias further description of a hypothetical person positively or negatively. As we say, it is not that the words 'warm' and 'cold' exist in the mind, but their meanings do. It is these meanings and their associations which would seem to be important in perception. Certainly the warm–cold opposition would fit with the kind of attitude model proposed by Argyle and others in which one axis is defined in terms of hostility–friendliness.

Although it may seem that some concepts are more important than others, it is still not possible to identify a definitive list of priority terms let alone relate them within some structure. The principle of having and using categories would seem to be acceptable. It is possible to agree about certain main categories such as male–female. But it is not possible to produce a neatly packaged list of everyone's categories and of terms within these, which act as consistent points of reference.

4.11 Stereotypes

This word identifies **a category which we refer to when making inferences about items such as attitude, role, emotion, motive.** The word is often used in an adverse sense, and indeed we will return to it used in this way in the last section. But you should realize that in principle stereotypes need not be a bad thing. They do act as a point of reference, somewhere to start when trying to make sense of people. **They represent especially dominant or important categories with strongly associated elements.** They offer generalizations about a group of traits or attributes, indeed they create the idea of the group being a group. It is the degree of exaggeration and simplification that we will criticize later. But again, commentators such as Brigham (1971) have argued that nevertheless stereotypes of people do have some basis in fact. This is not to defend the intellectually and morally bankrupt uses to which stereotyping is put (you can find examples in the media). But it is to recognize the positive use of associating information and experience when trying to make sense of other people. For example, a stereotype of old people might include the attributes of being doddery and grey haired. Now, if one dealt with people over the age of 60 it might be very arguable as to how doddery they are. But it is likely that a considerable number will in fact be grey haired. And in terms of media stereotyping it can be pointed out that the elderly Miss Marple character created by Agatha Christie in detective fiction runs counter to typing of both old people and of women as being woolly headed and intellectually incompetent. Her perceptions are very acute!

So stereotypes are not bad in principle. They are **salient categories with a high degree of cohesion, and represent powerful cognitive structures** within the process of perception. It is the **social values** attached to categories and stereotypes in particular which cause one to pass judgement on their uses. The value themselves represent a kind of pre-judgement. Making pre-judgements is dangerous – they are assumptions until proved, and may be proved wrong.

4.12 Conclusion

So it is clear that **perception is a process operating as part of communication when we interact with others.** It contains at least two major points of reference. One is the verbal and non-verbal signs offered by the person perceived. The other is the categories within the mind of perceiver. These categories may also be called sets or schemata or stereotypes. These points of reference have to be used by the perceiver. Types of use, or perceptual activity, have been described above. They include selecting, assigning, comparing, integrating. Another common word for describing perception and making sense of others' behaviour is 'attribution'. The categories we refer to are useful for making rapid judgements and for calling up related pieces of information. But they may also lead to bias in the sense that they represent assumptions about what piece of information is connected with what other piece of information. They enable us to make guesses about the internal state of the other person, and to make predictions about how they will continue to behave and communicate. But they also enable us to be lazy. It is easy to make generalizations. There is a certain pressure on us to do this when we are meeting someone for the first time, and we need to make decisions about them quite quickly if we are to carry on interacting successfully. There is another kind of pressure in that communication is dynamic, can proceed rapidly, and offers a great deal of information. It is sometimes difficult to digest the full meaning of what someone had said when they are waiting for a reply, and when both people want to get on with the conversation. Nevertheless, **it is within our powers to reserve judgement and not to jump to conclusions.** If we wish, **we can consciously pay closer attention to what people are saying.** You should refer forward to the section on perceptual skills for a summary of this view that to a degree perception is controllable.

KEY QUESTION

Perceiving and Communication

Using the model on page 67, Fig. 2.2, explain the process of perception of a person who is watching people in the following situations and roles: (1) a model displaying *haute couture* fashions, (2) a teacher in a school class, and (3) a salesperson in an electrical good shop.

5   WHAT AFFECTS PERCEPTION?

This section will look at the main elements which affect how we perceive other people. Some of these ideas have already been referred to because they also relate to earlier topics.

We will look at these factors in terms of **context** – the physical and social environment; **physiology** – the physical competence of participants in the interaction; and **psychology** – mental competence and activity. It is worth remembering that one always comes back to psychological factors because sense and meaning are constructed in the mind.

5.1 Contextual Factors

■ *Physical Context*

In the first place these may be entirely physical. If we go to visit someone not known to us, and see in their house various expensive possessions then we may be inclined to attribute wealthiness to them. There are a great number of possible examples in which physical context is read in terms of cultural symbols. To take one more instance, if one was interviewed for a job in an office that contained little furniture but did have telex links and a desktop computer, then one might make inferences about the traits of the interviewer. That person might be seen as being severely practical, competent in use of technology, and so on. We assume that people create a physical environment around them which is an extension of their personality and their beliefs.

■ Social Context

In the second place, there is the social context. If one has been invited over to someone's house in order to socialize, then in this situation people obey certain conventions of social behaviour. They assume that social rules include making an effort to get to know people and to be pleasant towards them. If people do behave like this then they are more likely to be perceived as friendly than they might be at, say, a business meeting.

■ Spatial Positioning

Perception is also affected by where people place themselves in relation to one another. This aspect of context is know as **spatial positioning**. In this case there are cultural factors which will affect where people stand or sit. To sit directly opposite someone may be taken as a sign of aggression or confrontation. To sit close beside a man if you are a woman may be taken as a sign of invitation. But there are also practical considerations in positioning. If you sit right beside someone it is actually rather difficult to see them. People forced into this situation end up twisting round in their seats to get a better look. So people who are seated perceive and communicate most effectively when they are at an angle of about 90 degrees to one another. When standing, an angle of about 45 degrees is the norm.

5.2 Physiological Factors

These refer to the physical characteristics of the people involved. In the first place these may affect perception in a mechanical sense. If one person is deaf, then they will be denied one channel of communication through which perception takes place. It limits the amount of information that they can receive.

Second, one could be talking about the inherited physical appearance of the person being perceived. People who fit culturally acquired ideals of beauty are seen as more attractive, are perceived more favourably than those who do not. This fact is implicit in the efforts which some people make to change their appearance so that they become more attractive to others. Hence the many occupations and industries such as those of beautician or even plastic surgeon, which are geared to making such physical changes.

The interpretation that we make of physiological factors leads to attribution. There are a great number of studies showing that various physical characteristics lead to particular judgements. For example, dark skinned people tend to be assigned negative attributes by fair skinned people – such as unfriendliness or lack of humour.

Together with physiological factors one might also consider **dress and display signs**. We read things into what people wear. Males who wear dark plain suits are perceived as being more authoritative and reliable than those who do not. Women who wear large or colourful jewellery will be perceived as being more extrovert (and even more 'feminine') then those who do not.

There is a considerable literature on non-verbal communication which you can read in order to extend these examples.

The fact that these signs appear to 'stand out' as being important is discussed below with reference to saliency.

5.3 Psychological Factors

■ Motivation and Predisposition

These factors work in conjunction with those described above. For example the **degree of motivation** that we feel in conducting the interaction will affect how careful or how selective our perception is. This has to do with self-gratification and our personal needs. So, if you are taking a college course which you very much want to pass then you will tend to pay good attention to what is being said by the teachers. If you want to develop a relationship with someone else, then you are likely to perceive their communication, especially in response to your own, with some care.

Unfortunately this will not stop you also having **predispositions**. These are preformed ideas about your Self and about others. These are incorporated within the schemata already referred to. So **perceptual sets** (also already explained) will operate with the effect of predisposing you to read things into the other person's behaviour. A simple example would be where as a male you have a set which incorporates favourable attitudes towards females with dark hair and a sense of humour. When you meet a brunette who laughs a lot you may then have a predisposition to like her.

■ Attraction

This is closely linked with the idea that attraction is an influential factor in perception. If, for the reasons just given, you are attracted towards someone then you are more likely to perceive them favourably than not.

■ Past Experience and Resemblance

The factor of **past experience** is also bound up with attraction, sets, and predispositions. For instance, if you were looking for someone to share an apartment with, then you would probably look for a person who had similar attributes to those of a known friend. If you met someone like this, you would be predisposed to believe that you would get on with them. You would make certain attributions, including those all important predictions. The phrase **resemblance criteria** is also sometimes used to describe details of behaviour and appearance which remind one of some previous experience. If you had to visit a dentist for the first time and that person reminded you of one visited in childhood for a painful extraction, then you might perceive this dentist unfavourably.

■ *Open and Closed Minds*

It is possible to see **open and closed mindedness** as factors which affect perception. Basically, these are about Self, the kind of person you are. If you are very concerned to maintain your view of your Self, then you will be inclined to perceive others only in terms of preserving your self-image. So you might edit out the full effect of critical remarks someone was making about you because this threatened your self-image. This would also be an example of ineffective listening. Equally if you have a secure self-image then you may be more honest in your assessment of what someone else is saying because you can cope with criticism and can accept praise without becoming arrogant.

■ *Role Relations*

Role relations will affect perception for the obvious reason that there are schemata associated with role. If you have to deal with your supervisor at work you will see them in a certain light just because they are your supervisor. You will expect to see certain attributes and behaviours associated with that role. The supervisor might be the same age as yourself, possibly known to have similar interests. But you still would not perceive that person as a potential friend, because you would also have perceived attributes of status and power that you would not associate with friendship.

■ *Saliency*

Saliency describes distinctive characteristics of the other person which will bias the way we collect information about them and the way that we form our judgements. What we consider to be salient depends on the situation and on what we have learnt to consider 'normal' (to be part of the social consensus). The fact remains that we do tend to notice salient features, and that thereafter they incline us to perceive the person in a certain way. For example, it could be that we believe that a beard is a salient feature when perceiving a male. It may be that we have a set with regard to beards, that we make associations with beards. If so, then the recognition of that beard will certainly influence our assessment of that male. Similarly, if someone starts shouting in a business meeting, this may well be perceived as salient communication behaviour. Judgements made by others at the meeting will be dominated by the fact that this person behaved unexpectedly. This also makes the point that unconventional behaviour automatically achieves saliency.

■ *Social Values*

Finally, let us consider **social values** as influential factors. We might also say that it is a matter of convention that some behaviours are preferred to others. Values are indeed about preferences, likes, dislikes, aversions. For instances, someone might converse in what they perceive to be a positive, firm manner. But we might see it as being overbearing. Specifically, we might observe a loud voice, close body proximity, emphatic delivery, assertive gestures. There is a close relationship between the social value placed on such behaviour and the inferences that we will make. If we believe that it is socially inappropriate this is much the same as saying that it is not valued socially. Because it is not valued socially, as well as because it may seem threatening to ourself, we dislike this style of communication and perceive the person unfavourably.

As we approach the end of this chapter, you may think that we have said much that is critical of the way that we perceive others. There does seem to be much room for error and misunderstanding. We shall go on to look at these errors in the next section.

KEY QUESTION

What affects perception?
Compare the importance of context, physiology and psychology as factors affecting interpersonal perception in the following situations:

- between friends meeting for an evening out
- between work colleagues
- between doctor and patient in the surgery.

6   ERRORS IN PERCEPTION

The list of errors that we may make in perceiving others is formidable! So much so, that it is almost a relief to remember that people do manage to communicate successfully with one another in spite of their mistakes. Of necessity we have already at least referred in passing to the various kinds of error that we can perpetrate. Basically, one can say that we do one of four things, separately or in combination.

- We miss out some piece of information.
- We make too much of something.
- We make false connections between one thing and another.
- We guess wrongly about the other person by making false association of traits or of experience.

Most errors in perception can simply be described as false assumptions, as will be seen from what follows. It may also be argued that if perception involves the use of 'labels' and categories, then error is built in to the system. Labelling an example of communication behaviour as meaning one thing tends to exclude it from meaning another. The categories we use may be incomplete. By including some information within a category we are presumably excluding other information.

6.1 Fundamental Attribution Error

This phrase, first used by Ross (1977), refers to **the tendency to attribute cause and blame to people rather than to circumstances**. It means that we really ought to find out about circumstances before forming judgements from what people tell us. Look and listen before jumping to conclusions.

6.2 False Consensus

This error was also tested by Ross (1977) and comes down to **a tendency to assume that other people agree with our own views**. It is part of a general tendency to suppose that others see the world as we do. This kind of perceptual filter is sometimes described as **Projection** – the mistaken projection of one's own values and beliefs onto other people.

6.3 False Consistency

In this case **we tend to assume that the behaviour of other people is more consistent than it is**. It makes it easier to deal with them, easier to predict what they will say and do next if we believe that they are consistent (see Nisbett and Ross, 1980).

6.4 Primacy Effect

This refers to a tendency to fix first impressions and to build on these rather than be open to changing our views of others. There is much evidence of this effect, built on the work of Asch in the 1940s. It has been suggested (Wyer and Srull, 1980) that this effect can be so strong that general impressions of others persist even when we cannot remember what led to the formation of these impressions in the first place. It appears that this effect may result from our desire to create a schema for another person and then to look for information that builds upon it. This initial creation of a schema may also be described as a **priming effect**. Hodges (1974) draws attention to the fact that negative first impressions seem to be stronger than positive ones, harder to get rid of or modify. This has some relationship to the strength of norms and values – someone whose behaviour is distinctly antisocial or unfitting to an occasion really sticks in our minds. Once more, the lesson seems to be that one should hold back from making snap judgements, and consciously look for information to modify first impressions.

6.5 Halo Effect

This bears close comparison with the primacy effect. It describes a **tendency to privilege one piece of information above others when forming an impression of someone**. The curious thing is that in some ways it seems to work the other way from the primacy effect in that in this case it is a positive factor that is sociably desirable which creates the halo and blots out clear judgement of other elements of behaviour. For example, if one perceives a member of the opposite sex to have looks, possessions, or even something as specific as a hair style which the perceiver believes is socially desirable, then this will cloud perception, and influence judgement of other characteristics. Other elements will be ignored or re-interpreted in the light of what is seen immediately to be an attractive and dominant feature. Again, there seems to be a dangerous tendency to see what one wants to see, rather than what is actually there.

6.6 Recency Effect

This bears some comparison with the primacy effect. Simply, this describes the alternative **tendency for people to perceive others in terms of the last thing that they have said or done**. Perhaps at the end of an argument the other person will say to you – *and I don't want to talk to you again unless you are prepared to apologize.* This last sentence may well prey on your mind. The issue of apology will be the one that dominates your perception of what the argument was about. It is well known in terms of communication practice that people tend to remember best information which comes at the beginning and at the end of the communication.

6.7 Preconceptions and Predispositions

Although we have described these already, **the effect of our internal states** is so powerful that it bears repetition and expansion. For instance even while we may be perceiving the **emotional state** of the other person, we ourselves will be in a certain emotional state. Moods of elation or depression will certainly affect how we interpret the cues given off by the other person. If we are much obsessed with how we feel then this will cause us to screen out cues from the other person. In colloquial terms, if we are feeling very sorry for ourselves then we may not be perceptive enough to see why we should feel sorry for someone else.

Cultural bias is another kind of preconception. We grow up within a culture and perhaps within a subculture in which certain kinds of behaviour are considered 'normal'. Normality is relative. Our idea of social reality is relative to our upbringing. It is notorious that the English are perceived as being 'cold' people, and that they perceive many other cultures (Italians for example) as being noisy and excitable. It has been demonstrated that indeed the English specifically gesture less than the Italians and offer far less body contact. This does not make one or the other kind of communication behaviour right or wrong. But it does explain how culture can distort perception if one is not aware of what is happening and does not consciously try to modify one's judgements. In these cases one should not fall into the trap of seeing what are only conventions of communication as reality. **The conventions of behaviour change from culture to culture.**

We will also have **pre-formed attitudes** as part of our schemata (discussed above). These cause us to interpret the other person's words and actions according to the beliefs and values which are associated with these attitudes. Attitudes can be triggered even by small details of behaviour, and like all pre-dispositions may be associated with stereotyping. For example, someone may have a habit of tapping their teeth with a pencil while they are trying to work out a problem. This repetitive behaviour causes you irritation because it breaks concentration. Your reaction may be summed up as – *I can't stand people who tap their teeth like that* – and then you begin to look for other things that you don't like about that person!

6.8 Self-Fulfilling Prophecy

You will remember that we have already referred to this in the first chapter. But it is worth reminding yourself that this is very much an example of communication in action. It describes what happens when we act on our perceptions. If we perceive someone to be pleasant and friendly, then we treat them accordingly. This means that they in turn get positive feedback from us. So they are even more inclined to be pleasant and friendly. If they do behave like this then our original assessment is confirmed – what we prophesied has been fulfilled.

6.9 Stereotyping

You can also refer back to the last section for other information on this way of making some categories more dominant then others. Stereotypes are quick, simple ways of classifying people. They are harmless if used only as a temporary rule of thumb, but lethal if taken as the last word on another person. Stereotyping usually starts with identification of a few salient non-verbal signs such as dress or expression. Then, by rapid association within the category, judgement passes on to make assumptions about that person's attributes and beliefs. Common stereotypical categories may be labelled in terms of race, age, gender, class. **What is lethal about stereotyping is the speed and intensity of the assumptions and predictions that are made about the other person on a slender basis.** These assumptions and predictions are also too often critical of that person. The associative power of stereotypes is such that we 'know' that women are no good with technology, that Russians are out to take over the world, and so on. Of course we don't know anything of the sort. But an associated problem is that of the self-fulfiling prophecy, because if women are treated as it they are incompetent at handling technology then they will perceive themselves as being like that. A rather neat vicious circle!

Stereotypes are such extreme generalizations about people that they miss out the individual variations, they ignore the gradation of attributes. One example of such simplistic judgements was seen by the authors recently in an English pub – a notice said, *Hippies cannot be served here*. We never did find out what it was that made the owner feel unable to serve the people so labelled, but we could make our own assumptions!

In some ways it could be said that stereotyping is the lazy person's perception. It means that they don't have to concentrate in order to distinguish features. Anyway if a stereotype is assumed in order to criticize some group of people then there is an assumed corollary that somehow the perceiver is better than the person stereotyped. In other words, the stereotype can have the payoff that one feels better about oneself – a cheap way to achieve self-esteem.

This bias in perception based on a desire to bolster one's self-esteem has been described by Argyle (1983) and others as a type of communication barrier separate from stereotyping. In this case one would be looking for the cause of the bias, as much as the way that it operates. The cause is to be found in our motivation. We have needs to see people in a certain way, **so we adjust the facts until they fit.**

Stereotyping has been described as **illusory correlation** (Hamilton, 1976). In other words the categories include associations between attributes which are not necessarily true.

It has been suggested that there are two kinds of bias at work in stereotyping. One is where **we simply make things up** – again perhaps because of personal needs. The other is where **we exaggerate traits** which actually do exist.

Another reason for making these distorted judgements may have something to do with our membership of groups. We tend to want to see our group as being better than the other lot, so we exaggerate or make up derogatory things about the group, and make up flattering things about our own group.

This can be seen in national stereotypes. There is a fund of jokes by the English about the stinginess of the Scots or the illogicality of the Irish – and of course vice versa. There is a fund of jokes by the French about the Belgians, by the Russians about the Polish, and so on. These jokes can lead in turn to people perceiving particular nationalities or groups in terms of those stereotypes.

This can also be seen in subcultural groupings such as social or professional groups, or in gender-based stereotypes.

People with black leather outfits, tattoos and motor bikes are proclaiming their membership of the group; they may also wish to impress people outside the group. Outsiders may despise them or fear them or simply draw mistaken conclusions about them from their different dress codes. There are for instance, groups of bikers who are professed Christians who seek to do 'good works'.

Accountants or lawyers who tend to dress soberly and adopt a serious demeanour whilst at work also get labelled stereotypically as dull and conservative. Again jokes are used to reinforce these outsiders' views – 'Auditors are accountants who found accountancy too exciting . . .' .

Stereotypes of male and female, men and women have been discussed and challenged in all quarters. There is now a large body of literature on the communication patterns of men and women which serves to understand and change these stereotypes. Some of these books are listed in Suggested Reading on page 86.

For effective perception of others we obviously need to guard against such stereotypical labelling.

KEY QUESTION

Errors in perception
Describe three different situations in which you feel you have fallen into one or more of the errors of perception listed here. If you cannot think of real situations, imagine situations in which you might make one of these errors.

6.10 Conclusion

As we have said, all this adds up to a long and dismal list of errors. Clearly our judgements on other people may be more fallible than we realize. What is significant is how these judgements affect our relationships with others because they affect the way we interact with them. We are going to look at social interaction in more detail in the next chapter.

As a matter of terminology you should also note that these errors in perception are sometimes called **perceptual filters**, and are a major part of what we have described elsewhere as **psychological barriers** to communication.

But we would like to end this chapter on a more positive note, believing that recognition of these barriers is half-way to doing something about them. Communication theory should lead to communication practice. So now let us look at perceptual skills.

7   SKILLS IN PERCEIVING OTHER PEOPLE

In this chapter, Perception of Others, we have dealt with the processes we use in perceiving other people. We have not sought to provide a general treatment of psychological theories and physiological experiments that seek to explain all of the ways in which we perceive and make sense of the world around us.

However, we have used the idea that all perceptual processes can be described in three stages: **selecting, organizing and inferring**. These can be seen as three general perceptual skills that we use when perceiving other people:

• Selecting: we have to choose certain features from all the possible sensory inputs – sight, hearing, smell, touch and general impressions – from another person. That choosing will depend on our own attention and the context and purpose of our encounter or interaction. If you and a friend meet a stranger and afterwards seek to describe the stranger to each other you are likely to have selected different features about that person. It is a perceptual skill to make this selection process more conscious. At this stage we can imagine we are perceiving another person as a 'physical object'.

• Organizing: the features we have chosen to notice will then be arranged within our own cognitive processes to enable us to make sense of the other person. We are likely to categorize them and need to use skill to avoid stereotyped categories as we place them into a particular group identity of gender, race, social class, occupation, nation, etc.

• Inferring: We will then draw conclusions about the person, for example, we might categorize them within opposites such as like me/not like me, friendly/not friendly, honest/dishonest, trustworthy/untrustworthy, confident/not confident, and other less personal inferences as wealthy/not wealthy, up to date/old fashioned. It is a perceptual skill to be aware of the evidence that leads us to such inferences. At this stage the other person becomes a 'psychological entity' with feelings, motives, personality traits, etc. and not just a physical object.

These processes can lead us into errors of selecting (e.g. one characteristic we give attention to above all others), of organizing (e.g. we fail to allow for cultural differences or our own emotional state), or of inferring (e.g. we form a judgement based on factors that are not to do with the other person).

We should watch out for the traps described in section 6 above. The main thing to realize is that perception requires a positive act of attention and the reserving of judgement as we categorize the noted features. The first rule is recognize the inferences you are making and avoid unfounded assumptions; the second is don't jump to conclusions and fixed unchangeable perceptions.

The following list of skills should help in making more accurate perceptions of other people:

■ *Attending to Detail*

This refers to making a conscious effort **to notice verbal and non-verbal clues which may provide information** about the internal states of the other person.

■ Withholding Judgement

This refers to **reserving one's opinions and decisions about the other person for as long as possible,** so that a proper range of information about them may be acquired.

■ Modifying Assessments

This refers to **being prepared to change one's view of the other person** when you find out more about them.

■ Checking Evidence

This refers to continually **checking speech and actions of the perceived to match these against opinions already formed.** This in turn suggests that you are always ready to modify your assessment of that person.

■ Comparing Information in Different Ways

This refers to **cross-referring various details** noticed in different ways in order to **avoid stereotyping.** If one tries various associations of information then one may either change judgements or perceive alternative judgements.

■ Looking for Alternative Causes

This refers to **consciously seeking different reasons for people's behaviour.** This kind of skill is about a deliberate attempt to explain why people talk and behave as they do in more ways than seem immediately obvious. This includes looking for cause and blame in situations as much as in people themselves.

■ Seeking Further Information

This refers to a **search for more information in what people say and do,** in order to support or reject opinions already formed.

■ Empathizing

This refers to **sympathetic projection of one's awareness and perceptions into the viewpoint of the other person.** This skill is about trying to understand the other person's point of view, and about trying to see the world as they see it. This must lead to a more honest perception of that person. It also counteracts our tendency to see the world only from our own point of view, and to become victims of our own preconceptions.

Practice and use of these skills has more to do with consciousness of Self and of the other person than anything else. They may be described as kinds of social skill (see next chapter). They are skills which may be developed with some mental effort and through awareness of what is happening when we perceive others and when we communicate with them. They are about consciousness of Self, not self-consciousness. Too much deliberation leads to artificiality. But equally there is an effort which can be made, and which counteracts our tendency to 'naturalize' perception. That is to say, we tend to see the way we perceive people as something naturally acquired, and practised equally and accurately by everyone. This is not so. **We can learn more about how to perceive, and more about forming more accurate perceptions of others.**

REVIEW

You should have learnt the following things from this chapter:

- What the term perception means and how it fits within the process of communication.
- How it affects interaction with others.

1 First Things
- Perception of others is defined as assessment of others, of their verbal and non-verbal communication, for our purposes.
- Perception predicts how we will carry on communication with others.
- Perception is about creating social reality in our minds.

2 Why Do We Perceive Others?
- to remember information
- to make sense of the other person's behaviour
- to organize social understanding
- to predict the behaviour of others
- to plan our own communication
- to maintain our Self and our view of reality
- to reduce anxiety
- to satisfy our needs

3 What Do We Perceive?
- the personality, attitudes and emotions of the other person
- attributes of the other person
- people's roles
- social reality
- presumed causes of behaviour and the motivation of the other person
- unexpected and predictable behaviour
- purpose – what we look for changes according to the purpose that we have in communicating with the other person.

4 Perceiving and Communicating
- All perception and communication must take place through the senses.
- We do form first impressions when perceiving. These need to be modified through further perception, but many examples of interaction do not allow time for this further perception.
- Perception and communication take place through the exchange of symbols.
- There are cognitive processes which carry out the assessment in perception.

- Perception involves acquiring data or information about the other person. We tend to make dangerous generalizations from this data.
- In handling data we look for distinctiveness, consistency and consensus.
- There are five types of validation used when checking this information: consensual, repetitive, multisensory, comparative and experimental.
- Perception can be described as stimulus–response behaviour up to a point.
- Attribution theory describes perception as a process of looking for reasons behind the way people communicate. We build up a view of what the other person is like as a way of explaining why they behave as they do.
- We have schemata, categories and sets in our minds which we refer to when trying to form these explanations. These are pre-formed groupings which associate traits and place values on them. We may describe six kinds of perceptual activity which take place.
- One dominant type of category used is also described as a stereotype.

5 What Affects Perception?
- physical and social context: spatial positioning
- physiological factors relating to the person perceived
- psychological factors within ourselves: our motivation, perceptual sets, predispositions, attraction to the other person, past experience, resemblance criteria, open and closed mindedness, role relations, saliency, social values.

6 Errors in Perception
These can be summarized as: the fundamental attribution error; false consensus; false consistency; the primacy effect; the halo effect; the recency effect; preconceptions; self-fulfilling prophecies; and stereotyping.

7 Perceptual Skills
These can be summarized as: attending to detail; withholding judgement; modifying assumptions; checking evidence; comparing information in different ways; looking for alternative causes; seeking further information; and empathizing.

CASE SITUATION

The Wrong Message

Carl is an extraordinarily handsome, well-built, thirty-eight-year-old lawyer who hates going to parties or social activities. Even though he seems to have it all – a nice home, a smart car and financial security – he doesn't seem to have any 'luck' with women, as he puts it. After much coercion by Michael, a colleague at his law firm, Carl relented and attended Michael's party after being assured that a lot of attractive single women would be there. Even though he felt uncomfortable, he was glad he had accepted the invitation as he noticed across the room a woman to whom he was immediately drawn.

He observed that she was vivacious and seemed to talk to everyone around her. She had a big radiant smile and appeared open and warm. Carl immediately went over to her and said, 'Hi, I've been noticing you from across the room, and you have a gorgeous smile.' The woman beamed and thanked him. He then noticed that she kept smiling and looking at him, which suddenly made him feel uncomfortable and self-conscious. Even though he started feeling awkward, he forced himself to shake hands with her and introduced himself. 'I'm Carl Templer,' he said, as his eyes shifted downwards, reaching out his hand. He still kept looking downward until the woman introduced herself as Jennifer Dalton. Then his eyes began darting everywhere. Since they were standing near a sofa, Carl said, 'Sit down. Let's talk.' The woman agreed, and continued smiling at Carl. When they were seated, Carl seemed to be taking up the entire sofa: his arms were spread out around the back, his legs jutted out in front, and he had adopted a semi-reclining position.

As he talked about himself and what he did for a living, he kept fidgeting and moving around. This made him appear uncomfortable. His gestures were broad and sweeping when he spoke, which made him seem overbearing. As he continued to talk to Jennifer, he hardly looked at her. Instead, he kept looking off to the side – which made him appear as though he was more interested in the other people at the party. He hardly looked at Jennifer's face when he talked to her, and whenever he did manage to look at her his eyes moved down and seemed to lock in on her breasts. When she asked him a question, he ignored it and kept on talking about himself and other subjects. Jennifer began to feel as though Carl was having a one-way conversation – with himself. Her presence didn't seem to matter. Eventually, she decided she had had enough.

She strained a phoney smile, got up and said that she would be right back. While making her way to the other side of the room she ran into her girlfriend, Cathy, with whom she had come to the party. This was their conversation:

Cathy	Wow! You lucked out! Who was that gorgeous hunk you were talking to?
Jennifer	Gorgeous hunk? Asshole is more like it!
Cathy	Are you serious? What did he do?
Jennifer	First of all the jerk orders me to sit down like a dog and then he kept talking to my boobs the whole time – not even looking up at me. Then, when he did manage to break away from them, he'd look to see who else was coming in the room. He had a cocky air about him and acted like he was so great. It was like he was looking down at me and judging me. What a snot! Then, all he kept talking about was himself, his stupid cases and his stupid car. Ugh! Forget it!
Cathy	Oh, no! What a geek! And to think I thought he was cute!

After realizing that Jennifer was not going to come back, Carl went to find Michael. When he found him, this was their conversation.

Michael	(*all smiles, patting Carl on the back*) See, I told you you'd meet some nice-looking babes here. Aren't you glad you came?
Carl	No, not really! That chick I was talking to . . .
Michael	Yeah. Boy, did she have a nice pair!
Carl	I guess. But what a bitch! Here I was being my nice-guy self, telling her all about what I do – and then she splits, like she couldn't care less. She probably figured out that I wasn't a partner yet and wasn't a millionaire. I probably didn't have enough money for her.
Michael	Don't lose any sleep over *her*. It's good you found out now. You wouldn't have wanted her anyway!

From *He says, she says – closing the communication gap between the sexes* (Glass, 1992).

KEY QUESTIONS

Using the above extract, answer the following questions:

• Describe what Carl was trying to present about himself and how he tried to achieve it.
• Describe what Jennifer actually perceived about Carl.
• What would you say to Carl to help him create the impression he wants next time he meets a woman?

Suggested Reading

There are many books which are relevant in parts to the material of this chapter. We have chosen just four which you can read selectively. It is also true that these books cover more than one chapter of this work. So you will find that these four have a more general use.

Argyle, M. (1973): *Social interaction*. London: Tavistock (see chapter 4).
Gahagan, J. (1984): *Social interaction and its management*. London: Methuen (see chapters 4, 5, 6).
Gross, R. D. (1992): *Psychology: the science of mind and behaviour*. London: Hodder & Stoughton (see chapter 17).
Patton, R. and Griffin, K. (1981): *Interpersonal communication in action*. New York: Harper & Row (see chapter 3).

C *Social Interaction – social skills in operation*

3

Social Interaction
and Social Skills

When you were growing up, adults taught you how to read, write, add and
subtract. Conversational skills were another matter. You were taught how to
pronounce words and to organize those words into sentences, but nobody ever
taught you how to communicate effectively with other people.

Alan Pease with Alan Garner: *Talk language: how to use conversation for profit and
pleasure*, 1989

1   INTRODUCTION

We spend almost all of our time interacting with other people: think back over
your last week, how many of your waking hours have you spent completely
alone? Perhaps at some of those times when you were alone, you were reading
or listening to the radio and hence involved in indirect interaction with others.

This chapter is concerned with face-to-face interaction – how we communicate with other people. We shall mostly concentrate on one-to-one relationships here since Chapter 6 will deal with communication in groups.

A great deal of time in schools and colleges is spent on developing language
skills even for those who are naturally fluent and precise in their use of spoken
and written language. Less time is spent on consciously developing the languages of social interaction, which include a range of non-verbal and social
skills such as effective self-presentation, perception of others, building of relationships and managing a sequence of interactions (speaking, listening, eye-contact, facial expressions and gestures, questioning and so on).

Making our knowledge of interactions and our behavioural patterns more
conscious can certainly result in our being better able to express our feelings
and achieve our personal aims (most of which can only be achieved through
other people) and to understand other people and their needs and feelings more
fully.

It has been suggested that 'All communication consists of reaction and counter-reaction' (Markham, 1993). Hence, closely observing our own and other people's reactions to each word and action and the context in which they happen can help us to manage those 'inter-reactions' more effectively. There is nothing inevitable about our responses to other people, and their responses to us.

You may have heard people say 'he and I don't get on, there's a personality clash.' It's true that the people involved may have different personal characteristics and different views of the world, but if they can develop techniques to manage their interactions their 'clash' could be developed into a greater level of mutual understanding, even if it serves to recognize the nature of their differences.

2   WHAT IS SOCIAL INTERACTION?

Quite simply, **it is everyday encounters with other people.**

Erving Goffman (1968), whose work we shall be looking at more closely in the next chapter, suggests social interaction is

> that class of events which occurs during co-presence and by virtue of co-presence. The ultimate behavioural materials are the glances, gestures, positionings and verbal statements that people feed into the situation, whether intended or not.

There are several elements here that we wish to highlight. First, that **social interaction consists of 'events', a sequence of happenings between two or more people when they meet face to face.** Second, that **it consists of physical behaviour,** we make sounds and visual signs to express our meanings to other people. Third, that **these signs may or may not have been 'intended'.** We may deliberately formulate our verbal statements to elicit a required response, but we may not be so conscious of our non-verbal statements which are picked up by the other person. As we shall see later in this chapter, **social skills training is concerned with making our verbal and non-verbal behaviour more conscious,** and with developing patterns of behaviour which in turn become unconscious. A parallel has often been made with driving a car: when we learn to drive we are conscious of all the behavioural sequences we employ, but when we are experienced drivers we perform these behaviours unconsciously.

Goffman (1963) draws a distinction between **social interaction as 'co-presence'** (for example, a group of people in a bus or in a waiting-room are aware of each other, but not necessarily involved with each other); and on the other hand **'focused interaction'**, in which two or more people are actually giving full attention to each other and developing a relationship built on verbal and non-verbal exchanges.

It is useful at this point to introduce the concept of a **'transaction'**, which indicates that an interaction is more than just awareness of each other and becomes a main focus of exchange and negotiation. At its simplest this can be built on a model of stimulus and response and we shall see how these notions are employed in the later chapter on Transactional Analysis.

Myers and Myers (1992) suggest that there are three components of a transaction: a transaction can be defined as 'two or more people who mutually and simultaneously

- take one another into account,
- figure out their roles, and
- conduct their interaction by a set of rules'.

The crucial issue in a transaction is that it consists of a two-way flow of messages and influence, of action and reaction that changes and develops the relationship. It can be visualized as a series of verbal and non-verbal statements and feedback loops that spiral forward in time.

There are, of course, an infinite number of possible occasions for private and public social interactions and transactions. During one day we, your authors, find ourselves in encounters with other people such as at home with wife, son and daughter; in the car, bus or train with neighbours, acquaintances and strangers; at work with colleagues, both managers and peers; in the classroom with colleagues and students; at lunch with friends; at a meeting with industrialists or other employers; at a public function with groups of people, and so on. You might like to review your typical day's interactions with other people.

The concept of social interaction has been so frequently studied and discussed that it has developed complex layers of meanings and associations. O'Sullivan et al. (1994), in their Key concepts in communication and cultural studies define it more fully: 'The exchange and negotiation of meaning between two or more participants located within social contexts'.

We wish to investigate briefly the four main components of this definition:

1 At the heart of the notion of interaction is **exchange or negotiation**, that is, two or more people must be engaged together, aware of each other and giving and receiving messages that are decoded. Interaction presupposes two or more people to interact.

2 The participants have separate existences before and after any particular moment of interaction and meet in **a specific social context which influences the nature of their interaction,** whether they meet at an informal party, a street demo or a job interview. The **personality and temperaments of the participants also influence the interaction,** but recent research suggests that the situation has more effect than the individual personalities. Patterns of behaviour are a result of the interaction between a particular social situation and the personalities of the participants. Also, **the participants will relate to each other according to how they perceive themselves (self-concept), how**

they wish to present themselves and what roles they adopt in relation to each other (e.g. submissive–dominant, friendly–hostile, formal–informal, etc.). These roles may be determined by the social context and its cultural expectations, for example if the participants are father/daughter in a family, or teacher/pupil in a school, or doctor/patient in a surgery.

3 Additionally, this definition stresses a location in a social context – **interaction cannot take place in a social vacuum.** Inevitably an interaction exists in a particular situation which may be familiar or unfamiliar. The situation may have clear, culturally prescribed expectations – e.g. a church service or a school class – or it may be informal and open – e.g. a party amongst friends. In any case, the participants are free to some degree to define the situation for themselves: an atmosphere can be created to fulfil their needs, e.g. a coffee morning can suggest certain expectations of appropriate clothing and behaviour, but participants can redefine it as more or less informal, more or less personal, and so on.

4 The fourth element in this definition is meaning. This is the element we shall be particularly concerned with since **the creation and generation of meaning from the exchange of verbal and non-verbal behaviours dictates the outcome of all interactions.** The message of an interaction is what the participants perceive to have happened between them. If communication has been effective then each participant will have closely similar perceptions of what took place.

We manage our social interactions and negotiate meanings between each other through a combination of the following:

- **Language** – words in sequences
- **Non-verbal behaviour** – paralanguage, posture, proximity and use of space, facial expression, gaze and eye-contact, gestures and body movement, bodily contact, clothes and appearance, physical objects
- **Relationship of participants** – adopted roles and attitudes to each other, mutual perceptions (see Chapter 2)
- **Social context** – physical place, atmosphere, cultural expectations, definition of the situation (see Chapter 4).

Let us investigate these separately. It is important to keep in mind that for purposes of analysis and explanation we need to separate these, but in practice they all inter-relate and overlap, for example the expectations about the context will influence the words considered appropriate and the words used will determine the warmth of the relationship and so on.

KEY QUESTIONS

Using the four main components of a social interaction described on pages 91–2, analyse the following specific examples of interactions:

- patient/doctor

- customer/salesperson

- prisoner/prison officer

- mother/son, or father/daughter

- child/teacher

3   LANGUAGE AND SOCIAL INTERACTION

3.1 Uses of Language

There are many ways of approaching a description of human language: what it is, how we use it, and why we use it. **Uses of language and speech are the primary distinctions between humans and other animals.** Language is our most sophisticated symbol system consisting of a vocabulary and structures (syntax and grammar). **We use it for generating meaning, for handling our experiences, for expressing our ideas, opinions and feelings, for thinking, for controlling other people, and for communicating with each other.**

Aitchison (1976) (after Charles Hockett) has developed a list of design features that characterize the nature of language. The key elements of these are:

■ Use of Vocal Auditory Channel
In social interaction **language is essentially a system of organized sounds.** Our individual patterns of speaking are personal to us and yet also share a common cultural and social inheritance.

■ Arbitrariness
Both sound and written forms of language are neutral symbols which have no connection with the objects or ideas they symbolize. We agree within a particular culture to invest specific sounds and patterns on the page with agreed meanings. Although we agree about these meanings, each symbol represents for us slightly different meanings according to our level of experience, knowledge and range of attitudes.

■ Semanticity
We use these arbitrary sound symbols to mean or refer to objects, actions or ideas. In social interaction, language is the prime carrier and creator of our

meanings – this is sometimes referred to as an **ideational function**; it is also used to carry and create the meanings of our relationship between the participants – **our choice of words reflects the nature of the relationship we wish to create and this can be referred to as an interpersonal function.**

A sequence of social interaction can be analysed on at least two levels of meaning: one is the content of the interaction, what it refers to outside the situation; and the other is actual relationship between the participants. We can perhaps visualize this in a simple diagram (see Fig. 3.1).

Another significant aspect of semanticity is that we invest words and structures with layers of meaning. We certainly do not have a language that exists as one word having one meaning. Even the simplest word, e.g. bird, will denote a

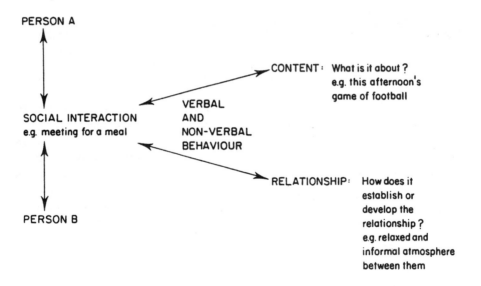

Fig 3.1 *A model for social interaction*

basic meaning, but will also connote a range of cultural and personal associations. These personal associations are often charged with an emotional response, for example, one could take words such as 'animal', 'money' or 'marriage' and illustrate their denotative and connotative meanings as in Fig. 3.2.

Words are repositories of personal perceptions and experiences – hence we talk about exchanging and negotiating meaning between each other. The same is true of non-verbal signs and symbols – they do not exist as 'one sign has one

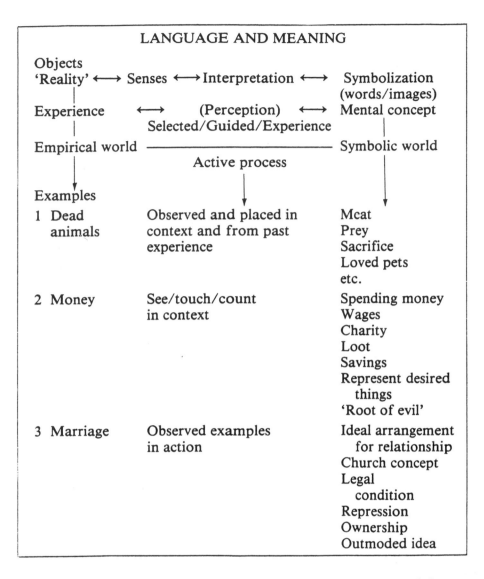

Fig 3.2 *A model to describe language and meaning, experience and the creation of symbols*

meaning'. We invest them with different meanings, according to our personal experience and the social and cultural context.

While discussing some aspects of semantics, we wish to spend a moment on what has been called 'metalanguage', which refers to the way in which words can be used so that the meaning goes beyond, or is hidden within, the accepted literal meaning of the words. Commercial transactions and advertising are a rich source of metalanguage examples, and, in particular, estate agents have developed a metalanguage of their own which the experienced purchaser has learnt to decode.

Pease and Garner (1989) have provided some amusing examples:

Metalanguage	Translation
Unique opportunity to purchase	We are having difficulty selling
Compact	Very small
Residence with great potential	Fallen down dump
In an exclusive quiet area	A long way from shops and schools
Ideal for the handyman	Will cost a fortune to renovate

In metalanguage, the words taken on specific contextual meaning. It is worth differentiating this from 'paralanguage' which refers not to the words themselves but how they are said, including stress, intonation, loudness, warmth and so on.

■ Cultural Transmission or Tradition
People hand language down from generation to generation and a major role of schooling is to enable young people to develop language skills. **The language also becomes a vehicle for containing cultural values and experiences and shapes people's thoughts into the ways of that culture**. A particular view of this process can be found in Dale Spender's book *Manmade language* (1980) which provides examples of how the vocabulary, structure and conversational use of language reflects a primarily male-dominated (man-made) view of the world.

■ Duality or Double Articulation
This refer to the fact that **language is organized into two layers**. The basic sound units (e.g. *c, a, t*), which are meaningless by themselves, become meaningful when combined into a sound sequence (e.g. *cat*).

■ Displacement
We use language to refer to things far removed in time and place. The words we use in social interaction are an important element of the actual relationship at that moment, as noted above. But they can also refer to events of thousands of years ago, or create imagined worlds in far-distant futures.

■ Structure Dependence
We recognize the patterned nature of language, and group sounds and words into meaningful structures. We have a notion of sentence structures, so that in a conversation hints given by an unfinished sentence can be sufficient to convey meaning. For example, a transcript of a phone call might look like this:

Receptionist:	Hello
	Curl up and dye
Caller:	Oh, hello

	Hello, this is Sarah Johnson.
Receptionist:	Hi, how are you?
	Long time no . . .
Caller:	Is that you Jane?
	Hi, no. I've been away for a month
Receptionist:	Where did you go?
	Was it Portugal, did you say?
Caller:	Yes, it was great, beautiful beaches, hot weather, and the hotel was good. Got a gorgeous tan. We didn't want to come . . .
Receptionist:	No, I know.
	It always goes so quick . . .
	I'm off next week – can't wait . . .
	I'd like to hear about it. We fancy Algarve next year.
Caller:	Yeah, OK
	Well I can tell you when I come in.
	I wondered if I could come in on Saturday. Have you got a gap?
	Just a cut and dry . . .
Receptionist:	Um, well. I think so. Let me see, a bit busy.
	But yeah, how about 1.30?
Caller:	Fine. I'll see you then.
Receptionist:	OK, so half-past one on Saturday
	See you then.

In reviewing this dialogue, you can see that rarely in a conversation do we use complete structured sentences. Also you might like to decide how much of the interaction was ideational (the purpose of the call was to make an appointment for a hair cut) and how much inter-personal (about the relationship between the participants).

■ Creativity

Finally, the most important and interesting characteristic of language is its creativity. We can talk about anything we like in any way we like. The phone call we just looked at was in some ways unpredictable and went beyond its simple, predetermined aim. However, creativity does not mean completely open licence, since if we wish to communicate with each other we depend on a level of orderly predictability. **We are creative within limits which we learn. These limits are both those of linguistic structures and of culturally learnt relationships.**

Having reviewed the characteristics of language in a rather abstract way, we now wish to concentrate on three uses of language that are important for understanding the use of language in social interaction:

- controlling a conversation
- influencing a relationship
- expressing a personal identity.

3.2 Language and Controlling Interaction

One of the prime areas of research in social interaction has been into how we initiate, maintain and close a face-to-face encounter. These are conscious, deliberate elements in an interaction and much of the overt communication in interactions is carried by our use of words. But as we shall see later in this chapter, non-verbal signals are also used to reinforce our verbal messages.

Peter Honey, in his book *Face to face* (1988), sought to help managers develop their skills in achieving objectives through face-to-face interaction. He stresses the need to establish clear objectives for any interview or meeting and to use verbal and non-verbal means to keep the total personal behaviour in step with those objectives. He uses transcripts and case studies to illustrate how effectively, or ineffectively, people manage their interactions at work. **Critical points in any interaction are the opening and closing moments.**

Typically, the opening sequence builds the relationship and clears the channels for communication:

– Hello
– Hello
– Nice morning
– Yes, better than yesterday
– Yes, we all feel better when the sun shines. Well, I thought we ought to meet today to . . .

These opening moments, in terms of the task in hand, are redundant. But they are also vital for establishing contact and for setting the mood and atmosphere for the interaction. At the outset we can determine how formal/informal, positive/negative, friendly/hostile the interaction is going to be. Notice also how the phase of opening remarks is neatly turned to the main business by the use of the word 'well' (other often used words for this are 'right', 'OK', 'now', 'anyway'). When you are next speaking on the phone, consciously listen for when either you or your caller use one of these words to mark the shift from one part of the interaction to the next. We use these language markers to identify the boundaries. As we come to the end of an interaction and one of the participants wants to wind up, the same device will normally be used:

– OK then. We seem to be agreed.
– Well, not really. I'm not clear about who . . .
– Right. I thought we agreed that you would . . . and I would . . . Anyway, we need to sort it out now.
– But surely we still need to . . .

We use speech as a cue or regulator of our interactions. In the extract here, one speaker is clear that he or she wants to close the interaction; but there is reluctance to do so on the part of the other – language cues usually make the participants' view unambiguous. If the point is not taken then gestures or eye-contact can be used to reinforce the point. Often before the commitment of 'anyway' or 'OK' to signal a shift in the interaction, some more ambiguous non-verbal cues might have been used (for example, shuffling documents, seeking eye-contact, shifting on a chair).

3.3 Language Influencing Relationships

We use speech as the main vehicle for referring to the task or topic in hand. We might of course also be using some written material or a picture or plans to focus the topic as well. We also use speech for controlling the stages of development of the interaction from the opening through the main business and to the closing. We also choose our words as a means of influencing the nature of the relationship and the roles we adopt with each other.

As we have suggested, one characteristic of language is its creativity. We have a wide choice in any utterance of the vocabulary and structure we use. For example, we could greet the same person in several ways:

1 Hiya, Nobby, how's tricks?
2 Hello Bob, how are things?
3 Good morning, Mr Clarke. How are you?

These three questions all carry the same information, but you would choose the more appropriate one according to the context and your previous relationship with the other person. You would not expect your doctor to speak to you in the surgery as in (1), but she might speak to you in the pub as in (2).

We use these different registers of speech according to how we perceive the situation and how we wish to relate to other people. One of our social skills is to be able to shift our language registers. Sometimes it is necessary to use a formal vocabulary and structure (for example in a court), but at other times such a register would be quite inappropriate (e.g. in a football crowd).

3.4 Language and Self-Presentation

Finally, in this section, we want to draw attention to how we use speech as a way of presenting ourselves. Register is not only chosen as a result of the situation, social context and the other person, but also as a personal choice, to reveal ourselves. We each have an individual language capacity resulting from our experience, upbringing, education and so on, which can be called our **idiolect**. We can be conscious of how we choose and pronounce our words, but also may not be conscious of our own particular word usage and accent until we receive feedback from other people or listen to a tape-recording of ourselves.

We develop a personal communication style which consists of a repertoire of behaviour patterns including verbal and non-verbal elements. As we shall see in the next chapter, this notion of self-presentation has been described in terms of a performance. **We play roles that we believe are appropriate for a particular situation and relationship**.

In face-to-face interactions, however, the language we use exists alongside a whole range of non-verbal features. Words are only one channel of communication and, it has been claimed, not the most important channel. For example Bandler and Grinder (1979), in a book that is a transcript from their seminars, quite baldly state:

> and while the record that follows may have contained enough clues for the participant in the seminar, only the more astute reader will succeed in fully reconstructing the earlier events. As we state explicitly in this book, the verbal component is the least interesting and least influential part of communication.

As we shall see in a later section, Bandler and Grinder provide useful information and theories about how to be more sensitive to people's non-verbal feedback. However, for conscious sharing of ideas and information with each other, rather than attitudes and emotions, spoken language remains a primary means of communication.

As we discussed in Chapter 1 (page 10), research in recent years has analysed gender differences in how men and women use language to present themselves and interact with others. Some of these studies in conversation have explored, and exposed, traditional stereotypes. Coates (1991) has surveyed some of this research and focused on what might have been called 'women's style' of presentation through linguistic interactions. Jennifer Coates highlights five general linguistic issues:

- **Verbosity**: there is a widespread belief in our society that women talk (chatter) more than men, yet research findings consistently contradict this.
- **Tag questions**: such questions, which often end a statement with a tentative question like 'isn't it? . . . or OK? . . . agreed? . . .', can seem to be used more by women and imply a less assertive position. However, tag questions are used deliberately to facilitate a conversational interaction.
- **Questions generally**: research findings so far suggest that women use interrogative forms more than men and that this may reflect women's relative weakness in interactive situations. However, women exploit questions and tag questions in order to keep conversation going.
- **Commands and directives**: men tend to use instructions and commands more than women whose linguistic style is more inclined to be non-hierarchical and more participative.
- **Swearing and taboo language**: there is little hard evidence on male/female

differences in swearing, though the folklinguistic belief that men swear more than women and use more taboo words is widespread.

3.5 Language and Subculture

In this section we want to draw attention to ways in which language defines the diversity of subcultures, gives them meaning, incorporates and endorses their values. It is, of course, true that many aspects of subcultures contribute to this sense of distinctiveness – for example dress codes, oral traditions and visual communication. But we are not trying to make a complete case study of a culture. Rather, we are trying to make the point that culture is in one sense a product of communication, or is realized through communication. **The meaning of a culture to itself and to other cultures lies in what it says and how it says it.**

Subcultures are all around us and part of us. Just as the notion of a mass audience for the media seems to dissolve the more exactly one tries to define it, so also the notion of a British (or any other) culture tends to dissolve on examination. There are many subcultures when one considers class, region, occupation, ethnicity, youth, leisure activities, and the groups such as Hell's Angels – so many that it is as if one has to define national culture as the sum of these varied parts.

Language used by subcultures helps define their sense of identity for themselves and to others. Language used about them also defines how they are understood by the society of which they are a part. This language use by them is often about creating distinctiveness and very possibly difference from society at large. Sometimes the intention is even to deal in conflict, because conflict involving threat from without causes the group or subculture to focus protectively on its identity, its values and its survival.

In any case, identity can in cultural terms be split when for example one is speaking Punjabi at home and English at work.

In terms of distinctiveness, the language of youth cultures, for example, may involve being privy to a secondary code that refers to clothing and music through words which are not understood by the culture in general. Words even become recycled, such as the present fashion for 'fab' as a term of approval. It appeared in the Sixties, became passé in the Seventies, and is now temporarily acceptable again, with its associations of kitsch and nostalgia. Youth cultures are also marked by paralinguistic features which in Britain are notable for the adoption of the London accent (even by speakers of RP), for slurred delivery with hesitation, for appended phrases such as 'y'know' and 'sort of'.

In fact in this case the identity is mixed up with class and with a notion that borrowing certain restricted code features associates one with working class values, with something 'genuine'.

■ Subculture and Values

Language used by and about subcultures also says things, directly or indirectly, about the values they hold and the values that others attach to them. We have just indicated that certain speech features may themselves be associated with values by referring to other factors such as class. Young Afro-Caribbeans in London have been re-using Creole forms to create a patois which serves the function of both giving them a distinct identity and enhancing their own sense of self-worth and value. And of course what they talk about is what they value. It is worth noting that what they are resisting is not only a dominant white culture in a general sense and what is seen as a threatening police force in particular – but also previous generations of West Indian immigrants, many of whom had sought to shed their patois in order to integrate. There is a whole set of oppositions set up on the issues of age, race, authority, all of which are implicit in language. This is true in terms of language used both by subcultures and about subcultures. In this case it is worth looking at the comments we make elsewhere about discourse in the section on gender and language.

3.6 Language and Gender – Females

In the first place it should be said that **there are clear differences in the use of verbal and non-verbal language by men and women.** These differences not only identify the gender of the speaker, but they also say things about the nature of the interaction, the nature of the situation, and the way that each of the genders tries to deal with interactions.

The significance of these differences tends to be interpreted according to the values of the interpreter. Borisoff and Merrill (1991) say baldly that 'Numerous studies have established women's superior abilities both as decoders and encoders of verbal messages when compared with men'. Whereas Spender (1981) takes a more implicitly critical stance when she says that 'language has been made by men and used for their own purposes'.

One may also distinguish between language used by women and language used about women. Both kinds of use identify gender differences and say things about the status of women, the social behaviour of women and the conduct of relationships between the sexes.

We are, of course, talking generally about Western cultures here. But it should also be realized that other cultures may show other kinds of difference in communication, in relation to gender. Some of these differences are extreme. For example, the speech of Carib women or of Siberian females is considerably different to that of the males in many respects. There are plenty of examples of words (like some social practices) being taboo to women in other cultures.

■ Acquisition of Gender Definitions

In the first place, if a 'special language' is acquired and used by women in particular, then it must come from somewhere. The same is true of language used about women. This language is a substantial part of the acquisition of gender definitions – what it means to be female, how one should regard females.

Females will learn to use certain kinds of talk and will learn to accept being talked to in certain ways because of their upbringing. We are talking about socialization, about address by significant others at home and at school, about peer group talk not least in the context of games, about models of talk represented in various media. For example, there are female characteristics of hesitancy in speech and deferral to males in conversation (not universal, but frequent). Children will see these communicative behaviours represented in movies and in television drama, and so will tend to internalize and 'naturalize' this behaviour as being acceptable and normal.

Language used about women, even by women, is often demeaning and belittling. More will be said about this in the section on discourse. But, for example, it is noticeable that diminutive forms of women's names are more common for women than for men and are more commonly used even when they are older. When women are emotionally distressed it is common to hear words such as 'hysterical' or 'emotional'. These words are used to imply that they are 'not coping' or are 'out of control'. Although there is a separate issue of how emotion is expressed differently according to gender, the same kind of behaviour in men is described as anguish or outrage.

■ Interpersonal Behaviour, Language and Gender

When one looks at how women use language there is evidence of differences in non-verbal behaviour. Females are touched more than men, they smile more and they use more eye contact. Indeed such differences are expected of them. For women the communication of gentleness, warmth, tact is seen positively. Women show more listening cues because they do more listening than men. It has also been suggested that listening is seen as a lower status, passive activity in a male-dominated world. This would tend to reinforce such behaviour. Women do of course have the difference of higher voices, but in fact some of the perceived difference is because they use a greater range of pitch than men. Females perceive, respond to and give off cues about feelings more than men. This is the more likely because this behaviour response is socially endorsed as being OK for females. In relation to talk it is more likely that women will use more of these cues because they talk more about feelings then men. Conversely, men have been found to talk about actions, and of course their related non-verbal behaviour (NVB) matches this.

This idea of a necessary connection between the two channels of communication fits in with similar points about the connections between role, relationships, perception and communication. In other words roles create expectations about speech, which are gender specific. Equally it can be said that gender patterns of speech represent gender roles. We make assumptions about how we expect mothers to talk, and how they talk defines them as mothers. Women are often better perceivers then men because they are better listeners: the fact that they use listening cues also elicits the information which helps them perceive others accurately. It is a kind of chicken and egg argument. The same logic applies to the fact that women disclose rather more than men (and disclosure helps improve relationships). Hargie *et al.* (1994) refer to this as well as to the work of Hill and Stull (1987) which identifies **four variables which affect disclosure by gender.** These are situational factors, strength of gender role identity, gender role attitudes, cultural gender role norms. For instance, in Western business circles there is a male-oriented view that control of emotion and of disclosure is desirable. Women who want to 'succeed' in business have to modify their usual gender role behaviour.

Generally, it has been found that men and women talk about different topics. Men tend to talk about work and sports activities. They are competitive. But women talk about family and friends and health matters. Also there is more than gender bias in the content of communication. The way women talk is also different. For example, their speech is usually more fluent and more accurate than that of males. Indeed they talk in more complex speech structure from an earlier age than do males. Argyle (1992) refers to research which identifies female characteristics such as hesitations, hedges (sort of), tags (didn't I?), and the greater use of 'doubt' words such as 'may' or 'might'. In mixed sex conversations men dominate in various ways (loudness and interruption), but also because women are in one sense more socially adroit at maintaining conversations and showing listening cues. They may, in effect, actually encourage men to talk more than they do. The related topic of assertiveness is referred to elsewhere (page 121), but in terms of gender one can identify the fact that men are more verbally aggressive than women. It has also been found that people are more assertive towards those of the same gender. Other differences are numerous and subtle, and perhaps culturally defined. For example, it is less acceptable for women use to swear words than for men, though things have changed a great deal in the last generation. Women tend to use more words to amplify descriptions of experiences, not least again in respect of feelings they have had.

■ *Female Gender and Discourse*

A discourse may be described as a selective use of language which produces particular meanings about the subject of that discourse. These meanings may usually be described as value judgements about that subject, whether it be children, news or in this case, women. Discourses are also part of our ideology. They contribute to the total view of the world and of power relationships which are major aspects of ideology. The notion of language can apply to pictures as much as to words. But given the framework of this book we are concentrating on words about women and the discourse that they help create.

Miller and Swift (1979) refer to **the naming of women** as a way of implicitly demeaning them. That is to say, women are often addressed by their first names, where men are not. Women lose their names (and identity?) when they marry. Many female names are derived from male ones, but rarely has it happened the other way round. They and other writers refer to words which describe the quality of gender and draw attention to the selective nature of these words. They cite a dictionary definition which includes 'gentleness, affection and domesticity . . . fickleness, superficiality and folly'. You may judge for yourself what such words say to people about the meaning of being female. In fact one can easily collect sets of words about women under headings such as appearance, occupation, sexuality, insults, and you can see that these words are largely specific to women as opposed to men. They often have **negative connotations,** or suggest some kind of limitation to female ability or potential or character. And so often such words define women in relation to men or as opposed to men. Women are 'attractive' – to men of course. And the words that are gender specific not only are used rarely about men, they may even be insults when applied to men – males don't like to be called 'pretty'.

Ironically in the light of what we have already said, part of the discourse is words about women which suggest they talk too much. Spender (1981) lists '*chatter, natter, prattle, nag, bitch, whine . . . gossip*'. This language criticizes and denies women talking, it devalues it. Such value-laden meanings of the discourse about femaleness extend into many areas of language use. For example, a women who is sexually charged and active may well be called a nymphomaniac. The word is not a compliment. There is no such equivalent for men, and anyway it is OK for men to be sexually active. One might even argue that simply the great number of terms identifying female clothing has a significance in that it contributes to that part of the discourse which says that being female ought to be all about owning clothes, being interested in clothes, wanting to be looked at for the clothes being worn.

Nor should it be assumed that the language of the discourse is used only by men. It is perfectly possible to hear a women calling another woman a bitch. Women inhabit the same discourse as men, they perpetuate the language, they operate within the same ideology. The discourse creates ways of women thinking about themselves as much as ways of others thinking about women and femaleness. It is true that women are defined as people-oriented and 'sympathetic', within the discourse. It does seem that women use conversation and devices of speech towards social and co-operative ends (where men's talk is often about competing and dominating). But this is unhelpful to sexual equality when such qualities and such talk are ultimately not valued through the power structure of our culture.

KEY QUESTIONS

Write down lists of words to describe feminine and masculine qualities.
What do the lists tell you about what it means to be female or male?

Suggest some ways in which we could change communication in order to change how females are defined and viewed within our culture.

With reference to subcultures that you know about, write down words and phrases which you think are typical of the way that they talk.

Explain how subcultural groups use words to represent their beliefs and values.

4 NON-VERBAL COMMUNICATION AND SOCIAL INTERACTION

So far in this section on 'how we manage social interactions' we have concentrated on verbal language – the use of words. However non-verbal 'language' is always present in interpersonal interaction and it has been suggested by many researchers that the non-verbal dimensions account for 80 per cent of the 'content' or meanings that are conveyed in face-to-face interactions.

Later in this chapter we shall describe some aspects of social skills that we develop more or less consciously and effectively; and at this stage it may be useful to draw a distinction between 'linguistic competence' and the wider concept of 'communicative competence'.

Linguistic competence refers to our ability to speak, read and write at least one language with understanding of accepted word meanings and with a knowledge of accepted grammatical forms. There seems to be continuous debate in Britain about the use of Standard English with 'correct' grammar and spelling and about Received Pronunciation. From a communication point of view, these forms of language are part of a range of forms and styles that are needed for linguistic competence, but non-standard forms may also be appropriate in some contexts.

Hence, **communicative competence** refers to our ability to use forms of verbal and non-verbal languages in ways that are appropriate to different situations and with an awareness of social and cultural expectations. Appropriateness is a key concept here, although someone with such competence can choose to challenge what may have become norms of cultural appropriateness, in the same way that a poet may challenge accepted forms of written language. The greetings used as examples on page 99 indicate verbal forms that reflect ideas of appropriateness in different social contexts and different interpersonal relationships.

In the last 20 years much has been revealed about non-verbal communication in academic and popular publications. The term 'body language' has become familiar enough to feature regularly in magazine articles and even in the UK for an advertisement for cat food.

The description and analysis of non-verbal behaviour in social interaction have been among the main reasons why notions of social skills and of social skills training (SST) have developed. One simple measure of this growth of knowledge is to compare the first edition of Michael Argyle's *Psychology of interpersonal communication* (1967) with the most recent fourth edition (1983). Argyle concludes this fourth edition as follows:

> I have tried to outline what has been found out, mainly by experimental research, in an important area of human behaviour. Interpersonal behaviour is a centrally important part of human life. Relationships with others are one of the main sources of happiness, but when they go wrong they produce very great distress and are one of the roots of mental disorder. Can our new knowledge of social behaviour help?

Argyle believes that the new knowledge can have practical benefits for individuals and groups to communicate and relate together more fully.

In this section, we shall outline briefly what are now considered to be the main functions of non-verbal communication and then focus on some aspects of non-verbal communication and its place in regulating social interaction.

The **principal functions of non-verbal communication** in social interactions can be categorized as follows:

■ To Convey Our Attitudes and Emotions

This may be deliberate as when we use gaze or physical proximity to indicate our feelings towards someone else. It may, however, not be deliberate, but rather our reluctance to be close to someone or to make eye-contact may give the other person the impression that we do not like them, which may not have been our intention. **The notion of non-verbal communication presupposes some intention to communicate. It is useful to distinguish this from non-verbal** *behaviour* **which may cause other people to decode messages that we did not deliberately or consciously encode.** Another way of describing this is to distinguish between communication (as a deliberate sharing of meaning with someone else) and information (as a message that is picked up by someone else). Another term that is useful here is **leakage.** This describes the way in which we might be aware of deliberately controlling our facial expression and hand movements to hide our nervousness in a situation, but we may be given away by leaked messages from our strained voice or shaking knees.

■ To Support Our Verbal Communication

We are quite often aware of using facial expressions or gestures deliberately to reinforce or complete what we are saying. Analysis of social interactions by video recordings and close observation shows that the whole body is engaged whilst speaking and listening. This was well expressed by Abercrombie (1988) in an article on '**paralanguage**' when he said, '*we speak with our vocal organs, but we converse with the whole body*'.

Pioneering work on body movements in social interactions, which he named **kinesics**, was done by Ray L. Birdwhistell (1968) who sought to break down movements, gestures and facial expressions into their component parts (kinemes). He has analysed body movements as a series of structures, comparable with analysis of language as a series of structures building from basic sounds (phonemes) which are built into sequences and paragraphs. He pointed out that non-verbal behaviour constantly takes place, both during speech and during silence.

> Kinesics is the science of body behavioural communication. Any person who has 'learned how to behave in public' and is at all aware of his response to the awkward or inappropriate behaviour of others recognizes the importance of body-motion behaviour to social interaction. It is more difficult to conceive that body motion and facial expression belong to a learned, coded system and that there is a 'language' of movement comparable to spoken language, both in its structure and in its contribution to a systematically ordered communicative system.

> Communication is a continuous interactive process made of multi-levelled, overlapping, discontinuous segments of behaviour. The interaction of communication does not cease when interactants lapse into silence, to begin again with the onset of phonation; other channels continue communication operations even when the auditory–aural channel is not in use. Humans move in relatively orderly fashion while they vocalize and when they are silent; they can perceive the regularity in the visible movement of others (or at least become aware when it is irregular) and proprioceptively in themselves. They can smell, taste, touch, and otherwise register perception of themselves and their surroundings. When regularities appear, they are not simply mechanical, 'automatic', or happenstantial. Research with visible body motion is convincing us that this behaviour is as ordered and coded as is audible phonation. Like language, infracommunicational body-motion behaviour is a structural system that varies from society to society and must be learned by the membership of a society if it is to interact successfully.

In describing social interaction we still tend to assume that speech (or 'audible phonation') is the prime channel of communication, and that non-verbal behaviour supports speech. It is important to remind ourselves that **in some circumstances, especially of intimacy or hostility, speech is replaced by non-verbal communication**. It has also been suggested by Mehrabian (1971) that of the messages received in a conversation, 7 per cent are verbal, 38 per cent are vocal (paralanguage) and 55 per cent are facial and non-verbal.

■ *To Present Yourself*

In discussing language earlier in this chapter, we referred to speech as a way of presenting oneself. But also our choice of clothes, bodily adornment (hairstyle, make-up, jewellery), the objects we surround ourselves with, and our general styles of behaviour, are very significant in self-presentation. We choose to present ourselves through a variety of roles and this theatrical metaphor of self-presentation will be explored more fully in the next chapter.

■ *To Regulate Social Interaction and to Provide Feedback*

As we saw above, we use speech to regulate and guide a conversation, especially in the opening and closing phases. However, in many situations, even before we speak, we need to catch someone's eye before we can begin the interaction. For example, in public places such as restaurants or shops we have to gain attention, usually non-verbally. Non-verbal cues are also crucial to the smooth management of interaction.

We signal our desire to speak by mutual eye contact. Having got the floor, the speaker will not maintain the gaze, but the listener will tend to keep looking at the speaker. The speaker will then make eye-contact as a signal that he or she is about to stop and pass over to the other. These turn-taking signals are mostly non-verbal. Whilst listening, the listener will provide feedback through head-nods or murmurings to acknowledge agreement or to encourage the speaker to continue. Alternatively, frowns or seeking eye-contact or murmuring '*yes, but . . .*' indicates a desire to take the floor.

In addition to non-verbal signals to help turn-taking, we also use non-verbal feedback signals to indicate the status relationship of the participants. The clearest examples of this are the use of physical space and proximity, and paralanguage (especially the tone of the voice). The positioning of participants in a room – who stands, who sits, their orientation to each other, how far apart they are – indicates the power relationship. Similarly, bodily posture and body tension are signals of the interpersonal relationship. Blushing can also be an example of leakage rather than communication.

The regulation of interaction is often tentative, i.e. one person is not necessarily in a clearly dominant power position, and so it is an asset to use non-verbal rather than verbal signals. Non-verbal signals often work by hints or innuendo and are therefore ambiguous. It is possible to retreat from a non-verbal message by saying '*Oh, I never intended you to get that impression*', but a consciously expressed spoken utterance is less easy to withdraw. For example, it is unlikely that you will say '*Will you come to the party with me on Saturday?*' unless you are fairly confident from non-verbal messages that have been exchanged that the answer is likely to be yes. Openly asking someone for a favour and openly being rejected is more difficult to cope with and more embarrassing than hinting at such things non-verbally.

KEY QUESTIONS

Record someone speaking on video.

Then use the recording to write down details of non-verbal behaviour used with speech. Comment on how these details affect your understanding of what is said.

5   MAKING CONVERSATION

- 'Where have you been?'
- 'Out.'
- 'What did you do?'
- 'Nothing.'

We learn, and are taught, how to talk to other people from an early age so that 'making conversation' comes to seem as 'natural' for most people as walking on two legs. We may also, as in the above quotation, practise the art of *not* making a conversation.

However, we recognize that the 'art of conversation' is a highly complex set of conventions, skills and attitudes when we find ourselves floundering as we try to talk to someone, or when we occasionally hear someone suggest that the art of conversation is dead, or when we become very conscious of our need to interact with someone to get something we want.

In a conversation lots of things are going on all at the same time. To put it more precisely:

But conversation is more than a co-operative form of verbal interaction rooted in a huge reservoir of background knowledge and assumptions, it is also the context in which multifarious channels of human communication operate and interact. (Ellis and Beattie, 1986)

The co-operative nature of conversation is fundamental. Two or more people use verbal and non-verbal signals to share something of themselves. The exchange given at the start of this section indicates a lack of co-operation on one side. One can easily imagine the non-verbal and paralinguistic signals accompanying those words. It is an everyday sort of exchange which is quoted in Argyle and Henderson (1985) who locate it as an exchange between 'parent' and adolescent'.

In the past 20 or so years, there has been a great deal of research into how people interact verbally and non-verbally. Techniques of observing, analysing and recording interactional sequences (especially using video equipment), have been systematized. What has previously been felt only intuitively can now be more scientifically described. Atkinson and Heritage (1987) observe that:

> Conversation analytic studies are thus designed to achieve systematic analyses of what, at best, is intuitively known, and more commonly, is tacitly orientated to in ordinary conduct. In this context, nothing that occurs in interaction can be ruled out, a priori, as random, insignificant, or irrelevant.

Every flicker of an eyelid can count in a conversation.

It is beyond the scope of this book to summarize all the findings of recent research in conversation analysis and sequential analysis of interactions, but the brief reading list at the end of this chapter offers further sources of information. There are now conversations for transcribing elements of conversation such as simultaneous or overlapping utterances, intervals between and within utterances, characteristics of speech delivery (e.g. falling or rising tone, animated tone, emphasis, quieter or louder volume, faster or slower pace, gaze direction, head nods, applause) – for details see Atkinson and Heritage (1987). We shall be discussing seven significant elements of conversation making: openings, turn taking, closings, questioning, listening, using non-verbal communication, and recognizing feedback.

As a background to these specific elements, it is important to remember that social interactions are carried out using various communication channels within a range of contexts and relationships (see section 3 in this chapter). They often also accompany other activities such as eating, dealing with children, mending a car, and so on.

5.1 Openings

In the Case Situation at the end of this chapter, we have an imaginary situation in which two people find it difficult to open an interaction. The opening moments of an encounter are commonly accepted as being very important. In advice for people attending interviews it is often suggested that 'You don't get a second chance to make a first impression'. Such advice may serve only to make the opening moments more nerve-racking.

We easily recognize that some of our conversational openings are difficult, but it is less easy to recognize how such openings are successfully negotiated. What skills are required to open a conversation?

Christine Saunders in Hargie (1986) defines openings as

> the interactors' initial strategy at both personal and environmental level, utilized to achieve good social relationships, and at the same time establish a frame of reference deliberately designed to facilitate the development of a communication link between the expectations of the participants and the realities of the situation.

This definition highlights a number of points:

• openings should be consciously managed

- at a personal and at a context level, the scene must be set
- the appropriate relationship must be established
- the expectations of the people and the task in hand must be kept in focus.

The essential move is to open contact and to greet each other. This is done non-verbally through eye-contact, eyebrow flash, open smiling expression, touch, handshake, embrace, kiss or simply beckoning, welcoming tone of voice, and body proximity. Verbally, there are standard greetings, of course – *Good morning, Hello, Hi, How are you?* The choice of vocabulary reflects the relationships, personalities, moods and context. One needs to set the tone for the rest of the interaction, and indeed perhaps for a continuing relationship. Figure 3.3 'The social skill of opening a conversation' summarizes these verbal and non-verbal components.

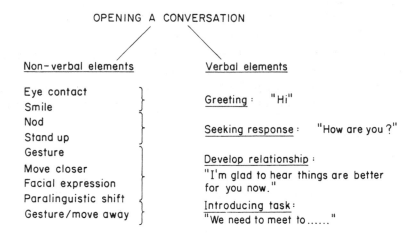

Fig 3.3 *A model describing skills in opening a conversation*

If the encounter is to be friendly and warm then a series of 'phatic' remarks might be exchanged on subjects such as the weather or controversial current events. If the encounter is to be cool and more hostile, then the opening can lead straight to the task or issue. '*I asked you to come and see me because . . .*' The choice of where you meet, whether you are sitting or standing, when you meet, and so on, will all create a mood and relationship.

If you know why you wish to open a particular interaction then all you do and say should contribute to the relationship you want to establish and to the task you want to achieve. If you are the recipient, rather than the initiator of this opening, then you still have the opportunity to influence the situation through your verbal and non-verbal contribution.

5.2 Taking Turns

A successful conversation is neither a monologue nor a babble of voices. Somehow, almost mysteriously, we take turns to speak and maintain a continuous non-verbal dialogue. In general, we take turns to hold the floor; one person speaks at a time; we do not talk simultaneously for any length of time; we manage transitions from person to person quite smoothly. Most of us succeed in this through a system of verbal and non-verbal 'cues' that regulate interaction.

In this section we shall briefly review some of the research that has been done into how we take turns in conversation. Such knowledge represents an important communication skill in managing conversations.

There are two main research traditions in studying turn-taking. Firstly, that we use *rules* in what we say and how we say it in order to manage the transitions from person to person. Secondly, that we use *signals*, especially non-verbal ones, to manage transitions. In practice, we intuitively use both rules and signals.

The *rule-based* emphasis suggests that we use particular units of speech to indicate possible completion points for another person to come in.

Clear examples of this are to be seen in questions that invite a response from another person. These may be specifically addressed:
– 'Bill, what do you think?'
or they may require self-selection by the next turn-taker in a group:
– 'Who can tell me why it happened?'
Such turns may not be so directly signalled by questions but may hint at a relevant point for transition. This can be done through treatment of the topic and through use of words such as *'Anyway'*, *'OK'*, *'Anything else'*. Conversation analysis indicates that we move the topic forward, sideways or backwards by a series of small steps and mark the boundaries of topics with transitional markers.

The 'next turn' indicates to the previous speaker what the recipient has understood and how he or she is guiding the topic. For example:
A: 'It's hot tonight'
B: 'I'll open the window'
This indicates that person B took the initial statement to mean a specific thing which was not necessarily intended.

When analysing naturally occurring conversations we find that they take a number of unpredictable turns. Studies in conversation analysis aim to expose what Harvey Sacks called 'the technology of conversation' (Atkinson and Heritage, 1987).

You can listen to conversations to identify how the interactants move from topic to topic, turn to turn.

The *signal-based* emphasis on conversation turn-taking stresses the non-verbal cues that lead people to 'take the floor'.

A good deal of research has been done on the use of gaze and eye-contact as signalling mechanism. In general, the speaker does not maintain eye-contact throughout his/her turn, but signals the final moments of the turn by making eye-contact for the next speaker to come in.

A deficiency in some of this research has been the concentration on one type of non-verbal signal without attention to the context of other non-verbal channels, and verbal and paralinguistic channels. Duncan (1972) listed the following behaviours as 'Turn Yielding Signals' to act as '*Cues*' for the next speaker to take the floor:

- Intonation: the use of any rising or falling intonation contour.
- Drawl on the final syllable, or on the stressed syllable of a terminal clause.
- Sociocentric sequences: the use of one of several stereotyped expressions, typically following a substantive statement, e.g. '*or something*', '*you know*', etc.
- Pitch/loudness: a drop in pitch and/or loudness in association with a sociocentre sequence.
- Syntax: the completion of a syntatic clause involving a subject–predicate combination (i.e. a completed statement).
- Gesture: the termination of any hand gesticulation or the relaxation of a tensed hand position.

It can be seen that there is a range of signals to indicate that you're handing over to the next speaker. We can of course accidentally or deliberately misread these signals. But the give and take of conversation will make it flow if all participants want it to continue.

As with all social interaction we manage this flow through a combination of attending to:

- the topic, task, context
- the relationship
- the verbal channels
- the non-verbal channels.

5.3 Closing

We do not usually simply end a conversation by stopping our talk and our listening. If we do so, then we give off rather a brusque and rude impression.

Quite often it is difficult to make a smooth transition to close an interaction. We can occasionally simply say: '*Well, that's it. We've finished now*' or, we may look at a clock and stand up to indicate that we have to be elsewhere. The nature of the relationship and of the context will dictate suitable closing strategies. There may be tensions between needing to leave and not wanting to separate.

As with turn taking, it is possible to observe verbal, topic-based conventions and also non-verbal, relationship-based signals for disengaging from an interaction.

Verbally, the participants can summarize the encounter or look forward to future actions and thus show that the conversation is coming to an end. There will then be formal exchanges, such as:

– 'Fine, OK. That's it then'
– 'See you next week when we'll check how it's going'
– 'Bye, see you'
– 'Bye, see you.'

A conversation needs to be concluded in the appropriate mood for future contact, or for future non-contact.

Non-verbally, there are a range of closing conventions. These include, breaking of eye-contact; clearing up papers; standing up; straightening clothes, hair, etc., ready for departure; smiling; shaking hands and so on. Early signals to end may be given, and then depending on the response, they can be adjusted to prolong the encounter, or may be continued in order to close it.

In long-standing relationships, as opposed to one-off encounters, the closing strategies are important moments not only to end the face-to-face contact, but also to set the tone for the next encounter. With someone close to you, there may be a bitter feeling on either side if one of the partners leaves without the ritual hug and kiss. With a working colleague, there would be uneasiness if you simply walked out without jointly signalling the close of the conversation.

5.4 Questioning

This is an essential skill for any type of interaction. Questions are used to obtain different sorts of information (the task) and to keep the interaction moving forward (maintaining the relationship).

As with many social skills, we may feel we know how to ask questions because we have been doing so since we could first talk. However, it is possible to refine these skills, especially for particular purposes whether interviewing, teaching, market surveys, counselling, interrogating or social conversation.

It is useful to think in terms of open questions (what were you doing last night?); closed questions (did you stay at home last night?); leading questions (isn't it true to say that last night was the best night of your life?); recall questions (were you at the party at 8.00 p.m.?); process questions (how could you have improved the party last night?); and affective questions (do you feel embarrassed about talking about last night?). It is easy to assume that because a question has been asked there must be an answer, but a useful text book on communication (*The dynamics of human communication* by Myers and Myers, 1992) suggests that there are 'unanswerable' questions. As examples, they cite two types of question – 'Is photography an art?' to which there is no definite answer, and for which the response is simply a matter of semantic definition. Secondly, 'does God exist?' to which again there is no definite answer and for which the response depends on personal values and beliefs.

5.5 Listening

As with questioning, we may well believe that we have been listening successfully to other people all our lives. However, we might also accept that often we *hear* other people talking but we don't always *listen* to what they are saying. In recent years several large business organizations in the UK have made listening a theme in their advertising campaigns. For example, we are told that one of the major British banks is 'the listening bank'. The implication is that if the bank listens to its customers it shows that it takes its customers seriously.

Listening, like all acts of perception, is an active, not a passive process. We need to attend to what is being said, select from it and then interpret it for ourselves.

Common **problems of listening** come from:

- merely taking note of the information and content and not taking note of the context and feeling behind it;
- allowing ourselves to be distracted and sidetracked into our own interests, which often leads us to hearing only what we want to hear;
- being put off by the context or by the speaker;
- preparing our response before the speaker has finished;
- not looking as if we're listening, i.e. failing to give verbal and non-verbal feedback to the speaker.

A useful discipline to develop our listening skills was devised by Carl Rogers, a psychotherapist and counsellor who developed a client-centred therapy method. At the heart of this therapeutic method Carl Rogers stressed the need to listen to what his clients were really saying through their verbal and non-verbal messages. To do this he believes you must empathize with the other person. That is, you must imagine how it would make sense to say what the other person is saying without filtering it through *your* own beliefs and experiences. In order to develop this skill he suggests that before you reply to a speaker you repeat in your own words what the speaker has just said to the speaker's satisfaction. This method certainly slows up a conversation or a meeting. But if you try it, it does make you listen, and usually shows that most of the time we do not listen to what other people are really saying.

As well as this technique of 'reflecting' or mirroring back what you have just listened to, an active listener will also be giving verbal and non-verbal feedback to **show** that she/he is listening to the other person. This can be positive head nodding or smiling or saying 'yes, I see' at appropriate points.

Like all other activities as part of interaction, listening is a mutual activity – all parties need to display the skills of listening. A conversation comes to an end if either partner stops listening. A good conversationalist spends more time listening than speaking and concentrates on what the other person says rather that what she/he will say next. An exercise in listening skill is to listen to a radio news broadcast with full attention and monitor the stories without taking notes. When it is finished, write down as much as you can remember. You can then gauge for yourself how fully you normally give full attention and listen actively without wandering into your own intrapersonal distractions.

5.6 Using Non-Verbal Communication

The clearest example of conscious learning of the social skills of non-verbal behaviour is in the training of an actor – the most important way of revealing a character on stage, film or TV is through non-verbal cues. Hence an effective way of observing non-verbal behaviour, especially facial expression, body movements and gestures, is to watch some TV drama with the sound off. As you would expect, the effect is generally more obvious and larger than real life and it is interesting to contrast such conscious acting of a part with the silent 'performances' of people in a factual piece of television such as a documentary, or news. We can thus analyse other people's non-verbal behaviour, consider how we normally 'read' people's behaviour in daily life, and compare our own use of NVB. It is possible with a video recorder to review the same sequences of social interaction several times and to concentrate on specific elements each time – e.g. gaze and eye contact, gestures, facial expressions and so on.

Another interesting and accessible way of developing increased sensitivity to one specific type of non-verbal behaviour is by recording from the radio. This medium of course has no non-verbal channel except paralanguage and the occasional 'sound effect' or 'background noise'. As with TV, you can listen to radio drama to concentrate on how a character and relationships are developed without any visual observation of non-verbal behaviour. And by way of comparison, also listen to factual radio programmes: at the very least it heightens one's awareness of how we place people through their use of language and paralanguage (i.e. in terms of age, gender, nationality, social class, temperament and even personal appearance). We attend to such things as their accent, tone, speed of speech, volume and pitch. We characterize a voice as friendly/unfriendly, cold/warm, educated/uneducated, young/old, all from aspects of paralanguage.

As students of communication we may engage in field observation of social interaction – shops, streets, waiting rooms, publications, sport, schools, cafes, pubs and so on provide rich data for analysing non-verbal behaviour. How do customers and salespeople negotiate non-verbally? How do couples or groups in a cafe interact non-verbally? You may try to draw conclusions about people's attitudes and relationships from their non-verbal behaviour – who's trying to impress whom? Who's dominant? Who's nervous?, and so on.

As well as observing others, try some experiments with your own non-verbal social skills by breaking conventions, e.g. whilst speaking to a friend maintain eye-contact or avoid any eye-contact. Try to note your 'normal' use of eye-contact.

The importance of eye-contact and the disturbance we feel when it does not follow our culturally programmed expectations was used as part of an advertising campaign by the Spastics Society, now renamed SCOPE, (see Fig. 3.4).

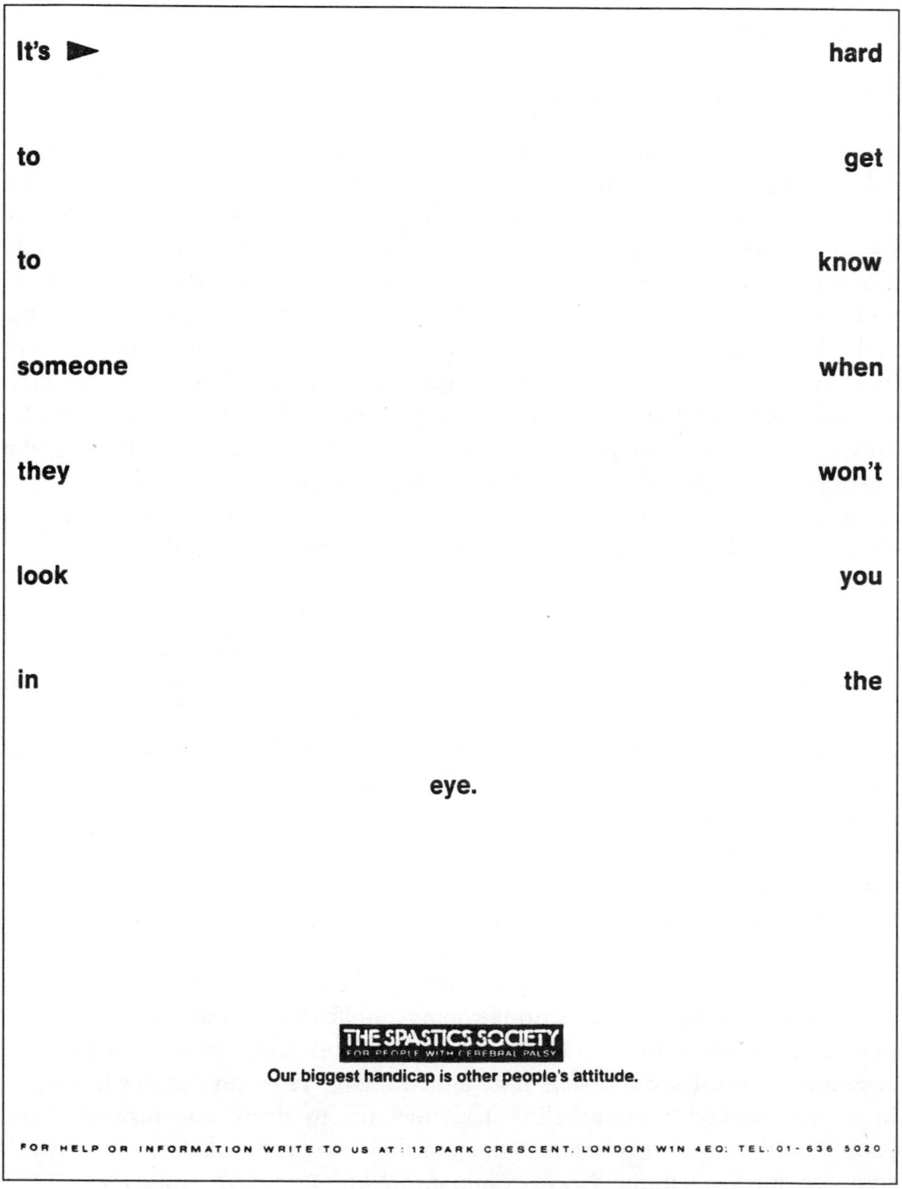

It's ▶   hard

to   get

to   know

someone   when

they   won't

look   you

in   the

eye.

THE SPASTICS SOCIETY
FOR PEOPLE WITH CEREBRAL PALSY
Our biggest handicap is other people's attitude.

FOR HELP OR INFORMATION WRITE TO US AT: 12 PARK CRESCENT, LONDON W1N 4EQ; TEL. 01-636 5020

Fig 3.4 *Advertisement for the Spastics Society – barriers to communication*

As we shall see in the next chapter, presenting ourselves to other people is about 'defining the situation' for other people and managing the impression that other people get of us. **Effective communication is about gaining the desired response from someone else.** Once again Bandler and Grinder neatly sum up this idea:

> The meaning of your communication is the response that you get. If you can notice that you're not getting what you want, change what you're doing.

If we can see and feel the way another person is handling their experience, how they really feel, and if we reflect that back to them through mirroring their use of words and non-verbal communication, then we will build an effective relationship for interactions.

5.8 Assertiveness

Assertiveness training has become a common phenomenon in the past 20 years: it's likely to be available as an evening class at your local college. Many people believe that these courses are aimed at women who stereotypically are portrayed as submissive as compared to the stereotypical male aggressiveness. Several books listed at the end of this chapter deal with male and female socialization which tends to create different linguistic and communicative behaviour for men and women.

However, the need for assertiveness as a communication skill applies to everyone. It is likely that any reader of this book had dreaded or sought to put off an awkward meeting with someone, or dreaded making a complaint about something even though they felt it was justified. Similarly many of us find it difficult to say 'no' when we are asked to do something by our partner or boss even though we do not want to do it.

Being assertive is not the same as being aggressive. It enables you to express your view in a clear and confident way without putting down the other person. Dickson (1988) draws the distinction between aggression and assertion very clearly:

> Aggressive behaviour is competitive, overriding, always lacking in regard for the other. It means winning at someone else's expense. Assertion is based on equality not superiority, co-operation not competition, honest and appropriate expression of feelings instead of ruthless expression of them . . .

All of the elements of interaction and social skill we have discussed here can be used to create encounters that are mutually assertive, in which people express themselves and are accepted as themselves.

But, how do we deal with difficult people?

Ursula Markham in her book, *How to deal with difficult people* (1993) has a great deal of useful advice on the difficulties you may meet and applies many of the skills outlined here. In particular she roots the notion of assertiveness in terms of 'rights'. As an assertive person you have certain rights:

- You are entitled to ask for what you want – but you also have to remember that the other person is entitled to say no.
- You are entitled to make decisions and choices for yourself.
- You are entitled to your own opinions and feelings, to acknowledge them to yourself and to express them to other people.
- You are entitled to make mistakes, bearing in mind that others must be allowed to make mistakes too.
- You are entitled not to know everything.
- You are entitled to decide whether you want to become involved in someone else's problems.
- You are entitled to change your mind.
- You are entitled to privacy.
- You are entitled to achieve.
- You are entitled to alter yourself in any way you choose – granting the same right to other people.

KEY QUESTIONS

Observe or videorecord a conversation.

Write down the cues used by the participants which influence how the interaction is carried on.

Explain how assertiveness might help someone improve their social relationships.

6   COMMUNICATION AND RELATIONSHIPS

Any relationship is conceived, affirmed, conducted and even broken by the use of communication. People build or destroy bridges between one another, and those bridges are built from communication. However, if the communication is a bridge then it is one that carries an immensely complex traffic of meanings. These meanings are about nuances of feelings in a relationship, about its condition, about where it is going. There is a great deal of non-verbal traffic which travels across with deceptively simple phrases such as, *I really like you.* The communication style of a given relationship is peculiar to its participants. It isn't possible to prescribe 'good communication' for a relationship, although in what follows you will find references of ways of talking which are more likely to lead to 'success' than others are.

6.1 Establishing Relationships

Obviously relationships are established when people make various kinds of communicative contact – eye contact, greetings and the like. Given different social conventions and situations, people have different expectations of the kind of relationship that they may wish to establish. There is, for example, the birth relationship of parents and child, the business relationship of worker and client, the personal relationship of one adult loving another. It is this last from which we will tend to draw examples in this section.

The social exchange theory suggests that people form relationships on the basis of rewards and gain. They will use communication to establish a bond with one or more other people because they see some rewards in it for them, and they believe that they will gain something. Deaux and Wrightsman (1984) also point out that 'people may measure the gains in a relationship against some baseline that they have come to expect'. This would support a view that people can find it more difficult to establish relationships as they get older; they have changed their 'baselines' as they get older, and have become more particular about the rewards they expect.

There is a view of adult love relationships known as 'love at first sight'. Certainly passionate relationships can develop quickly. Unfortunately the evidence is that this is an indicator that such relationships will be short term. Also, the cues for initial attraction between people do not of themselves predict long-term stability in the relationship. There is also evidence that the 'arranged marriage' is not a bad way of establishing a relationship. This evidence comes from research which makes it clear that in many cases similarities of age, education, intelligence and attractiveness are good predictors of the survival of a pair bond. It has also been found that common interests, common values and similar personalities are a fair predictor of success in forming a relationship. The work of dating agencies confirms this. In fact many people do use their perceptual skills to search our similarities. People have a 'preference for the familiar over the unfamiliar' (Duck, 1993).

6.2 Developing and Maintaining Relationships

The quality of any relationship depends on the positive use of social and perceptual skills. People who try to empathize with one another are likely to relate successfully. By the same token, people who play games with one another are likely to destroy a relationship. To make one more link within this book, assertiveness within a relationship should be a healthy thing because it includes the honest expression of feelings and needs. Of course this may not work out if one partner has a poor sense of self-esteem and sees the assertiveness as being threatening.

Poor perception of others is broadly based on false assumptions. Such assumptions are likely to be dangerous and even prevalent in early stages of a romantic relationship because of the force of attraction. We can project on to others, we can believe that the other person has the same attitudes and values, likes and dislikes as ourselves because we want to believe it. These assumptions actually lead to a lack of communication. Hence the finding that many married couples have never clearly discussed intimate matters such as whether or not to start a family, let alone when and how many children they would like to have. Once a relationship and communication is well established between a couple then a degree of assumption may not be a bad thing. Being able to be quiet with a partner does not mean that feelings do not exist. Older couples may justifiably make some assumptions and communicate accordingly, precisely because they have done a lot of careful perceiving. But again, **it is the quality of communication in the early stages which establishes the quality of a relationship long term**. Even a long-term relationship lacks quality if it is in fact based on long-term false assumptions.

In one sense a relationship is developed by using communication to establish information about the other person which reduces uncertainty. The more one is sure about another person's background, activities, beliefs, the more one is able to be sure that the relationship is or is not likely to develop. It has been observed that couples will often 'test' one another to sort each other out or to sort out which stage of the relationship they are at. Testing might be about words used to provoke statements of belief, or might be about intimate gestures used to test the 'trust' and 'liking' stage of the relationship as far as the other person is concerned. Relationships are always developed through degrees of self-disclosure in which the participants gradually reveal information, feelings, attitudes to each other through their communication. By definition, self-disclosure involves trusting the other person, and when such trust is reciprocated then one feels that much more intimate with and bonded with the other person.

Duck (1993) says that 'interdependence of the two individuals in a relationship is an essential element to relationships and to relationship development'. He also refers to Hinde's ideas about the features of a developing relationship. These are:

- The content of interactions – what people talk about. The more a relationship develops, the more personal is likely to be the subject matter.
- Diversity of interactions – different kinds of situation and communication between people. The more activities a couple share the better they are likely to 'get to know' one another.
- Qualities of interactions – the style of talk. Words whispered into someone's ear betoken a kind of trust different from the same words spoken across usual body space.
- Frequency and patterning of interactions – how often we communicate. A lot of interaction and communication that is patterned according to the needs of both partners signifies a positive relationship.

- Reciprocity and complementarity – whether people respond as they are expected to socially or whether they respond in a way that matches the other person's need. Those who respond in a complementary way are more obviously considering their partner and are signifying a degree of intimacy in their relationship.
- Intimacy – the personal closeness of communication actions. There is well-established work on the significance of intimate touching in relationships.
- Interpersonal perception – mutual judgements and self knowledge. Successful relationships include the ability to have an accurate view of how one is seen by one's partner.
- Commitment – the degree of time and trouble that one is prepared to go to for the other person. Commitment includes sexual exclusivity with a partner, but more generally is about putting the needs and interests of the other person before one's own.

In terms of the **continuation of a relationship** there are a number of factors that will affect this, not the least of which is the partners' relationship to others. Duck talks about 'ways in which interior aspects of relationships are communicated to others'. It is also true that how others communicate their view of a relationship will affect its stability. A relationship may not even progress if, for example, parents express strong opposition to a couple getting together. On the other hand, just the act of sharing talk with other people helps validate the relationship. But that talk must be a positive experience. Public disagreements and negative feedback can be as damaging to a relationship as private quarrels. Connected with this is the idea that having a variety of activities, having friends, exchanging activities is a positive thing. It seems that social experience for couples is on the whole concerned with kinds of play and is helpful. Private experience – running a home and so on – can be pretty much routine, and doesn't do much to make life exciting. At the same time, sorting out roles and responsibilities through which to run a relationship does seem to be important to its survival.

In fact, Argyle and Dean (1965) proposed an **equilibrium** model for relationships. This would seem to be a development of Heider's earlier theory in which people balance liking and disliking in their evaluation of others. The equilibrium model is about the balance between wanting to approach people and wanting to avoid pressures from others; about needing relationships but fearing rejection. In particular they proposed that often the balancing was carried out by using non-verbal behaviour to 'compensate' for what was said. One person might suggest a meeting with another using words. The other person doesn't want this closeness, and balances the relationship by making non-verbal signs to indicate 'distance'.

However, it does seem that in terms of how people actually do maintain their relationships (as opposed to how some people might think they should do this), it isn't just a matter of seeking a balance at any stage of intimacy which preserves some kind of *status quo* at that time. It has been found that some couples maintain by using avoidance techniques, i.e. there are things that they don't talk about, by tacit agreement. On the other hand, some work successfully by being very direct and always talking about issues and feelings. Equally, being direct can become a kind of fetish and not take account of sensitivities. In general it would seem that directness, disclosure, open-ness are more likely to maintain than are other ways of using communication.

Howitt *et al.* (1989) talk about an attraction–dependency theory. They see attraction as being about qualities which make a current relationship better than anything that has gone before. Dependence they see as identifying the fact that our present relationship is better than anything else that is possible. One consequence could be that if the quality of the relationship drops below previous experience, or if a better relationship becomes possible, then the existing one is threatened and may not be maintained.

6.3 Ending Relationships

In one sense what has been said so far explains why and how communication may end. A lack of social skills, a lack of equilibrium, a lack of social networking are all factors which may well lead to the breakup of a relationship. One never knows for sure. Sometimes relationships are maintained (but not quality) when people stick together simply because the alternatives are uncomfortable. This is especially true of marriages, where the economic and social interdependency of a couple is such that splitting up would cause huge practical problems as well as personal discomfort.

Relationships may break up before they are well established because partners are aware of a lack of development – it wasn't going anywhere. It had also been found that men tend to have greater needs for power in a relationship than do women. In this case there is a correlation between the degree of male power demanded and expressed, and the likelihood of the relationship breaking down. On the other hand, women are more likely to actually end the relationship than are men.

Research carried out by Noller (1980) also suggests gender differences in terms of effective communication. This indicates that men are less effective than women in sending clear messages and in respect of a tendency to interpret the female partner's communication adversely in some way, when this was not the intention. It is not surprising that one can then argue that poor married relationships are about poor communication. However, there is also an argument about symptom and cause. One view is that failures of communication are symptoms of underlying causes. On the other hand, one needs to remember the view that one doesn't actually know anything about the other person than through their communication. So in a sense it is pointless talking about hidden feelings or attitudes which may be relevant. They remain hidden precisely because either one partner does not express themselves clearly or because the other partner is incompetent at picking up relevant signs of communication.

Baxter (1986) describes **eight elements of a relationship which partners value.** The loss or absence of one or more of these elements tends to predict the breakdown of the relationship – though this can only be a generalization. The elements are:

- a degree of autonomy (personal freedom)
- a certain amount of similarity (in views, interests, likes)
- mutual support
- loyalty and good faith
- honesty
- time together (both private and public)
- fair sharing of efforts and resources (goods, time, money)
- a sense of something special between them.

Duck (1993) recognizes **four phases in the dissolution of a relationship,** all of which can be seen as being very much about communication.

- Intrapsychic phase: in which one or both partners have intrapersonal reflections on the other, on the negative aspects of the relationship, on the possibility of breaking it up.
- Dyadic phase: in which there is talk between the two people about what is wrong and what might happen. The relationship can be repaired at this stage. But a lot depends on how open and constructive the talk is.
- Social phase: in which the partners actually talk to each other about breaking up, with each other about the realities of this, in which they begin to reorganize things in their heads to make themselves feel better about it all.
- Grave Dressing phase: in which the breakup has occurred or is about to, and communication is all about getting over it and about public versions of what has happened and why.

The essence of our social experience is that of the relationships which bind us to other people. The life cycle of human beings all the world is bound up with the formation of pair bonds. These relationships happen because of communication. The nature of the communication defines the nature of the relationship, its qualities, its continuance, or indeed its collapse.

Describe (with examples) the kind of communication that would be good in keeping a relationship going.

7 CULTURE AND COMMUNICATION

> And as a black child growing up in London I was baffled by the frequency and the poignancy of my father's complaints that I and my brother had no 'respect'. It took thirty years and the chance to visit and observe the rural Jamaica where he grew up for it to dawn on me what cultural and social resonance the word had for him and why it mattered.
>
> Foreword by Diane Abbott in *Transcultural counselling in action*
> by Patricia d'Ardenne and Aruna Mahtani, 1992.

Throughout this book we have made reference to the importance of 'culture' as a factor in the development of the self and in the ways we use language and non-verbal communication and also as the determinant of the world view we each develop. In this section we shall explore some of these cultural, or subcultural, issues and in particular some aspects of communication between people from different cultural backgrounds.

7.1 Interpersonal Communication and Culture

We can summarize the key elements of IPC as we explore them in this book as follows:

- **Our concept of self is the product of socialization and enculturation processes throughout our life.** These processes are explored through studies in social psychology, anthropology, sociology and media studies.
- **This self uses forms of communication – language , non-verbal behaviour, personal resources and skills – to share meanings with other people.** We use the word 'meaning' to indicate that what is shared is based on inferences and judgements and is not simply information or fact. There are always degrees of ambiguity and subjectivity and levels of meaning from simple denotation to personal and cultural connotations, for example, if someone said 'Isambard Kingdom Brunel designed the Clifton suspension bridge' the meaning and implication of that statement would vary according to the way it was said and the context in which it was said. We leave you to consider different emphases and different situations that could affect the meaning of that statement.
- **The forms of communication we use are the creator, and product of, relationships between individuals.** As children we learn and experiment with these forms and go on exploring them more or less consciously throughout our life.
- **Personal relationships are in turn part of a wider life that creates, and is the product of, a particular culture in which we operate.** We experience this culture directly through personal contact and indirectly through books, the media and other people's experience which they recount.

Figure 3.5(a) illustrates the way in which interactions between people involve these elements. This diagram indicates that these two people, their communication forms and relationships are within a common cultural frame in which they share common values and assumptions, a 'common sense'.

Figure 3.5(b) illustrates the way in which interactions between people from different cultures, or subcultures, have to cross cultural boundaries.

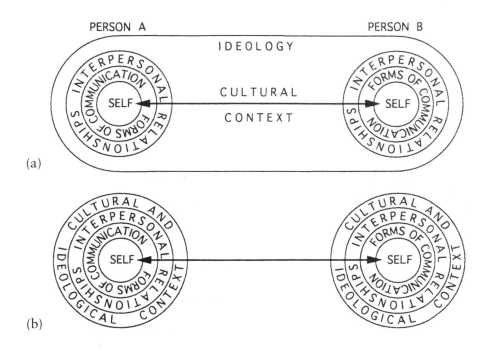

Fig 3.5 (a) *Culture, context and communication, (b) interpersonal, intercultural communication*

7.2 What is Culture?

It is important at this point that we briefly make explicit what we understand by the term culture and the way we are using the term here. Williams (1983) considered that 'culture is one of the two or three most complicated words in the English Language'. It has been invested with layers of meaning well beyond its origin in the sense of 'growing process' (a sense in which it is still used in the phrase 'a test tube culture').

Jenks (1993) describes the genesis of our concept 'culture' through four sources:

• Culture as a cerebral, or certainly, cognitive category which is a general state of mind. It carries with it the idea of perfection, a goal or an aspiration of individual human achievement. We sometimes speak of a 'cultured person'.

- Culture as a more embodied and collective category which reflects a state of intellectual and/or moral development in society. In this sense culture is linked with notions of 'civilization'.
- Culture as a descriptive and concrete category, viewed as the collective body of arts and intellectual work within any one society. This is probably the meaning of the word in everyday language – and sometimes it is given a capital letter: Culture.
- Culture as a social category; culture regarded as the whole way of life of a people: this is the pluralist and potentially democratic sense of the concept that has come to be the zone of concern within sociology and anthropology and latterly, within a more localized sense, cultural studies.

Here, in the context of communication studies, we are using the term culture primarily in the sense of section four in Jenks's typology: 'the whole way of life of a people'. Hence, if you are communicating with someone who is in the whole way of life a different set of people the forms of communication, the expected relationships and the world view are likely to be different.

There are issues around where the limits of a culture might be delineated. This in turn leads to the notion of culture in which there are subcultures. The most familiar examples of this are based on different ethnic groups living within what is sometimes called a 'majority culture', or generational groupings with different dress and behaviour codes from the majority.

We are not using culture here in the sense of High Culture, *'the best which has been thought and said in the world'* (Arnold, 1932). In fact, his nineteenth century view of 'the best' would have excluded a number of cultures and societies which we would now, with a knowledge of twentieth century anthropology, not consider as 'primitive or inferior'. Every culture is complex.

Scollon and Scollon (1995) sum up the usefulness of the concept of culture for analysing interpersonal and intercultural communication:

> . . . we want to mention that there is an intercultural problem in using the word 'culture' itself. In English there are two normal uses of this word: high culture, and anthropological culture . . . . In studies of intercultural communication, our concern is not with high culture, but with anthropological culture. When we use the word 'culture' in its anthropological sense, we mean to say that culture is any of the customs, worldview, language, kinship system, social organization and other taken-for-granted day-to-day practices of a people which set that group apart as a distinctive group. By using the anthropological sense of the word 'culture', we mean to consider any aspect of the ideas, communications, or behaviours of a group of people which gives them a distinctive identity and which is used to organize their internal sense of cohesion and membership.

At its simplest then, we use the term to refer to areas of commonality, the taken-for-granted. It is helpful to label cultural differences as, for example, national, racial, ethnic, generational, gender, religious and so on, which then indicates the roots of what creates different worldviews.

Before leaving this discussion of 'what is culture?', we wish to refer again as elsewhere in the book to the concept of 'discourse'. Again, discourse is now a widely used term that carries different meanings according to the context. Originally it referred to a system of language use, and discourse analysis was, and is, the study of how a certain type of language use naturally occurs within a specific group.

Stubbs (1989) provides a useful working definition:

> The term discourse analysis is very ambiguous. I will use it in this book to refer mainly to the linguistic analysis of naturally occurring connected spoken or written discourse. Roughly speaking, it refers to attempts to study the organization of language above the sentence or above the clause, and therefore to study larger linguistic units such as conversational exchanges or written texts. It follows that discourse analysis is also concerned with language in use in social contexts, and in particular with interaction or dialogue between speakers.

Hence we might talk of 'academic discourse' to signal the way that words are chosen and arranged amongst academics, or 'TV discourse' to signal the way that language is used within television.

We have referred elsewhere to discourse analysis as a technique for analysing the flow of conversation (see page 102) and here the analysis goes beyond the purely linguistic to include non-verbal patterning signals. These are also called 'speech events'.

It is easy to see how the link has been made between a 'culture system' and a 'discourse system'. The latter is the distinctive ways in which a particular group uses language and other forms of communication to share their meanings and cultural traditions and values.

Scollon and Scollon (1995) have developed the useful concept of 'interdiscourse communication' to analyse the difficulties that individuals from different cultures or groups meet when they try to share meanings even when using the same 'language' such as English:

> When as Westerners or Asians we do business together, when as men or women we work together in an office, or when as members of senior or junior generations we develop a product together we engage in what we call 'interdiscourse communication'. That is to say, the discourse of Westerners or Asians, the discourse of men or women, the corporate discourse or the discourse of our professional organizations enfolds us within an envelope of language which gives us an identity and which makes it easier to communicate with those who are like us. By the same token, however, the discourses

of our cultural groups, our corporate cultures, our professional specializations, or our gender or generation groups make it more difficult for us to interpret those who are members of different groups. We call these enveloping discourses 'discourse systems' (see Fig. 3.6).

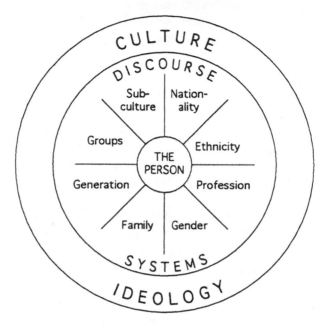

Fig 3.6 *Culture discourse and communication*

In recent years there has been considerable study of the different language/discourse systems of men and women especially in the US and UK societies (see page 102). Technically, one might want to describe these groups as 'male subcultures' and 'female subcultures' within an overall culture.

The view we wish to take here is that each culture or subculture is to be seen on equal terms. As students of communication we wish to avoid a particular 'ethnocentric' norm which might suggest, for example, that male patterns of language use are the cultural norm and female use is a deviant subculture.

It is the recognition of differences, the consciousness that each individual is the product of a particular set of experiences and processes of socialization that can help us in effective interpersonal communication within the same culture and across cultural differences.

7.3 Cross-Cultural Communication

We have chosen to use the term cross-cultural communication to describe the process of communication from one cultural group to another: elsewhere you will also meet the terms 'intercultural' and 'transcultural'. D'Ardenne and Mahtani (1992) have deliberately chosen the word 'trans':

> We have chosen the term 'trans' as opposed to 'cross' or 'inter' cultural counselling because we want to emphasize the *active* and *reciprocal* process that is involved. Counsellors in this setting are responsible for working across, through and beyond their cultural differences.

It is also important to stress that we are not talking about one culture communicating with another, but rather individuals communicating across cultural differences. Our focus is as always in this book on interpersonal communication. Cultures do not talk to each other, individuals do.

When you are trying to communicate across a cultural divide there are a number of issues to keep in mind:

■ Fundamental Differences in World View

It is easy at this point to fall into over-generalizations or even stereotypes. But with this caveat, it can be helpful to try to identify some of the basic values of your own and the other person's cultural background. For example, one of the differences often cited is whether a culture is basically 'individualistic' or 'collectivist'.

Triandis (1985) has studied some collectivist and individualist cultures and notes that people from the former tend to lay greater emphasis on factors such as age, gender and religion. They look for their own cultural group's norms and authority, and they are concerned with group loyalty and cohesion. People from individualist cultures tend to be less sensitive to the views of others.

Another significant value difference can be whether a culture tends to be more scientific/rational in its approach to life; or more led by religious belief systems. Another could be whether people are considered to be fundamentally 'good' or 'bad'. The Judaeo-Christian worldview is that 'man' is basically evil and needs to be saved in order to act with love and kindness. The Analects of Confucius, on the other hand, begin with the words: Man, by nature, is good; people's inborn natures are similar, but learning makes them different'. One could go on with other cultural value and philosophical differences, but these examples indicate the sorts of assumptions that may underlie people's communication acts.

■ Language and Discourse Differences

We have referred to these elsewhere in this book, for example see page 110, Making Conversation.

The ways in which verbal and non-verbal forms of communication are used between two people can vary, and the differences may not be recognized. For example, studies such as Tannen (1991) suggest that men use language more for information giving and receiving, whereas women use it more for establishing and maintaining a relationship.

With regard to NVC, Kinesics and Proxemics and Time concepts can be quite different, see page 106.

A short case situation from Scollon and Scollon (1995) illustrates how discourse system differences can affect cross-cultural communication:

> Two men meet on a plane from Tokyo to Hong Kong. Chu Hon-fai is a Hong Kong exporter who is returning from a business trip to Japan. Andrew Richardson is an American buyer on his first business trip to Hong Kong. It is a convenient meeting for them because Mr Chu's company sells some of the products Mr Richardson has come to Hong Kong to buy. After a bit of conversation they introduce themselves to each other.
>
> *Mr Richardson*:   By the way, I'm Andrew Richardson. My friends call me Andy. This is my business card.
>
> *Mr Chu*:   I'm David Chu. Pleased to meet you, Mr Richardson. This is my card.
>
> *Mr Richardson*:   No, no. Call me Andy. I think we'll be doing a lot of business together.
>
> *Mr Chu*:   Yes, I hope so.
>
> *Mr Richardson:* (reading Mr Chu's card): 'Chu, Hon-fai.' Hon-fai, I'll give you a call tomorrow as soon as I get settled at my hotel.
>
> *Mr Chu* (smiling): Yes I'll expect your call.

When these two men separate, they leave each other with very different impressions of the situation. Mr Richardson is very pleased to have made the acquaintance of Mr Chu and feels they have gotten off to a very good start. They have established their relationship on a first-name basis and Mr Chu's smile seemed to indicate that he will be friendly and easy to do business with. Mr Richardson is particularly pleased that he had treated Mr Chu with respect for his Chinese background by calling him Hon-fai rather than using the western name, David, which seemed to him an unnecessary imposition of western culture.

In contrast, Mr Chu feels quite uncomfortable with Mr Richardson. He feels it will be difficult to work with him and that Mr Richardson might be rather insensitive to cultural differences. He is particularly bothered that Mr Richardson used his given name, Hon-fai, instead of either David or Mr Chu. It was this embarrassment which caused him to smile.

This short dialogue is, unfortunately, not so unusual in meetings between members of different cultures. There is a tendency in American business circles to prefer close, friendly, egalitarian relationships in business engagements. This system of symmetrical solidarity, which has its source in the Utilitarian discourse system, is often expressed in the use of given (or 'first') names in business encounters. Mr Richardson feels most comfortable in being called Andy, and he would like to call Mr Chu by his first name. At the same time, he wishes to show consideration of the cultural differences between them by avoiding Mr Chu's western name, David. His solution to this cultural difference is to address Mr Chu by the given name he sees on the business card, Hon-fai.

Mr Chu, on the other hand, prefers an initial business relationship of symmetrical deference. He would feel more comfortable if they called each other Mr Chu and Mr Richardson. Nevertheless, when he was away at school in North America he learned that Americans feel awkward in a stable relationship of symmetrical deference. In other words, he found that they feel uncomfortable calling people Mr for any extended period of time. His solution was to adopt a western name. He chose David in such situations.

When Mr Richardson insists on using Mr Chu's Chinese given name, Hon-fai, Mr Chu feels uncomfortable. That name is rarely used by anyone, in fact. What Mr Richardson does not know is that Chinese have a rather complex structure of names which depends upon situations and relationships, which includes school names, intimate and family baby names, and even western names, each of which is used just by the people with whom a person has a certain relationship. Isolating just the given name, Hon-fai, is relatively unusual and to hear himself called this by a stranger makes Mr Chu feel quite uncomfortable. His reaction, which is also culturally conditioned, is to smile.

In this case there are two issues of intercultural communication we want to use to introduce our discussion of intercultural professional communication: one is the basic question of cultural differences, and the second is the problems which arise when people try to deal with cultural differences, but, like Mr Richardson, actually make matters worse in their attempts at cultural sensitivity.

■ Self Presentation

Chapter 4 discusses aspects of this in the context of the general cultural values of the US and Western Europe. However, in cross-cultural communication, we need to be aware that different cultures have different traditions about how the self is presented to others. Indeed, people from the USA are likely to be much more 'personal' in their disclosure and informal in their language use and behaviour than the traditionally more reserved British. Differences can also be seen in how much people involve others or remain independent. Within the same culture people can interpret the communication acts of others as being over-friendly or 'distant'.

Many languages, but not English, have different sets of informal or formal pronouns which signal the closeness of the relationship. For example, in France it would be unusual to address another adult on first meeting as 'tu' instead of the more formal 'vous'. Such uses of language, or non-verbal behaviour, that are considered odd by the other person can be interpreted at the very least as impolite.

■ Interpersonal Skills and Relationships

The range of what are considered to be appropriate interpersonal behaviours is culturally determined and will influence how people build relationships with others.

Each culture will have its own ritual greetings and behaviour patterns for farewells. These can include shaking hands, kissing one or more times on the cheek, bowing, hugging and so on. Axtell (1991) describes what seem to a person brought up in a non-contact culture as an exotic variety of different greeting rituals, for example:

> Greetings can be downright physical too to the point you may want to wear a football helmet and shoulder pads. Eskimos greet each other by banging the other party with a hand either on the head or shoulders. Polynesian men who are strangers welcome each other by embracing and then rubbing each other's back. Among the Matavai, friends who have been parted for some time scratch each other's head and temples with the tip of a shark's tooth often drawing blood.

Another area of difference is how one expresses personal feeling such as anger. The section on assertiveness (see page 00) is written from a 'western' point of view but in some religious or cultural groupings submissiveness on the part of one sex is expected. Issues of respect and treatment of elders are other examples of values that are shown through interpersonal behaviour.

■ Stereotypes

We wish to end with a note of caution. When dealing with cross-cultural communication it is easy to categorize other people into overgeneralized groupings. Cultural influences are just that, they are not determinants of behaviour or language use. It would clearly be nonsense to think that 'all men are task oriented and ignore other people's feelings', in the same way it would be nonsense to say that 'all women are submissive'. The word 'all' is a dangerous word when describing people and cultures.

Our brief treatment of intercultural issues in IPC does no more than indicate some of the issues. An appreciation of cultural differences can help in effective communication. We can draw inferences and interpret meanings from words and non-verbal behaviour that are quite mistaken if we fail to take into consideration different group behaviours and worldviews.

Language is itself an ambiguous form of communication. We each draw our own meanings from the same word as we discussed on page 94.

We will give the final word to Scollon and Scollon (1995) on whom we have drawn for much of the inspiration of this section. We recommend the book for those of you who wish to explore the topic further.

> In the contemporary world of international and intercultural professional communication, the differences between people are considerable. People are in daily contact with members of cultures and other groups from all around the world. Successful communication is based on sharing as much as possi-

ble the assumptions we make about what others mean. When we are communicating with people who are very different from us, it is very difficult to know how to draw inferences about what they mean, and so it is impossible to depend on shared knowledge and background for confidence in our interpretations.

8   SOCIAL SKILLS

Social skill is the sum total of our ability to interact with other people. It is the ability to take appropriate social initiatives, and understand people's reactions to them and respond accordingly. . . . Individual social skills include all of the various components of the behaviour we use in these social interactions – the right patterns of eye contact, the right facial expressions, gestures and tone of voice, saying the right thing, using humour and so on. Like any skill, we can learn these and get better at them with practice.

This extract from *Eye to eye: how people interact*, edited by Peter Marsh (1988) neatly sums up the idea of social skill – it is the result of learned patterns of behaviour and consists of verbal, non-verbal elements and responses to and from other people. In this book, we might have avoided the adjective 'right' since there is no absolutely right behaviour but rather behaviour that is considered mutually appropriate and effective in enabling people to share meaning.

In essence, **interpersonal social skills are the range of verbal and non-verbal behaviour patterns we have learnt that enable us to manage our encounters with other people.**

It is possible to refine and analyse these behaviour patterns down to minute moments of action and reaction. In this section we wish to provide an overview and a variety of perspectives on social skills. In the reading list at the end of this chapter you will find references to further sources of more detailed information.

Whatever the approach to describing interpersonal skills, we wish to stress that any social skill is more than a sequence of 'right' actions. A person-to-person interaction is rooted in the relationship that is built between those people; it is not the same as a person-to-machine relationship. This relational aspect has been stressed by us previously and sets a context for this section:

Interpersonal communication skills are also social skills which are used in various social relationships:
- Social skills can make communication with others effective and satisfying. It is a skill to make sense of others' feedback and to make appropriate responses. Key social skills are: to show approval to others, to empathize with others, to listen effectively, to present oneself appropriately, to perceive ourselves and others accurately, to control verbal and non-verbal

behaviour to good effect.

- Listening skills use non-verbal communication.

Key listening skills in social situations are: to acknowledge the person who is talking, to maintain the conversation effectively, to show approval of the other person.

- Perceptual skills are present in three stages of perception – recognizing, reflecting, and acting.

Key perceptual skills are: to make accurate observations of the other person, to avoid jumping to conclusions, to make careful judgements, to make appropriate responses to what is perceived about the other person.

From Dimbleby and Burton (1992).

A more comprehensive and detailed list of 'core social skills' can be found in *A handbook of communication skills*, edited by Hargie (1986). These are:

■ Non-Verbal Communication

Research usually divides non-verbal behaviour into seven dimensions or categories:

- **Kinesics**, which embraces all body movements such as hand, arm, head, foot, leg posture, gesture, eye movement and facial expression. The term 'body language' is often used for this.
- **Paralanguage**, which includes all sound patterns that are content free, that is the way words are spoken as well as pauses and speed.
- **Physical contact**, which ranges from touching to embracing.
- **Proxemics**, which describes space and distance between people and also the setting of territory.
- **Physical characteristics of people** including skin colour, body shape, physique and judgements such as attractiveness.
- **Personal adornment** such as perfume, clothes, jewellery, make up and hair style.
- **Environmental factors** that come from the physical setting in which the behaviour occurs, such as indoor or outdoor, type of room and how it is designed and decorated – an office is not usually also a kitchen.

A skilled communicator will use all of these in presenting themselves and in perceiving and responding to other people. An unskilled, or unaware, communicator will take all of these factors for granted and not use a range of choices in their use. There are obviously degrees of sensitivity to these factors – someone who stands very close shouting and poking their finger at another person is clearly using deliberately staged non-verbal behaviour to reinforce their words.

■ Questioning

Everyone knows how to ask a question, but asking questions that obtain the answers you want or gain the effect on other people that you want is a question of knowledge and skill.

There are clearly professions such as teaching, the law, personnel management, selling or social work where the effective use of question techniques is essential. In teaching, for example, questions may be used to check memory recall, to elicit knowledge, to solve problems, to speculate on the unknown and so on. A factual question is likely to be a closed question – 'when did Columbus discover America?' – expects a known answer. A speculative question is likely to be an open question – 'why do you think there is life after death?' expects a range of possible responses.

The context of interpersonal communication will strongly influence the appropriateness of questions. For example, a doctor or nurse while on duty can ask personal and private questions that would be socially unexpected, or unacceptable, in any other context.

Questions are also the energy that maintains, or extinguishes, a conversation. They are your means of showing interest and empathy. Pease (1992) notes that starting with a 'difficult question' can ensure that the communication process never flows easily:

> A real estate agent once revealed this trick of the trade. 'When a potential client walks in the door, I don't ask him what he has in mind. That's too hard a question to start out with. He'd become nervous and withdrawn. And if I pressed him, he would probably withdraw all the way out of the door. Instead I ask him what type of home he's living in right now. That puts him at ease, gets him feeling comfortable around me. After a while, either he or I will shift the conversation around to what he's got in mind'.

Pease comments, 'This advice also applies to social occasions. It's usually best to start with simple questions about topics in which others are likely to be interested . . .'.

This questioning technique is likely to show another person that you have empathy for them and help the interaction along. But, there is a general issue here about the whole notion of social skills.

The estate agent's 'trick of the trade' suggests the use of a skill to give yourself a manipulative power over others – in that well-known tradition of which Dale Carnegie's *How to win friends and influence people* is the best known example (Carnegie, 1938). We leave you to recognize such manipulations in your own or other people's behaviour: there is a difference between a genuine interest in the answer to your question and a question that is purely manipulative. However, there are shades across this spectrum: is the defence lawyer questioning the prosecution witness seeking the truth about an incident, or seeking to prove his/her client's innocence regardless of what actually happened? The nature of the questions is likely to reveal the motives.

■ Reinforcement

An effective communicator 'naturally' gives feedback to the person or people she/he is interacting with – this acts as reinforcement to the other person to keep on as they are, or if it's 'negative reinforcement' to ease off from what they are doing. Such feedback may be verbal or non-verbal – a gesture to carry on, a smile of encouragement, a maintaining of eye contact, nodding of the head or use of questions to maintain the flow and so on.

Such techniques are important in maintaining an encounter with someone else, and in building a relationship.

■ Reflecting

Elsewhere (see page 116) we have referred to the work of American Psychotherapist Carl Rogers, who is credited with coining the term 'reflecting' to refer to the action of paraphrasing what has been said by the other person in your own words. At its crudest it is simply a repetition of the other person's words, but the purpose is to seek to ensure a genuine empathy with the other person by seeking to reflect his/her feelings as they have just been expressed. It is also a technique to aid active and careful listening of what the other person has actually said.

To conduct an interaction such as an interview using this technique all of the time could be very tedious, but also could be effective in an emotional counselling interview. Used occasionally, it can be effective to ensure a genuine understanding of the other person's views.

■ Opening and Closing Sequences

These are important moments in any interaction for establishing the social relationship and for introducing the content or purpose of the interaction. In some cultures there can be elaborate greeting or parting routines that are expected. We discuss these elements more fully in later sections of this chapter.

■ Explaining

The ability to make something plain to someone else is clearly an important communication skill. Someone who has a passionate interest and knowledge of a topic can often find it difficult to explain that knowledge to others who do not share the passion. This skill depends on careful choice of words and linking of ideas, but also an empathy with the other person and a means of recognizing levels of interest and understanding, e.g. through feedback.

■ Self-Disclosure

We have introduced this skill in Chapter 1 (see page 37). In an interaction the levels of self-disclosure will reflect and determine the nature of the relationship.

In an intimate relationship self-disclosure of experience and feelings as well as opinions and ideas is a key factor. In a professional relationship levels of personal disclosure will be less. In the caring and medical professions the skill of one-sided disclosure built on professional trust is developed. Such self description may lead to the carer having more extensive knowledge or theories about the client than the client him or herself.

■ Listening

Listening is more than hearing. It is an active process of deliberately attaching meanings to sounds and calls for high levels of attention and concentration to interpret what is actually said by the other person. It is easy to hear what you think was said rather than what was actually said (see section 5.5).

■ Assertiveness

This skill will was discussed more fully earlier in this chapter. Here we want to stress the link between assertiveness and self-esteem (see page 11) and the differentiation of assertion from aggression.

Anne Dickson (1988) in her book *A woman in your own right – assertiveness and you* caricatures four stereotypical women (but it could also be men) who are either aggressive, passive, manipulative or assertive. Each of us exhibits these behaviour patterns in different situations. The assertive type of behaviour is described as follows:

> And so to Selma, the assertive woman. Selma respects herself and the people she is dealing with. She is able to accept her own positive and negative qualities and, in so doing, is able to be more authentic in her acceptance of others. She does not need to put others down in order to feel comfortable in herself. She does not believe that others are responsible for what happens to her. She acknowledges that she is in charge of her actions, her choices and her life. She does not need to make others feel guilty for not recognising her needs. She can recognise her needs and ask openly and directly – even though she risks refusal. If she is refused, she may feel rejected – but she is not totally demolished by rejection. Her self esteem is anchored deeply within herself; she is not dependent on the approval of those around her. From this position of strength, she is able to respond sincerely to others, giving herself credit for what she understands and feels.

Such a feeling of self-confidence enables one more easily to develop the range of social skills we are describing here, neither to manipulate or be manipulated but to encounter people with mutual respect.

The above are some of the core interpersonal communication skills. In addition to these, Hargie (1986) goes on to discuss others such as: interacting in groups (see Chapter 6); chairmanship (*sic*); negotiating and bargaining; case conference presentation; humour and laughter; handling strong emotions; and showing warmth and empathy.

This list of social skills reflects the types of skilled attainment and competence that a professional such as a teacher, social worker, nurse, doctor, salesperson or counsellor will seek. In recent years, it has become accepted that people who are involved in interpersonal interactions as part of their professional life require some social skills training. Social skills training (SST) focuses on the coding and decoding of non-verbal behaviour. If we wish to be able to express ourselves and present ourselves favourably, and to understand other people sensitively, then we can benefit from a clear understanding of how non-verbal behaviour is central to all social interactions.

At its most general, **we can describe social skill in terms of having the ability to control and monitor the information we give off to others and to read the information others give off to us.** If we are more socially skilled we should be able to manage our encounters with other people more positively.

These social skills can be of general use to enable us to cope with a range of life encounters with friends, with family, at work, formal and informal, friendly and hostile, and so on.

The term 'skill' in the context of human relationships may seem rather off-putting since it has connotations of a mechanistic process. Argyle and others have compared a social skill to a motor skill, such as riding a bicycle, in that both have:

- Specific aims and definite goals: for example in social interaction we might wish to convey knowledge, information or understanding; to obtain information; to change attitudes, behaviour, or beliefs; to change the emotional state of someone else; influence another person's personality, temperament; to work at a co-operative task; to supervise another person's activities, or to supervise and co-ordinate a group task.
- Hierarchical structure: small units of skill are built up into broader units, for example, being able to ask questions, to listen and to provide feedback are all specific skills which need to be combined to conduct an interview or to carry on a conversation.
- Perception of others' reactions: reading cues and monitoring feedback are both essential to social skills and for performing a physical action.
- Timing of responses to synchronize a smooth operation.

However, there are also fundamental differences between social skills and motor skills:

- Dealing with other people and their idiosyncrasies and changes is different from dealing with a mechanism.
- Empathizing with the other person to try to imagine how she or he feels is never necessary with a machine.
- Presenting yourself to another person is a dynamic process. Both they and the relationship are changing whilst a machine is a static object.
- Rules of social behaviour are not as rigid as the rules of a game or the rules for operating a machine.

We take the view that social communication skills are not the same as mechanical motor skills because they are people-based (predictable and unpredictable), because they are dynamic (changing personalities and relationships) and because they exist at various levels (conscious/unconscious, overt/covert). At the heart of social skills is a conscious sensitivity to our own and to other people's intentions, emotions, experience and verbal and non-verbal behaviours. Understanding of our social skills also depends on our paying attention to various theoretical analyses and practical explanations of interactions, such as those of Eric Berne and his notions of games (see Chapter 5), or those of Erving Goffman and his notion of public performance (see Chapter 4).

Social Interaction – a Skills Checklist

Verbal Skills
- Are you speaking too loudly or softly for the situation?
- Are you varying your tone, pace, etc.?
- Are you pitching your voice too high or low?
- Are you speaking clearly and aware of whom you are talking to?

Non-Verbal Skills
- Are you standing too close or too far away for the situation?
- Are you showing your attention to the other person?
- Is there any way in which your appearance may be inappropriate for the situation?
- Are you using facial expressions to express interest and provide feedback?
- Are you catching the other person's eye too much or too little?
- Is your posture too relaxed or too rigid?
- Are you using appropriate gestures?
- Does your body language match what you are saying?

Social Skills
- Is your speech too formal or relaxed for the situation?
- Do you give and receive feedback?
- Are you using appropriate questions to maintain the interaction?
- Do you show that you are interested and listening?
- Do you spend the appropriate time on opening and closing the interaction?

REVIEW

You should have learnt the following things from this chapter:

1 Introduction
Patterns of social interaction are learnt.

2 Social Interaction (SI)
The ability to interact with other people is an essential everyday skill.
   The main aspects of social interaction are:

- negotiation and generation of meanings
- self presentation and use of communication channels
- creation of a relationship in a social context.

3 Language and Social Interaction:
People in each culture have developed a language system that has a number of identifying features: use of vocal auditory channels, neutral symbols, meanings attached to sounds, cultural tradition, structures of sounds, ability to refer to concepts, ideas and things that are far removed, dependence on conventions of use, creativity.

Language and Controlling Interaction: We use language to control face-to-face encounters and to influence the relationships we wish to develop and to affect the ways we want to present ourselves.

Language Influencing Relationship: We use language (vocabulary, structure, register) to influence the nature of our relationship and the roles that we adopt.

Language and Self Presentation: We use language to present ourselves in different ways in different contexts to different people, with the intention of affecting how we are 'seen' by others.

Language and Subculture: What culture means is defined by the use of words within that culture. Subcultural groups define their identity and their values through the words that they use.

Language and Gender: Our understanding of what it means to be female is defined by particular uses of language. To some extent men and women use words in different ways. This affects the ways in which they interact. Special uses of language that define femaleness are said to be part of a discourse.

4 Non-verbal Behaviours and Interaction:
When in the presence of others our body language never stops. This non-verbal activity may be conscious, deliberate communication or it may be unconscious giving off of information. In any case, it fulfils several functions:

- conveys attitudes and emotions

- supports (or denies) or replaces verbal communication
- presents ourself to others
- regulates interaction through cues and provides feedback.

5 Making Conversation

We take conversation for granted, but it is a highly complex interaction between people. Openings to conversations are about making first impressions and offering greetings. These are often represented through a conventional set of verbal and non-verbal utterances. Turn-taking in conversation is seen as being rule based and signal based. Proper use of these rules and signals allows the interaction to flow smoothly.

Closing conversations also obeys conventions, has to recognize the relationship of the participants, and may predict later interactions.

Questions in conversation are used to obtain information and to develop the interaction. They may be described as: open, closed, leading, recall, process, affective.

Listening is an active process and is often helped by 'reflecting' back phrases used by the speaker.

Being sensitive to feedback from other people is a social communication skill. This includes noticing minute non-verbal signs which are given off unintentionally as a result of what has been called Neurolinguistic Programming. This supposes that we deal with experience in three modes: auditory, visual, kinaesthetic.

Assertiveness is about saying what you feel and what you want, but with consideration for others.

Assertiveness is not about being aggressive.

6 Communication and Relationships

Communication is crucial to the establishment, maintainance of and ending of relationships.

Interpersonal skills are important to good relationships.

Good relationships depend on elements such as trust and self-disclosure.

7 Cross-Cultural Communication

The Self is a product of the culture in which it is formed.

Personal relationships are also formed within the context of a given culture.

Culture is defined through the beliefs and behaviours shared by a given group of people.

The ideas of culture systems and of discourse have much in common.

Communication across cultures is best looked at on the level of individual, interpersonal communication.

Different cultures have different beliefs and values: one is not inherently superior to another. These beliefs include differences in the ways that communication is carried on and what it means to the participants.

One should not generalize about different cultural beliefs and behaviours, especially at the level of the individual.

> **8 Social Skills**
> Social skills involve the use of appropriate verbal and non-verbal behaviours which carry on an interaction that is successful for the people involved.
>
> Social skills include the controlled and sensitive use of non-verbal communication, questioning, reinforcement, reflection, explanation, self-disclosure, listening and assertiveness.
>
> Social skills are not as 'cut and dried' as manual skills.

CASE SITUATION

> Read the following short extract, then either:
>
> • Write approximately 200 more words of the conversation including his intrapersonal dialogue and their non-verbal behaviour.
> • Write the same situation from the woman's point of view.

Getting Started

It wasn't the first time she'd ignored him.

He first saw her when they were queuing for their grant cheques. He was in the A–L queue and she was next door in the M–Z. She looked just his type: tall, slim, short cropped hair – brown gently streaked blond, bead earrings, subtle make-up, student clothes. He'd tried to engage her in a smile. She resolutely avoided seeing him, but he knew that she knew that he was giving her the eye. She had that self-conscious, avoiding-seeing him look – she held her head just a little bit higher, she laughed to her friends just a little bit louder.

Now it's getting silly. Every time I see her she knows I'm looking but she doesn't look at me . . . It was twice yesterday. Three times the day before. I don't yet even know what course she's on.

Next time, I'll speak to her.

OK. This is it. There she is, at the bar with the same girl she was with yesterday.

Walk, purposefully but casually, next to her, money out to attract the barman. Not to be seen to be deliberately moving over to her. Now, half turning, obviously seeking the barman, but really just catching her eye – got it –.

'Hi. Can I get you a drink?'

She turns, looks, half smiles, 'I don't know, can you?' (Oh no! Bloody clever. She's probably doing the English Course.)

'I haven't managed it yet, and I've been here for ages', she smiled and lifted her eyebrows. (Oh, Oh, not putting me down, but ready to talk.)

'I don't expect so then. If he didn't notice *you*, he won't notice *me*', mutually gazing. (Blimey, did I really say that? Puke. Obvious flattery – probably put her off. You've gone too far, no, she's smiled, she's accepted it. Keep calm. The barman's seen us, he's coming over.)

'What do you want?'

'Half lager, please.'

'Two halves of lager, please, and . . .' leaning over her to see her friend, '. . . what do you want?'

'Gin and tonic. Thanks.' (Oh, my God – glad I like the lager girl. Good thing my grant cheque came last week.) 'And a gin and tonic.'

'Thanks.' Pay money. (Now what next? Keep calm.) Casually, my arm brushing hers, 'I saw you in the grant queue last week.'

'Yeah, I saw you too.'

Suggested Reading

Argyle, M. (1973): *Social encounters*. London: Methuen.

Argyle, M. (1983): *The psychology of interpersonal communication*, 4th edn. Harmondsworth: Penguin.

Argyle, M. (1988): *Bodily communication*. London: Methuen.

Atkinson, J. M. and Heritage, J. (1984): *Structures of social action: studies in conversation analysis*. Cambridge: Cambridge University Press.

Bolton, R. (1986): *People skills – how to assert yourself, listen to others and resolve conflicts*. Sydney: Prentice-Hall.

Coates, J. (1991): *Women, men and language: a sociolinguistic account of sex differences in language*. London: Longman.

Dickson, A. (1988): *A woman in your own right – assertiveness and you*. London: Quartet.

Dimbleby, R. and Burton, G. (1992): *More than words: an introduction to communication studies*, 2nd edn. London: Routledge.

Ellis, A. and Beattie, G. (1986): *The psychology of language and communication*. London: Weidenfeld & Nicolson.

Gahagan, J. (1984): *Social interaction and its management*, London: Methuen.

Glass, L. (1992): *He says, she says – closing the communication gap between the sexes*. London: Piatkus.

Hargie, O. (ed.) (1986): *A handbook of communication skills*. Beckenham: Croom Helm.

Markham, U. (1993): *How to deal with difficult people*. London: Thorsons.

Marsh, P. (ed.) (1988): *Eye to eye: how people interact*. London: Sidgwick & Jackson.

Montgomery, M. (1986): *An introduction to language and society*. London: Methuen.

Myers, G. and Myers, M. (1992): *The dynamics of human communication*, 6th edn, New York: McGraw-Hill.

O'Sullivan, T., Hartley, J., Saunders, D., Montgomery, M. and Fiske, J. (1994): *Key concepts in communication and cultural studies*, 2nd edn. London: Routledge.

Pease, A. and Garner, A. (1989): *Talk language: how to use conversation for profit and pleasure*. London: Simon & Schuster.

Scollon, R. and Scollon, S. W. (1995): *Intercultural communication: a discourse approach.*
    Oxford: Blackwell.
Tannen, D. (1991): *You just don't understand: women and men in conversation.*
    London: Virago.
Tannen, D. (1992): *That's not what I meant: how conversational style make or break
    your relations with others.* London: Virago.

See also the reference list at the end of this book.

Ulay Beauty Cleanser reveals the softer you.

Now, from Ulay, comes Ulay Beauty Cleanser to clean off your make-up and cleanse your face gently, thoroughly, perfectly.

And being uniquely Ulay, it leaves your skin softer, smoother, without a trace of greasiness. They say it helps you stay younger-looking.

What other cleanser dare say that?

D *Self Presentation – we put up a mask to front our public performances*

4

Self Presentation

> And indeed there will be time
> To wonder, 'Do I dare?' and 'Do I dare?'
> Time to turn back and descend the stair,
> With a bald spot in the middle of my hair –
> (They will say: 'How his hair is growing thin!')
> My morning coat, my collar mounting firmly to the chin,
> My necktie rich and modest, but asserted by a simple pin –
> (They will say: 'But how his arms and legs are thin')
> Do I dare?
> Disturb the Universe?
> In a minute there is time
> For decisions and revisions which a minute will reverse.
>
> From 'The Love Song of J. Alfred Prufrock' by T.S. Eliot

1 INTRODUCTION

As we have suggested in Chapter 1 of this book, our notions of **self-image and self-esteem** are crucial to our ability to participate in human communication transactions. Our communication processes – encoding and decoding meanings through shared symbol systems – begin and end in intrapersonal communication.

In this chapter we are turning our attention to the public display of self. In order to do this we shall be relying heavily on the work of the late Erving Goffman, an American social anthropologist and sociologist whose publications reflect his fieldwork in the UK and his USA. His first book, *The presentation of self in everyday life,* has become a classic, and the metaphor he adopts there of a '**dramaturgical performance**' provides an established terminology for describing the public performances that we play in our daily social interactions. The booklist at the end of this book provides a note of Goffman's other publications which reflect his further research into behaviour in public places and enclosed institutions. He was always concerned with observing, describing and analysing the details of how people behave in front of each other how they treat each other.

Let us begin with a note of how Goffman views some of the basic concepts we are exploring in this book and then move on to review some aspects of self-presentation using his terms to do so. The terms we shall be using include **Persona, Performing, Staging, Teams and Roles.**

Chapter 1 of this book provides a background of how people have come to define the concept of self and the next chapter on transaction analysis will be using a psychological model of the self and **ego states** as a tool for analysing transactions between people. Goffman's view of the self is based on our ability to project a self-image to other people:

> When an individual plays a part he implicitly requests his observers to take seriously the impression that is fostered before him. They are asked to believe that the character they see actually possesses the attributes he appears to possess, that the task he performs will have the consequences that are implicitly claimed for it, and that, in general, matters are what they appear to be. In line with this, there is the popular view that the individual offers his performance and puts on his show 'for the benefit of other people'. (Goffman, 1959)

Elsewhere, Goffman has succinctly expressed one of his concerns in the phrase *'a chief concern is to develop a sociological version of the structure of the self'* (Goffman, 1961).

Later in this chapter we shall review how far each of ourselves is a social construction.

In Chapter 3 we have explored some aspects of social interaction and social skills. At this stage it is worth quoting Goffman's definition of an interaction:

> Interaction (that is, face-to-face interaction) may be roughly defined as the reciprocal influence of individuals upon one another's actions when in one another's immediate physical presence. An interaction may be defined as all the interaction which occurs throughout any one occasion when a given set of individuals are in one another's continuous presence; the term 'an encounter' would do as well.

We are concerned with public actions, observable behaviour rather than private motives or 'hidden' personalities. The key words in this chapter are performance and role.

Let us briefly explore some of the concepts which Goffman uses to analyse self presentation.

2   PERSONA

Essential to the notion of the presentation of self in everyday life is the belief that each of us in our daily life is playing a series of parts. We learn roles for real-life as actors learn roles for make-believe. There are, of course, differences between real-life and 'the stage'; for example, in real-life we believe in the part we are playing and create the part for ourselves, in real-life we are performers and audience at the same time, and in real-life we write our own scripts.

Goffman consciously took some of his terms for discussing the presentation of self from the work of the American sociologist, Robert Ezra Park and refers to this quotation from one of Park's books:

> It is probably no mere historical accident that the word person, in its first meaning, is a mask. It is rather a recognition of the fact that everyone is always and everywhere, more or less consciously, playing a role. . . . It is in these roles that we know each other; it is in these roles that we know ourselves.
>
> In a sense, and in so far as this mask represents the conception we have formed of ourselves – the role we are striving to live up to – this mask is our truer self, the self we would like to be. In the end, our conception of our role becomes second nature and an integral part of our personality. We come into the world as individuals, achieve character, and become persons.
> (Robert Ezra Park, *Race and culture*, 1950)

We select our behaviours in order to create a desired impression in other people. Hence, we internalize the roles we choose and create a public self. Goffman believes that, as individuals and as teams, we are seeking in our interactions to 'define the situation' so that others will accept our definition of ourselves, of them and of the situation and thus we can control other people's responses to us. Other people are led to accept our definition of the 'reality'. For example, in a selling situation the salesperson wants to be able to convince a potential customer of the truth of what the salesperson says; in a teaching situation a teacher wants to be able to convince a student about the validity of his or her arguments.

In order for someone to create the impression they wish, they need to manipulate their conduct, their appearance and the social setting. Other people generally take our behaviour on trust, they infer and attribute to us the qualities that we deliberately give off. **This notion of 'giving off' an impression is essential to understanding self presentation.** Goffman draws a distinction between the impression that a person 'gives' and the expression that a person 'gives off'. He draws a distinction as follows:

> The first involves verbal symbols or their substitutes, which he uses admittedly and solely to convey the information that he and the others are known to attach to these symbols. This is communication in the traditional and narrow sense. The second involves a wide range of action that others can treat as symptomatic of the actor, the expectation being that the action was performed for reasons other than the information conveyed in this way.

It is clear that this idea links closely to that of social skills discussed in Chapter 3. If we are scoially skilled, we have learnt to control the apparently coincidental impression that we 'give off' about ourselves. We can, of course, only know people by their behaviour, hence we use the team attribution in describing our perception of others. We have to attribute causes to other people's behaviour. These questions of perception of other people have been discussed in Chapter 2.

Before leaving this section, we wish to note further this idea of 'mask'. In Western cultures, in contrast with some other cultures, we do not wear physical masks except in carnival and masquerade. Dark glasses, especially mirror glasses, can be used as a depersonalizing mask and some people have also argued that make-up, hairstyling and dress are used as forms of mask. We may wish to hide or protect our real selves, or we may wish to create a projected impression of how we want to appear. Fashion magazines provide a regular rich source of available masks for people to wear in order to face other people.

Smiling has also been described as a mask (Fast, 1970). We may keep smiling through the day, but the smile may hide our real feelings of anger, stress or annoyance. We just have a public face we must maintain.

Similarly, we use clothing to mask the body. This masking may cover what we are embarrassed by – both men and women may feel their body shape does not conform to the cultural ideal they would like. Or masking through dress may be used to make a declaration of group allegiances and professional identity. Such dress could be the graffitied leathers of a biker or the dark suits of bank workers.

This masking may have a lot to do with cultural values. For example, many women of the Muslim faith (say, Bangladeshi) wear clothes to mask the physical signs of their gender, and to show modesty and restraint. The priests of many cultures, including British Christians, wear robes and regalia which both emphasize their distinctive role and mask the ordinary human being within.

Also, some professions mask the individual person to create an impersonal social role. In the case of surgeons and their teams, the physical mask is used for hygienic reasons, but it also has the effect of hiding the person and helping their professional performance. A surgeon performs operations on other people that are so disturbing to contemplate that the ritual of hospitals serves more than just medical purposes. The whole paraphernalia of the place licenses behaviour that would be intolerable anywhere else.

Controlling our performance, both verbally and non-verbally, and hence defining the situation and leading the audience to adopt our view of the situation is what we now want to explore.

KEY QUESTIONS

Describe what are in your opinion four key characteristics of the Persona of a school teacher. Compare your answers with those of other people.

How does the concept of Persona relate to ideas about self?

3   PERFORMANCE

This term, taken from drama, implies some notion of deceit, i.e. seeking to appear to be something that we are not. However, this is not the sense in which we wish to use the word here. **We can present a performance that we believe is true and sincere and which we want observers to believe.** Goffman rather unnervingly writes that '*one finds that the performer can be fully taken in by his own act; he can be sincerely convinced that the impression of reality he stages is the real reality*'. Surely this is true for most of us for most of the time. We believe that we are presenting ourselves, our attitudes, ideas and actions. We are playing an unconscious role, we believe we are being ourselves. We believe in the impression that is being fostered by our own performance.

Certainly at the other end of the spectrum it is possible to conceive of a 'cynical' performance in which an individual has no belief in his/her own act and no concern with the beliefs of the audience. He or she is merely and deliberately putting on a performance to deceive – things are not what they seem. An example of this is, of course, the 'Confidence Man' who sets out to deceive to rob his victim. Another example, of a 'con' that is played because the audience demands its, would be the doctor who prescribes a placebo because the patient demands some treatment.

A moral dimension does come into this of course. We can expect that things are as they appear to be. Or as Goffman puts it, '*society is organized on the principle that any individual who possesses certain social characteristics has a moral right to expect that others will value and treat him in an appropriate way*'. In any particular performance, of course, we do not reveal ourselves completely and may indeed deliberately not disclose certain parts of ourselves. This issue of managing our self presentation and our perception of identity is fully described in Goffman's book *Stigma: notes on the management of spoiled identity*. People who are stigmatized or labelled in some way as 'abnormal' will manage information about themselves and not disclose information about themselves to some observers.

Goffman's contention is that without being dishonest or insincere, we do put on a performance to create a desired impression whenever we are in the presence of others. His observations of these performances were largely carried out in work situations, total institutions (mental hospitals, prisons or the armed forces), or in domestic situations where groups or individuals are consciously seeking to create an impression on other people. If we want to succeed in creating this impression we need to perform not only verbally, but more especially non-verbally where our 'real' feelings may leak. As we have noted in Chapter 3, people tend to rely more on non-verbal messages about other people than on the more consciously controlled verbal messages.

It is perhaps useful to think in terms of degrees of performance. You might like to reflect on your own communicative behaviour – are there moments when you feel you are not engaged in any sort of performance and can you define degrees through which your performance becomes more consciously played as the audience and social situations change? There are structured situations as in an interview, a first date or a formal occasion when your performance to create the desired impression is at its most staged. The idea of presenting performance suggests that an audience is needed: do you think we also perform for ourselves? Or when alone (or with a very intimate partner) do we drop the performing mask? Perhaps our giveaway is when we are conscious of being on stage and then retreat back stage where we can relax. Let us next look at this idea of staging.

KEY QUESTIONS

Performance

Describe two contasting performances displayed by an individual in two different situations (for example when receiving a ticket for a parking fine or when making complaints about the lateness of a train).

How does the concept of Performance relate to ideas about Attribution and the use of Strategies?

4   STAGING

As we manipulate our conduct and our appearance, our verbal and non-verbal communication channels for a personal performance, **we also manipulate our physical contact to create the appropriate setting.** On a theatrical stage we have make-believe performers playing roles in front of a real audience. In real-life the situation is rather different because participants are both performers and audience at the same time. This can lead to difficulties and Goffman spends a good deal of time discussing the **front stage** and **back stage** performances. The front stage is the public performance area where a careful manner and appearance are maintained. This front will provide the appropriate setting (of furniture, decor, physical layout and other items) for the desired performance. We can observe such staged fronts most deliberately created in, for example, shops, office reception areas, living rooms, or on ceremonial occasions. For example, devout Jewish families mark their Sabbath with a formal laying out of the table, including relevant symbolic 'props'. There is a breaking of bread and other ritual behaviours.

Key notes for front stage performances are politeness and decorum. The notion of front presupposes an area back stage where different norms of behaviour and decorum operate. This is the area where performers can drop their public mask, where different language norms can be used. Here the stage props are kept. A particularly clear example of this front/back can be found in restaurants where the stage door from private kitchen to public restaurant can mark a rapid change of decor, atmosphere, language and behaviour. One well-expressed example of this can be taken from George Orwell's *Down and out in Paris and London* (1951):

> It is an instructive sight to see a waiter going into a hotel dining room. As he passes the door a sudden change comes over him. The set of his shoulders alters; all the dirt and worry and irritation have dropped off in an instant. He glides over the carpet, with a solemn priestlike air. I remember our assistant maitre d'hotel, a fiery Italian, pausing at the dining room door to address his apprentice, who had broken a bottle of wine. Shaking his fist above his head he yelled (luckily the door was more or less sound proof) 'Tu me fais – do you call yourself a waiter, you young bastard? You a waiter! You are not fit to scrub the floor in the brothel your mother came from. Maquereau!'
>
> Words failing him, he turned to the door; and as he opened it he delivered a final insult in the same manner of Squire Western in Tom Jones.
>
> Then he entered the dining room and sailed across it dish in hand, graceful as a swan. Ten seconds later he was bowing reverently to a customer. And you could not help thinking, as you saw him bow and smile, with that benign smile of the trained waiter, that the customer was put to shame by having such an aristocrat to serve him.

It is comparatively easy to accept the idea of staging a performance in a public place such as a shop or a restaurant. We can also accept that in private work-places people are on stage – a supervisor is likely to dress differently, have a separate space, and use props such as worksheets, instruction manuals, pens, measuring rules, desks and so on depending on the nature of the work; an executive is likely to have a personal stage area with props such as desk, special chairs for him or herself and visitors, tables, cabinets, personal computers, executive toys, pictures on the wall, plants, bookcase, magazines, and so on as well as a secretary/PA to create a team performance.

These examples are all, of course, semi-public. Do we also use our home as a stage? We believe that we do. Certainly, homes have areas of front and back stage and some audiences are admitted to different stage areas. We wear different costumes in the bedroom, bathroom, kitchen and we have carefully chosen the props in each room according to our own tastes, self-image and financial state. In the presence of guests and visitors, the members of the household may be expected to act as a united 'cast', which creates problems sometimes for young children who do not maintain the role. They may fail to understand why a meal is being eaten in a different room on different plates with different cutlery and with different norms of behaviour than an everyday meal – *'use your napkin, dear'* – *'I don't usually have one'*; *'wait until everyone is finished before you get up dear'* – *'I've finished eating, why can't I get up?'*

Staging by one or more performers for an audience (who in turn are performers) is of course all calculated as a means of **'impression management'**. Many of the examples cited by Goffman are from shops where the sales-people are at pains to create a particular impression for their customers. A long-running comedy series on British television, *'Are Your Being Served?'* depended for a good deal of its humour on the subcultures of front and back stage in a department store. The communication behaviour in front of customers was rather different from that when the performers were alone. These performers acted as a team when on stage. We now wish to look at this idea of teams.

KEY QUESTIONS

Staging
Describe ways in which a living room or a receptionist's office can be set up as a 'stage' for a 'performance'.

Explain how the staging of a performance might affect the outcome of an interaction.

5　TEAMS

Teams are concerned not only with the presentation of self, but with a united presentation of a social establishment. In order for a social establishment, whether a family, a school, a hospital, a shop, a church or a business to manage the impression it gives off, it must create teams that can perform together. This team has the task of co-ordinating their individual activities to maintain a given projected definition of the situation. When an outsider enters the establishment, the team wants its definition of this situation and the interactive relationship to be the controlling one, the one accepted as real. For example, in a school teachers and head are expected to present a front to angry parents who may wish to complain. A member of the team will not criticize another colleague in front of the parents, but may do so later back stage. For a team to maintain a staged performance they need to maintain loyalty as team members; discipline to cope with any *fauz pas* that may occur and to keep up the public performance; and circumspection to plan ahead and to maintain the audience's perceptions in line with the desired impressions. Embarrassment may occur if the team is caught in some sort of false presentation, in the same way that an individual may feel embarrassed if he or she is caught out in performance. The team will, of course, share secrets not divulged to non-team members and may develop its own secret codes. One nice example given by Goffman which refers to a store is as follows:

> Now that the customer is in the store suppose she can't be sold? The price is too high; she must consult her husband; she is only shopping. To let her walk (i.e. escape without buying) is treason in a Borax shop. So an SOS is sent out by the salesman through one of the numerous footpushes in the store. In a flash the 'manager' is on the scene, preoccupied with a suite and wholly oblivious of the Aladdin who sent for him.

> 'Pardon me, Mr Dixon,' says the salseman, simulating reluctance in disturbing such a busy personage. 'I wonder if you could do something for my customer. She thinks the price of this suite is too high. Madam, this is our Manager, Mr Dixon.'

> Mr Dixon clears his throat impressively. His is all of six feet, has iron grey hair and wears a Masonic pin on the lapel of his coat. Nobody would suspect from his appearance that he is only a special salesman to whom difficult customers are turned over.

> 'Yes,' says Mr Dixon, stroking his well-shaven chin, 'I see. You go on, Bennett, I'll take care of Madam myself. I'm not so busy at the moment anyhow.' The salesman slips away, valet-like, though he will give Dixon hell if he muffs the sale.

For a full account of teamwork in presenting a social establishment we suggest you read the appropriate sections of Goffman's *The presentation of self in everyday life* or *Asylums*. The latter book, dealing with total institutions, shows how staff and inmates both develop sophisticated team performances. Particular examples of impression management by mental hospital staff are staff/patient parties, theatrical performances, institutional displays or open days.

We suggest that you observe team performance in action when you are in shops, restaurants and other social establishments. It may be possible to observe interesting cultural nuances, for example the busy working cafe at lunchtime contrasted with a more upmarket restaurant in the evening, or an Italian-run pizzeria contrasted with an English-run pub. Try to identify front and back stage areas, how the staging of the physical context has been managed, and how the performers treat their audiences.

6　ROLES

Earlier in this chapter we drew attention to the notions of persona, mask, role, character and person. We present ourselves, our personalities through performing roles in the presence of others. So far we have reviewed the idea of performing individually and in teams and the idea of staging. Now we wish to look at the concept of roles which Goffman defines as follows:

> Defining social role as the enactment of rights and duties attached to a given status, we can say that a social role will involve one or more parts and that each of these different parts may be presented by the peformer on a series of occasions for the same kinds of audience or to an audience of the same persons.

The way we play a role via our parts suggests some consistency based on the personality and self-image of the person. We engage in roles which are patterns of behaviour considered appropriate for a specific audience and a specific social context. For a general discussion of role-playing you could refer to *More than words* (Dimbleby and Burton, 1992). In this section we shall be concentrating on the nature of roles played in team performances for managing an impression.

There are three crucial roles to maintain a team performance:

- those who perform
- those who are performed to
- outsiders who neither perform in the show nor observe it.

Those who perform know the impression that is to be fostered and possess the secret information of the establishment and have access to front and back regions. In addition to these three prime roles in a performance, Goffman also notes what he calls **discrepant roles** which bring a person into a social establishment in a false guise. These include:

- The role of informer who gains access to back stage and secret information then openly or secretly shows it to the audience.
- The role of shill who acts as though he or she were a member of the audience but is in fact with the performers. He/she normally presents a model for the

type of audience response that the performers want. Such shills may be a part of an occasion such as a sale to provoke customer interest or response.

- The role of inspector who pretends to be a member of the audience but is in fact checking on the performers. Would a writer of a restaurant report reveal his or her identity to the waiter before eating the meal?
- The role of agent from another team spying on the performance.
- The role of go-between who learns the secrets of two teams on different sides. For example, a factory supervisor may have to play as part of the management team and also as part of the workers' team.
- The role of service specialist who specializes in the construction, repair and maintenance of the show which their clients maintain before other people. These include architects and interior decorators, hairdressers and others who deal with personal front and others, such as economists, accountants, lawyers, who provide factual information for the display.

The descriptions of these suggest almost conspiratorial games and more will be said about another view of games people play in the next chapter. The final comment in this section about roles and games concerns the audience. Often the audience for a performance will have access to a back region or access to secret team information, but will tactfully not acknowledge or exploit this in order to maintain the performance and the definition of the situation which has been projected by the performers.

7   PERSONAL STYLE

In our discussion of self-presentation so far it is possible to lose sight of the self in our recent concentration on performance, staging and teams. However, **within these public behaviour patterns there is a consistency of personal style and identity.** We play a role in our own personal way revealing our own attitudes, experiences and responses to the situation. We draw our own conclusions about how we can individually create the impression we desire. Goffman concludes his study of the presentation of self in everyday life with the following significant comments:

> In this report, the individual was divided by implication into two basic parts: he was viewed as a 'performer', a harried fabrication of impressions involved in the all too human task of staging a performance; he was viewed as a 'character', a figure, typically a fine one, whose spirit, strength and other sterling qualities the performance was designed to evoke.

This 'chapter' is equated with the concept of self and in turn the self is a product of performances and other people's reactions to them. It results from one's social interactions. For futher details about this you are referred back to Chapter 1.

Similarily, we create an identity of the self from a life history which is a single continuous record of social and biographical facts. A chilling sequence in Goffman's book *Asylums* concerns the stripping of personal identity of someone taken into a total institution whether a prison, a religious institution, mental hospital or the armed forces. The term which Goffman uses to label this process is '**self-mortification**'. By this term he means the way in which personal possessions, clothes and the freedom of action whcih we take for granted for an autonomous adult are taken from the individual. The individual may be a willing participant in this in order to redefine their self-identity in line with what they want or feel they need or in line with what their close associates feel they need. In the context of a mental hospital this effect is summarized as follows:

> I am suggesting that the nature of the patient's nature is redefined so that, in effect if not by intention, the patient becomes the kind of object upon which a psychiatric service can be performed. To be made a patient is to be remade into a serviceable object. . . .

Time spent in a total institution is a disruption of a life career by which self-identity is shaped. Each of us can review our life career and draw conclusions from it which confirm or deny our self-image.

The self is a private matter only known, and not fully, by oneself through intrapersonal communication. But it is also a public construct, a result of public performances and interactions with others. We all seek to present ourselves by creating a specific desired impression and by defining the social situation. Questions of controlling people and situations are fundamental to the notion of communication. In the next chapter we shall be looking at another perspective on the controlling games people play, but before we close this chapter, we want to create a checklist of skills arising from the ideas outlined here.

8   PRESENTATION SKILLS

So far we have been describing, analysing and giving some examples of how individually and in teams we present ourselves in social interactions. In terms of effective communication it is possible to identify a number of presentation skills.

- Reflect on the other person's view of you, on the persona which you wish them to perceive. It might even be possible for you to find out something about the other person or other people involved. Think how they may respond to you.
- Reflect on what you would like the outcome of the interaction to be (apart from the matter of your image). Consider what you can do to achieve that outcome.

- Reflect on the social situation involved, think about what would be appropriate for you to do and say in order to be seen in a positive light. This idea may include factors like the roles of others, or the role which others might assume you to take on.
- Reflect on yourself, on your strengths and weaknesses. Determine to build on your strengths and to overcome your weaknesses.
- Consider the stage where you will present yourself, and think about how you can use it to help put across what you want. This might even include organizing the props on that stage.
- Consider what verbal and non-verbal behaviours you can use to represent your desired persona, and then of course use them.
- Perhaps try practising your performance in some private back stage area.

Again, it may be thought that this kind of reflection, decision making, and deliberate action seems rather calculating. But if your motives and the preferred outcome of the interaction are positive, then there is no moral problem. Also remember what we have said about that fact that all humans do carry on this kind of organized behaviour in many ways – for example when trying to form intimate relationships, when trying to carry out their jobs successfully.

In order to contextualize this list of skills it is worth taking into account a number of situations in which we wish to present ourselves. An obvious one is an interview, where clearly we wish to be seen in a positive light. Many people prepare what they wish to say at interviews in terms of facts. But it is also relevant to consider how you wish to be perceived, and therefore how you should behave to achieve this image in the eyes of the interviewer. Thre are also relevant work situations for many people who have to deal with the public or with clients. Again the skill of self presentation largely depends on control of communicative behaviour, to control the impression that is formed by the other person. A more intimate situation is one where one wishes to present postively to someone with whom you want to form a good social relationship. The same principles of personal management skills apply, as people are subconsciously aware when they spend time choosing what to wear and even rehearse what they might say. Presentation also may include more formal performances in education or in work when talking to a small group of people. Although there are particular needs here to prepare the content and structure of what one is going to say, presentation skills still apply.

If you are in a college or school situation then you might benefit from having a group brainstorming session on what you all think are the qualities and abilities that make a person an effective communicator and presenter. When we have done this exercise, in addition to language skills, non-verbal and social skills, often a phrase such as 'personal confidence' emerges. Perhaps the three main sources of confidence (a belief that you can succeed in interactions with other people) are these.

- a positive self image
- a knowledge of communication processes
- being prepared and rehearsed for performing and presenting yourself to others, especially in front of a group.

REVIEW

You should have learnt the following things from this chapter:

Self Presentation
The importance of self-concept in communication and ways in which we seek to present ourselves in everyday life.

The terminology used by Goffman is based on a dramaturgical metaphor including performance, staging and roles.

Persona
Persona suggests the idea of mask, of a way of performing roles which in turn lead to a notion of self-identity – a consistency of role performance.

Performance
We can perform sincerely or cynically. We can regulate our verbal and non-verbal behaviour, our conduct, appearance and objects around us to create the impression of ourselves that we believe to be true. We inevitably perform and display public behaviour patterns when in the presence of others.

Staging
We manipulate physical context to create a suitable stage for our performances.

We perform differently in front stage and back stage regions. The back stage is kept secret from the audience and from other teams.

Teams
In social establishments we perform in teams which develop patterns of behaviour and secret languages to maintain a team presentation in order to manage the impression that the audience receives. Examples can be seen in any social organizaton from family to factory, from hospital to restaurant.

Roles
Teams presuppose performers, observers, and outsiders who neither perform nor observe.

Additionally, there are specialist or discrepant roles to aid the team or a rival team or the audience.

Personal Style

Within this notion of performance, lies a concept of self-identity which is a social product of other people's reactions to our role-playing performances.

Each of us has created an identity based on a life history or career that is both private and public. Total institutions disrupt the individual's social public identity kit in a mortification of the self.

Presentation Skills

These skills include, defining desired outcomes, awareness of self and of context, control of communicative behaviour to present a desired persona.

CASE SITUATION

Privacy

Mrs Purvis' mouth was an inhuman orifice, packed out with cotton wodges focused on the damaged tooth. The gum tissue had a distinctive tinge where the anaesthetic had turned it into unfeeling flesh. She shifted uneasily in the chair as he started to drill once more in order to finish undercutting the section he was working on.

Peter Collins smiled reassuringly and muttered something soothing as he started on the now nearly finished cavity. His patient rolled her eyes. His hands smelled of pale disinfectant and were perfectly clean. She tried to ignore the gurgling instrument in her mouth and gazed at the crocodile in the poster on the ceiling, with its disconcerting smile and clean, clean teeth.

Peter finished his work as briskly as ever, though it was the end of his working day. He sneaked a look at the clock and hoped that his stomach wouldn't betray his humanity as he leaned over the patient to finish the shaping of the filling with deft, quick scrapes. His legs were beginning to ache, but only he knew that. His white medical coat encased him protectively. His assistant had dark rings under her eyes. But she also maintained a firm pleasant manner. She admired him, his coolness in the face of daily dental crises, his certain manner as he asked her for things, his patience in dealing with the laboratories and the suppliers.

Mrs Purvis left at last, with a lopsided smile. He was pleased. He knew that he had done a good job. Her gratitude was appreciated. He complimented his assistant on her share of their good day's work, and they cleared up the instruments and the debris. Finally, she too left and he was able to shut up the rooms at the front of the house and to retire upstairs to his sitting room and the tree-clad view over the little park where he had once played with his children.

His children were now grown up, he was divorced and he lived on his own.

It was a kind of pleasure to let his body slump into an armchair. He enjoyed the lonely privacy of his room where he was not on view, where no one expected anything of him. Which is why he was not pleased when a minute later the telephone rang.

It was a colleague, who should have known better than to ring him at this time. But still, the call was only a matter of enthusiasm. She had been to a conference on conservation techniques, and soon Peter found himself out of his chair and pacing up and down, asking her questions. A curious observer from the park might have seen this tall, rather stooping figure crossing and recrossing the window frame, shaping the air with his hands.

When you have read the case situation, try answering the following questions:

What kind of things do you think that Collins would say to his patient that would be consistent with his self presentation?

How does the extract illustrate the ideas of back stage and front stage?

In what ways does the extract show connections between the ideas of role and performance?

Suggested Reading

The following books by Erving Goffman provide a number of perspectives on how we present ourselves and interact with others in a variety of contexts. In several of these books he deals with the 'problems' of self-presentation and interaction in total institutions, in public places and for people who feel in some way stigmatized:

The presentation of self in everyday life (1959). Harmondsworth: Penguin.
Encounters: two studies in the sociology of interaction (1961). Indianapolis: Bobbs Merrill.
Behaviour in public places: notes on the social organisation of gatherings (1963).
    New York: Free Press.
Stigma: notes on the management of spoiled identity (1963). Harmondsworth: Penguin.
Interaction ritual (1967). New York: Anchor Press.
Asylums (1976). Harmondsworth: Penguin.
Gender advertisements (1979). London: Macmillan.

E Transactional Analysis – the parental ego state may operate outside the role of parent

5

Transactional Analysis

> By far the greater part of all social intercourse is in the form of play.
>
> Eric Berne: *Transactional analysis in psychotherapy*, 1961.

1 INTRODUCTION

1.1 Why Examine TA?

In the first place, the simple answer to this question is, because it works.

We have been looking at various approaches to interpersonal communication in this book: at ways of explaining why we communicate in the way we do, how we carry on that communication, what conditions it, what regulates it. Transactional Analysis offers another approach which provides some very plausible answers to these questions of why, how and what. They may not be the only answers, nor is it the only approach. But it is useful in that it makes sense, and in that its ideas can be put into practice. **Understanding of TA may enhance one's own communication skills, as well as be used to understand the communicative behaviour of others.**

1.2 Transaction and Communication

The starting point for TA is the transaction. The assumption is that Berne has identified a basic fact of interaction which may be recognized and then built upon. We might say that in effect he has identified building blocks of communication.

In *Games people play* he describes these as follows:

> The unit of social intercourse is called a transaction. If two or more people encounter each other . . . sooner or later one of them will speak, or give some other indication of acknowledging the presence of the others. This is called the transactional stimulus. Another personal will then say or do something which is in some way related to the stimulus, and that is called the transactional response.'

1.3 Transactions and Culture

In what follows there are unresolved cultural issues behind the concepts and the communication which seems to reveal them. The main issue is to do with how far TA concepts can apply to all people in their dealings with one another, and how far they are only valid for the 'Western' culture which Berne experienced.

For example, in the next section the notion of Parent has qualities which one could say 'ought' to apply across class and ethnic group – caring or controlling. And yet one also has to account for the fact that parenting is based on rather different values if one is, say, immigrant Vietnamese Australian as opposed to high caste middle class Indian. One has to balance the importance of seeking general truths and insights against the dangers of making culturally arrogant assumptions about values and associated behaviours.

It can be seen that culture makes a difference if one just thinks quickly about greetings as a kind of transaction (see earlier references to ritual and strategy). In a business context, Western cultures are used to getting down to discussion after very brief introductions, and may well not refer to families and personal matters. In most Arab cultures and situations this would be considered to be rude. It is important to take time to ask after family. Communication may still be built on transactions. But the nature of these and of the meanings behind them are different in terms of culture. And this has to be taken into account when trying to make sense of that transaction and the people involved.

2 EGO STATES – PARENTS, ADULT, CHILD

Fundamental to TA are these three terms used as a description of personality. Encoding and decoding of communication starts and finishes with what are described as **three ego states.** Everyone has something of **Parent, Adult and Child** in them. **The presence of these ego states affects communication** in a given situation, depending on which state or combination of states predominates at that time. Particular verbal phrases and non-verbal behaviours are associated with given ego states. Someone who bangs the table and says 'I won't' may be said to be **Child-like** *but not childish*. Berne makes an important distinction here when refusing use of the colloquial term and so trying to avoid the value judgements associated with a word like 'childish'.

So it is important to understand that adults can be Child-like, and children can be Adult-like. Certainly it is true that the Child ego state (with its associated behaviours) is the one that is first laid down in early years, and the Adult comes later. But it is also true that people of young years are perfectly capable of behaving Adult- or Parent-like. Indeed, Harris (1970) argues that the child learns both Child and Parent from the moment of birth, and has learnt most of the associated attitudes and behaviours by the age of five. He suggests that learning of the Adult starts only a little later, at the age of 10 months. One of the dangers in misusing TA theory (and in assessing people generally), is to assume that Child, Parent and Adult are necessarily associated with certain ages or roles. This is a useful thing to bear in mind (see also Perception), because too often our communication is founded on assumptions about others, based on careless readings of their communicative behaviour. There is also the matter of the self-fulfilling prophecy being involved here – that people who are treated Parent-like may respond by being Child-like, but that young people who are treated Adult-like may indeed respond by being Adult-like themselves, even at the age of, say, 7 years.

Description of these ego states may be summarized as follows:

2.1 The Child

The Child is impulsive, instinctive, emotional and full of feelings. The Child may have negative manifestations such as temper and sulking, but it will also have positive aspects such as love and fun and curiosity.

The child state is one in which emotions and reactions are on the surface. In effect, we re-live the young person (Child) that we once were, when the Child takes over. Not surprisingly, this state tends to take over at times of high emotion or stress. People also flip into the Child state and its patterns of communication because in their experience it gets them what they want. Grown people lose their temper in arguments, sometimes because they feel that uninhibited rage is so disturbing to the other person that they will give in to them.

We are describing these ego states in a book in sequence on the page. But it is important to realize that, as with the communication process in general, things don't happen separately in sequence. All of us have all three ego states within us. All of these may manifest themselves in a conversation. It is not the case that one exchange has to happen in one ego state. So if one considers the example of an argument again, one person may also switch from Child rage (shouting) to Parental admonition (perhaps using the threatening finger), and then to Adult reason (saying, *yes, but let's look at the facts*).

■ Variations on the Child

TA theory also recognizes that ego states may have their own variations. In the case of the Child one may recognize at least three common variations, described as the Natural Child, the Adapted Child and the Little Professor. In the first case of the **Natural Child** our original description above still largely applies. This child is uninhibited in its behaviour: it is both fearful and curious, affectionate and aggressive, sensuous and self-indulgent, enjoys games but is also self-centred.

But **the Adapted Child** has been trained through contact with grown-ups. It has learnt strategies for coping with grown-ups around it that are still within the realm of Child, and which reflect its view of itself and its self-esteem (of which more later). The Adapted Child may be described as compliant (it gets by through obeying grown-ups passively without question): or withdrawn (it avoids others or perhaps 'dreams' its way through life and its problems): or procrastinating (it defers decisions and actions). If you think that you know grown-up people like this then you are probably right! People learn behaviours young. People in various kinds of work may behave like this because they are reacting to the boss in this Adapted Child state. They learned to cope with adults with status in these ways at a young age, and they keep on doing this with comparable adults when they are older.

The Little Professor is, on the other hand, most likely to be recognized at a young age. This version of the Child ego state is one in which the Adult is emerging. To an extent, it comes out of the curious and self-centred aspects of the Natural Child. In this case, one recognizes creative qualities, use of intuition as the rational mind develops, and attempts at manipulation (*I promise to be good for a week if you let me have . . .*).

■ Child Behaviour

So the characteristics of these three versions of Child may be said to construct personality: the Self from which communication comes and which adjusts to communication received. But then these characteristics are themselves inferred from communicative behaviour. So what are these behaviours?

To make a brief selection (which you may add to through observation), there are the following typical uses of speech. *Hey! Wow! Great!* and other exclamations – *She made me do it. I didn't do it. – You'll be sorry. I'm going to tell X about you! – Nobody loves me. Everyone's looking at my new outfit! – That was all right, wasn't it? – You're just trying to upset me – Go on, do it just for me – He's no good for you – Let's have some fun – I've had enough of this.* And of course any kind of baby talk fits this category – as used by owners to pets, lovers to lovers, and even adults to children.

Non-verbal behaviours might be those such as the following . . . paralanguage in which the speaker is whining about injustice, complaining about someone else, trying to aggravate, wheedling their way into someone's favours, exclaiming loudly as they excuse some mistake. The ingratiating tone of someone asking permission for action is probably the sign of an Adapted Child. Raw laughter and fast talk is the enthusiasm of the Natural Child. These behaviours may be matched and reinforced by kinds of body language. When found out in an error, people sometimes throw a temper tantrum as a kind of defence. When things go wrong they may slump in despair and look tearful. Adult women have been known to try and get their own way by fluttering their eyelashes and putting on a naive wide-eyed expression. Insulting gestures and faces are part of this Child state. Putting up a hand at a meeting for attention is a reversion to a Child state gesture. Pouting and nail biting are non-verbal signs of the negative aspects of this state, whereas jumping around and looking animated is a sign of the positively excited and enthusiastic child.

You should have grasped the point that a lot of these Child behaviours are to be seen in adults. To behave like a Child is not necessarily a bad thing. Indeed many would argue that it is healthy to express the Child within us if this means giving space to our curiosity, and expression to our positive emotions towards others.

2.2 The Parent

The Parent ego state is one in which we behave like a parent, a figure with status who directs the life of another (originally the young child), and who establishes standard and values. The beliefs and consequent behaviour patterns which we inherit at an early age are accepted uncritically (it is in an adult function to criticize). To this extent, while TA firmly believes in the capacity for growth and change, it also recognizes the heavy influence of the parent. Parental ego state, attitudes and behaviours are learnt from our parents. We absorb them and re-use them, often unconsciously, usually uncritically. The epitome of this state is to be seen in utterances such as – *it was good enough for my father so it's good enough for you*. This is of course no logical basis for any belief or a justification for any behaviour. Still one may even observe children repeating parental utterances as part of their play, and hence their process of socialization. Many a hapless doll has been admonished to sit still and behave or it won't get any candy. That same person, older in years, will practise the same threats in the same ego state on real children in order to obtain compliance. Parents may threaten to withdraw favours or reward in order to get their children to do what they want. Grown people may use the same device in order to influence the behaviour of others around them. In each case it is the Parent speaking, and the arguments and attitudes were laid down in childhood.

■ Variations on the Parent

In fact the Parent is not always directive or even punitive. **Two types of Parent may be recognized: the Nurturing Parent and the Controlling Parent.** The former may, broadly, be seen in a positive light. This Parent is caring, offers rewards, and protects the child. The behaviour of this Parent is sympathetic and comforting. These characteristics are important when read in conjunction with the later section which explains feelings of being OK or not OK. A Nurturing Parent can help the child to feel OK about itself and its relationships. Obviously, an over-protective parent can smother a child and can inhibit the growth of the Self. A child who is smothered cannot achieve autonomy. Misplaced protection and reward may be seen in parents who, for example, over-feed their children. In effect they may try to feed away anxiety and distress, and of course merely create another set of problems. But if qualities of true care are present then this kind of distorted Nurturing Parent should not emerge. A truly Nurturing Parent does not give a child everything that it wants when it wants.

The characteristics of the Controlling Parent are less attractive. There will be firm and immediate opinions about the child's behaviour and motivation. This Parent will be proscriptive, and will make quick judgements about the child. This Parent is authoritarian and punitive, moralizes and makes heavy demands of the child. Such a Parent ego state will pre-judge a child's behaviour, shaping a sense of guilt as much as of conscience. This kind of Parent is the one which generates things like the work ethic, and worst of all, makes the child feel guilty about failing even when it has done its best. This is the Parent who drives the child to succeed on the parent's terms. This is the parent who is prone to say – *it serves you right* – or – *I told you so* – when perhaps the child needs comfort rather than admonition.

■ Parent Behaviour

Once more, we may read the ego state through the communication.

The Controlling Parent will have a stock of do and don't phrases. They will tend to use imperative utterances such as *you must eat up your greens – you really shouldn't do that – for goodness, sake be good when your aunt comes – you ought to do your homework now* – and so on. Or – *come on, try harder now, don't be such a coward – you really are a bad girl – you stupid boy! – that's very naughty – how could a child of mine grow up to be such a little wretch!* Perhaps the most identifiable phrase which all parents will have delivered at some time or another, at least in exasperation, is the infamous – *because I said so!*

On the other hand, the Nurturing Parent will also have typical utterances. *Don't be afriad, it will be all right – here, this will make it better – don't worry. I'll talk to your teacher.* Or again – *why don't you let me help you do that? – if I were you I would try the blue crayon* – as well as terms of endearment in address such as *darling, honey* and terms of compliment such as – *that's a really good idea – you really are an angel – what a good boy/girl – that's pretty smart* – and so on.

These verbal utterances are of course paralleled by non-verbal behaviours. The Controlling Parent has a repertoire of expressions of disapproval which may be described as frowning, hostile, disdainful and the like, with all the specific associated uses of lowered brows and fixed gaze.

The Nurturing Parent will look happy, admiring, encouraging and use a lot of smiling.

Other body signs might be characterized in terms of lack of contact and of 'locking off' in the case of the Controlling Parent, but in terms of open gestures and touching in the case of the Nurturing Parent. The latter gives strokes, and so teaches the child to do likewise. The Controlling Parent points the finger, uses height, looks down the nose, or shakes the head. The Nurturing Parent will give the pat of approval or the hug of comfort. Similarly, one can compare paralanguage, where the Controlling Parent offers the gentle tones of sympathy or the bright tones of encouragement.

From what we have said about social skills, it will be very clear that TA is to be associated with these – or lack of them. The Parent ego state is very much alive in the grown-up. People try to win arguments or intimidate others by employing Parent communication behaviour. People comfort others in distress by replaying their memories of Nurturing Parents and what they did for them. As we point out elsewhere in this chapter, it is not uncommon for communication problems to be explicable in terms of people communicating Parent-like when the other person does not want to play along with this. Wives don't take kindly to husbands trying to be the Controlling Parent when trying to argue them out of the proposed purchase of a new car. And even the Nurturing Parent can irritate if it is a colleague at work saying *let me help you* when the other person wants some straight adult discussion of a problem.

Again, the value of this approach to interpersonal communication is that you can observe it at work for yourself. You can look for the utterances, and can consider whether or not barriers to communication are set up through inappropriate utterances out of an inappropriate ego state (see also crossed transactions).

2.3 The Adult

The Adult ego state is one which is characterized by detachment and logic. It is, one might say, most obviously represented through the character of Mr Spock in *Star Trek*, whose dominant characteristic is that of being logical. The Adult is a calculator, a reasoning person, one who is not swayed by emotion. In one sense the Adult is attractive because it is about truth and objectivity, and because it is a state of self that most obviously signifies sense and maturity. But it is worth remembering that the whole person has something of all three ego states in them and available to them. The Child, with its feelings and curiosity, is important as a foil to the moral arbitrator of the parent and the impersonal reasoning of the Adult.

In the Adult state there is no room for assumptions or dreams. The Adult is an information handler and decision maker. The Adult part of us gives and takes in information relevant to the interaction or situation being experienced at a given time. It listens actively as part of that information gathering. It correlates information and evaluates it. It calculates possibilities and probabilities. It thinks about cause and effect. It constructs models of physical and social reality from data. It weighs up new information against previous data and previous models. The Adult state comes into play when we are problem solving, which happens most obviously when we are at work. But the Adult may be there at any time, and probably should be there at times when it tends to slip away from us – such as when we are making our minds up about buying some expensive item of clothing which attracts us, and when logic as well as emotional response should come into play.

■ *Adult Behaviour*

In terms of characteristic verbal utterances, the Adult asks questions, explores and analyses. The Adult is likely to ask – *how did it happen?* – *where is your evidence?* – *why did you do that?* – *who says that is so?* The Adult will deal with problems by saying – *let's look at the facts first*, rather than, for example, making a Child utterance such as – *I'm fed up with this thing always going wrong*. The Adult will recognize false argument and say something like – *Fair enough, you're expressing an opinion, but that doesn't make it a fact*. Or *OK, that's decided then. We'll meet on Thursday at 10.30*.

The non-verbal communication of the Adult is restrained and neutral. It may underscore some point of logic, but will not attempt emotional inflection. In terms of paralanguage it is level, using emphasis for meaning, to underline questions, to signal a change of point in an argument.

The body language used in this ego state is also marked by an absence of features, as much as by active distinguishing signs. Posture is alert and responsive, matched by even eye-contact which obeys social conventions already referred to (e.g. turn-taking). Gestures are used to describe, say, physical characteristics. Gaze provides feedback and acknowledgement of the other person. One would expect to note reflective listening techniques. This state is one in which the person is attentive, clearly thinking about what the other person is saying, and shows confidence in their own abilities and their own worth.

KEY QUESTIONS

Ego States
Describe the behaviour of a grown person who is acting like an Adapted Child.

In what ways may a Controlling Parent or a Nurturing Parent have a negative effect on another person?

3   TRANSACTIONS

We have already described **the transaction as a basic unit of social interaction in which some verbal or non-verbal signal is offered, recognized and responded to.** Transactions may be as brief and ephemeral as that nod of recognition which British people offer one another as they pass each other in their place of work for the nth time. Or one may have an elaborate series of transactions through an animated conversation, with switches of ego states and their associated types of utterance.

The point of looking at transactions in communication terms is that they are the act of communication itself. Description of transactions also leads one to understanding of why conversations may have positive or negative outcomes. There are two dominant types of transaction recognized in TA theory, the **complementary and the crossed transaction**. Berne describes these as working on one level. But he also recognizes those transactions involving a sense of irony, innuendo, and phatic communication (see glossary). He identifies these as working on two levels and calls them **angular or duplex transactions**. To best understand these four types of transaction you should refer to Figs 5.1, 5.2, 5.4 and 5.5 and to the first two Case Situations. But they may also be

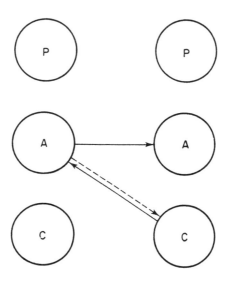

Fig 5.1 *A model for an angular transaction (after Berne, 1972)*

readily explained through verbal examples. Just bear in mind that each person in an interaction has the three ego states present, each with the potential to influence the style of communication that is used. The key question is, will the styles adopted match one another or not? Will they continue to match through the interaction?

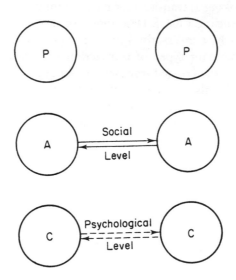

Fig 5.2 *A model for duplex transaction (after Berne, 1972)*

3.1 Complementary Transactions

A complementary transaction is one in which the styles do match because the ego states are complementary. Someone opens a conversation out of a particular ego state: the other person recognizes this and feeds back communication which complements that first utterance. And so it goes on for as long as the participants choose. They have adjusted to one another. This is not to make any judgement on what they say or how well they express themselves. Nor is it even to approve how they choose to match one another. So, for example, one might have complementary Adult to Adult talk between two engineers discussing the cause of a pipe-line failure. Or one might have a Parent–Child transaction in which a Supervisor speaks as Controlling Parent and a Clerk responds as Adapted Child – *You ought to pull yourself together. You can't go on coming in late – I'm sorry, you're right. I promise it won't happen again.*

You might feel that the Clerk shouldn't have responded in this way. But the fact is that the response matched and the communication continued smoothly. With reference to the model we have a transaction in which the lines remain parallel. You might consider what other kinds of complementary transaction there could be and work out appropriate communication behaviours. For example, two people swapping zany jokes might be thought to be operating as Child to Child. Two people exchanging instant (but unsupported) opinions about the moral decline of the young could be Parent to Parent.

3.2 Crossed Transactions

A crossed transaction is one in which our model's lines cross and the ego states are not complementary. Because it can illustrate and explain breakdowns in communication it is one of the most useful pieces of TA theory. In this case the response to an utterance, whether at the beginning of or part way through an exchange, does not match the style and ego state of that utterance. This is the case where the young person does not respond as expected to some parental injunction such as *Don't fiddle with that toy or you'll break it!* A reply such as *I'm trying to find out why the motor isn't working* is perfectly reasonable and Adult. Sadly, it is quite likely to invoke a hardening of the parental approach – *Don't argue with me! Put it down when you're told to.* Such are the opening gambits of family rows. Looking back to the Supervisor and the Clerk you decide the nature of the cross if the Clerk says – *I am together. But I've had some problems to deal with.* Ask yourself if it would still be a cross if the Clerk says – *Get off my back. Anyway you're no angel about timekeeping yourself. So don't preach to me.* Is there also a switch of ego states here?

3.3 Angular Transactions

An angular transaction is one in which on one level the speaker talks as if to one ego state, but covertly is addressing another ego state. People who try to wind up others are practised in this kind of double dealing. On the face of it, a statement such as *Charlie was having a good time at last night's party* may sound innocuous. But if the speaker is talking to Charlie's girlfriend who thought he was at home, then they may not get an Adult response such as – *Oh, I wonder why he didn't tell me that he was going.* We leave you to imagine what the more likely reply would be, and what ego state it comes out of!

3.4 Duplex Transactions

The duplex transaction is one in which the exchange takes place in parallel on two levels. These may be described as the overt social level, and the covert psychological level. In this case two people may appear to talk to one another as Adult to Adult, but in fact there is another level of meaning and exchange in operation. For example, consider a group of people who are trying to help one of their members install an alarm system in his or her home. Two of the group may be coming up with all kinds of adult utterances – *why don't we try wiring the sensors round this way?* – or – *I heard it was best to put the pressure pads under a window.* Now this kind of talk exchanged between the two seems unexceptional. But if it happens at a considerable rate, and if the other group members know that the two concerned both pride themselves on their practical knowledge, then they may perceive that unspoken psychological level of transaction which is basically about competition. They are talking Adult but on a Child level are saying, *I'm smarter than you are*!

The most common example of a duplex transaction is the 'girl meets boy, and they are attracted towards each other' situation. In this case the conversation may be on an apparently Adult social level – *what did you think of that TV show about the couple who adopted a child?* – and so on. But the two people concerned may be very well aware that underneath the reasoned talk they are also operating an emotoinal transaction.

In fact, this is where an all-embracing communication approach is helpful, because we would say that for this covert transaction to take place there must still be some communicative signs that make this transaction, and which one could identify. In other words it isn't just a matter of vague intuition that the couple are communicating emotionally, Child to Child, saying, I like you and would like to know you better. The covert level would be non-verbal. The couple would be talking through two channels and in two ego states at once. The reasoned verbal level justifies the contact. But the important messages, so far as they are concerned, are being fed back and forth through body language. In effect, it is like carrying on two conversations at once. There are two sets of transaction, or two levels and means of communication. In this way principles of Transactional Analysis and of communication are complementary, and inform one another.

KEY QUESTIONS

Transactions

Write a conversation which illustrates a crossed transaction.

Explain how an understanding of transactions would be useful for a trainee teacher.

4   HUNGERS

Just as Berne's notion of a transaction bears close analogy with a single act of communication, so also his idea of **hungers** looks very much like the notion of communication needs. In both cases the essential idea is that any act of communication, including those that may be defined as social, must be motivated by something. There must be an impulse, a drive to initiate that communication or transaction.

We will summarize analogies between TA and communication study at the end of this chapter. For the moment it is enough to say that the three hungers which, Berne argues, drive all transactions can be easily compared with types of communication need.

4.1 Sensation Hunger

The sensation hunger assumes a need in all humans for stimulus. Social interaction provides such a stimulus and satisfies the hunger.

4.2 Recognition Hunger

The recognition hunger is described as a need for sensations provided by another human being. It is perhaps rather more personal than the general sensation hunger. It is about personal recognition from an individual.

4.3 Structure Hunger

The structure hunger is about a need to create order and be a part of social structures – hence the drive for humans to form groups.

One could say by way summary that these three points may explain why people have an in-built need to talk to one another, why they want to form special relationships with one other person and why they want to be part of groups. In other words this is an explanation of why communication takes place.

5 TIME STRUCTURING

Another premise of TA is that social interaction is organized by people over periods of time in various ways. These ways of organization have at least two general characteristics: one is the time period of the interaction, long- or short-term: the other is the degree of habit or predictability involved in the interaction.

Transactions occur within these various types of time-structured activity. You should read the books referred to if you are interested in going into this in detail. We intend looking at one kind of short-term and one kind of long-term activity in the next sections. But still it is worth grasping the point of time-structures here because once more we can see useful analogies with mainstream communication theory.

■ Time-Structures Relate to Communication

For example, the principle of time-structures does suggest that communication is organized within units of activity. These units are more or less predictable in their content, in the nature of interaction, in the use of communication. For instance, Berne describes rituals as a short-term activity, and there is no doubt that these are characterized by extremely repetitive patterns and uses of communication. Work is described as another short-term activity, but this is less predictable in communication terms.

In one sense TA theory and Communication theory reinforce one another's ideas. In another sense they throw light on basic processes of social interaction which concern both approaches. Berne sees rituals as being 'highly stylized exchanges': we might say, entirely bound by conventions. They are, he would say, a safe form of interaction which may have the merit of giving **strokes** as part of the behaviour, but which is also limiting. In Communication terms we would be interested first in the fact that Berne effectively confirms the proposition that much communication is learnt (nurture not nature!). We would be interested in the content and treatment of relevant exchanges – *Morning, Mrs Brown. How are you this morning? Terrible weather again isn't it? – Thanks.* There are covert messages beneath these habitual exchanges. There is information about relationship, understandings, social bonding – whether one calls these exchanges transactions or communication. We may be more interested in the production, process and effect of such exchanges. Berne may be more interested in the psychology behind these, and in its implications for those involved. But in the end the one approach informs the other.

So, to take one last example, Berne refers to **pastimes** as the kind of social action typified by people's fairly predictable exchanges when meeting each other at social events – *Hello, my name's Michael. I'm a client of Peter Mountford. Do you know him? –* or something like this.

Berne is interested in the way that we organize such interactions, in the extent to which we may put ourselves in a kind of straitjacket by repeating some formula of conversation. This is very useful because it deals with matters of consequence: with the significance of certain kinds of use of communication. Again, we might also see this as a way of recognizing **conventions** in practice, or of exploring **covert messages**.

So now let's move on to look in more detail at two particular kinds of time structuring which can tell us quite a lot about how and why we use communication.

6   GAMES

There is no substitute for a reading of Berne's deservedly popular book *Games people play*. It offers many examples of different types of games, and says a lot about human interaction and motivation. It talks about ways in which we try to manipulate each other, or try to achieve some sort of psychological victory or satisfaction – what Berne calls the **payoff**. But the main characteristics of games can be explained fairly easily, so that one can then see how they are superb examples of communication in action. As examination of games tells us a great deal about how and why we use verbal and non-verbal language.

Games are an example of short-term structuring of time. They are a form of social interaction. **Berne describes games as 'sets of ulterior transactions, repetitive in nature, with a well-defined psychological payoff'.** He says that '*all* *games involve a con'* because the players, or the initiating player, are pretending to say and mean one thing, when in fact they are really manipulating the interaction and the other person towards some kind of conclusion which pleases them. **Usually a game does involve one person trying to 'put something across' one other person.** Berne has actually created a whole vocabulary to describe game elements.

6.1 Game Terms

The victim in a game is called the **mark**. A weakness in the mark which is used to **hook** the mark is called the **gimmick (G)**. This gimmick may be something like ill temper or fear of conflict which the manipulator arouses and uses in order to 'put one across' the mark. The **switch (S)** describes the point in the interaction when the manipulator uses some phrase which changes the direction of the conversation so that the mark is caught out and feels that he has been made to feel stupid or inferior in some respect. It is also at this point that the **crossup (X)** occurs. This describes the confusion that the mark feels at having been caught and may also be represented by confusion and breakdown in the conversation itself. The end of it all is the **payoff (P)** when the manipulator has scored a point (their payoff) and the mark collects a feeling of inferiority (their payoff).

The two important communication elements are first the **Con (C)**, which is what the first player says to the other one when trying to hook them. Then there is the **response (R)** which the second player makes if hooked.

So, picking up on our key letters above, one can actually express a game in terms of a formula that summarizes how one game element leads to another. That is:

$$C + G = R > S > X > P$$

6.2 Examples of Games

Berne gives his games colloquial titles which summarize their dominant characteristic, and which employ some key phrase from the game – perhaps the switch line.

The archetypal game is called WHY DON'T YOU – YES BUT.

In this simple game the manipulator uses an excuse or objection to every suggestion which the victim makes, so that eventually the victim is blocked into silence and is made to feel powerless or useless. He may also feel angry at having been drawn into what in the end seems to be a pointless conversation. If he expresses that anger then the manipulator has gained a double payoff by making the victim lose his temper as well. What of course the manipulator does not want is for the victim to say something like – *I don't think you seriously want help*. In this case the game is blown, and to an extent the victim has turned the tables on the manipulator. To be able to do this we need to able to recognize when others are playing games with us.

The conversation for this game might run something like . . .

I'm feeling really depressed. I owe three assignments and I just can't seem to get down to any of them.

Why don't you take a break and go out for a good time? It could make you feel better.

Yes, but I'm so broke I really can't afford to go out this week.

Well, why don't you go and see the teachers and ask for a postponement?

Yes, but I did that before. I can't ask them again.

So why don't you ask Jane for some help? I know that she's up to date with her work.

Yes, but she's got problems of her own. She just split up with her boyfriend.

. . . and so on, until the conversation dies with the victim feeling a failure and the manipulator feeling smug and vindicated in the excuses for not attempting the assignments.

Berne groups games in various categories, such as **life games**. In all groups one can see certain archetypal forms of game which give rise to versions special to that group. One archetypal game is called NOW I'VE GOT YOU, YOU SON OF A BITCH in which the manipulator 'catches out' the victim in some way, almost always as a result of a situation which has been deliberately engineered. The victim is led to the edge of an elephant pit. One variation of this as a **marital game** is called FRIGID WOMAN. This one is an interesting example because it certainly may not depend on a conversation, though talk is likely to enter into it. So, explained in narrative form because it can be dominantly about non-verbal communication, the sequence look something like this.

The wife makes it clear that sexual realtions are out of bounds and repugnant to her. The husband accepts this situation. The husband is the **mark**. The wife then proceeds to use her **gimmick** to hook the husband. She offers non-verbal signs of sexual availability, but nothing too overt. These signs, which are often ambiguous in meaning, such as bath towel that may or may not intentionally have been allowed to slip, increase in frequency and effect. Finally the husband decides that an offer has been made and proceeds to take it up. At this point the wife **pulls the switch**. It may even be the first time that a verbal transaction takes place. She asks him what he thinks he is doing, or something like this. This payoff for him is that he is left looking stupid, is guilty of breaking the 'rules' of their relationship, and may even feel guilty about his sexual drives. The wife's payoff is that she has 'caught him out' and got a moral buzz from doing this. The point of the payoff is emphasized if he starts protesting.

One interesting aspect of the switch is that it puts the victim in what has been called elsewhere a 'double bind'. The victim is damned if he does and damned if he doesn't. If the husband persists in his advances after the switch, he may not be playing the game as perceived by the wife, but he is still likely to feel guilty, and his behaviour can be used by her against him, perhaps in some later argument. Equally, he can't win by saying nothing or even by apologizing. It is too late. Even trying to expose the game by discussing her behaviour and their relationship is likely to lead to a destructive argument if she persists in her moral position.

6.3 Game Role

We have been using words like 'victim' to describe the behaviour of people in games. In fact, it is proposed that **there are three main roles one can see in Games and indeed in scripts** (see section 7).

There are **Persecutors** who are usually the initiators and manipulators in a game, who try to make someone else suffer. There are **Victims** who may be the victim of a manipulator, but who may also try to manipulate others by claiming victimization when this isn't actually true. There are **Rescuers** who can be helpful people, but who again may actually manipulate others by trying to make them grateful and dependent by doing things that are not wanted or asked for.

In fact, manipulative game roles can always be described as **illegitimate roles**. But there are also **legitimate roles** and role behaviour in life, where the role player isn't getting some kind of secret 'kick' and payoff from the transaction. People really are victims if they are denied promotion because of their gender. Counsellors are legitimate rescuers if they are helping other people to sort out their lives. And, although it seems a strange way of putting it, people who have a socially endorsed position which demands that they control the behaviour of others are actually acting legitimately. For example, a judge, a teacher or a parent may be seen as Persecutor, but it is accepted that it is OK for them to behave this way as part of 'agreed' socialization.

6.4 Games and Relationships

Games are negative and are destructive to relationships. The game initiator does not feel OK about themselves and is trying to create a relationship which helps them take out anger on others, which helps them feel better by making others feel worse, which reinforces their negative feelings because these are what they want to wallow in.

Games are about dominance and submission in relationships. They may be about the struggle to achieve this on the part of one person or another. They may also be about attempts to reinforce an existing situation. Those who use an illness or a disability in order to get a payoff from others are enacting the illegitimate role of Victim. They are exploiting their condition. When it is an ageing parent who is the person that is ill it can be hard for their carers to acknowledge that they are the victim of a game. But still this may be the case.

It is also hard for people to admit that relationships based on habitual games are also flawed. It is very easy for others especially to say something like – *Oh, they're always like that. He doesn't mean to hurt her. They always kiss and make up after it is over.* But this doesn't alter the fact that games are being played. It also suggests that the people involved are locked into bad scripts, which we will go on to talk about.

KEY QUESTIONS

Games

Write the dialogue for a game which you have had experience of (perhaps a variation on one that you have read about!). Try using the formula given in this book.

Why do people play games, and why shouldn't they?

7   SCRIPTS

■ Definitions

Scripts are an example of long-term structuring of time. A script is described by Berne as a *life plan*. Like other TA elements they are developed in one's formative years, and thereafter shape all our actions and interactions. It is important to emphasize that scripts are not pre-ordained though they are very explicable if one looks at the individual's experiences when growing up. They can be changed or modified. Again it is the case that recognizing one's life script is half-way to changing it. The script does of course affect our communication style, how we use communication, and how we interpret communication offered by others. People's feelings about themselves and about others will be written into their scripts. These attitudes are also formed through early experiences.

A script in a general sense comprises a view of the self, a view of others, and a view of the world, implicit in the plan of action which it represents. It also follows that such views and such a plan will affect attitude and the individual's overall communications style. **Scripts might be described as model stories which the person carries in the head and which will influence every interaction.** So a script shapes the way in which communication is used, as well as the purposes for which it is used.

■ Payoffs

Scripts like games may have payoffs for their uses. And like games, Berne has some alluringly colloquial titles for scripts which, he says, are rather like slogans printed on the script owner's T-shirt. For example, one such slogan is 'You Can't Trust Anybody'. The contention is that people who live by this script actually seek situations where this thesis will be proved. Then comes their payoff because they can turn round and say, I told you so. (This person is also saying in effect, looking to the next section, I'M OK BUT THEY ARE NOT OK.)

■ Script Types: Winners and Losers

In general terms, one could say that **scripts fall into paired categories.** One pair is about optimism and pessimism, in which people write themselves positive or negative views of themselves and of the likely outcomes of any action they may take. Another pair would be described in terms of fatalism and determinism, where the person would script themselves as being either more, or less, in control of their lives and actions. Again this will have a lot to do with communication style, and with the inflections of paralanguage and body language in particular. Berne refers to **Winners and Losers.** It is likely that those who see themselves as Winners from an early age will have qualities of confidence and drive in their social interaction. These qualities, being about attitude and emotion, are most powerfully expressed through non-verbal behaviours. In other words, we are back to situation where it can be argued that TA principles and terminology only become real, can only be tested, through observing and interpreting communicative behaviour.

Berne argues that we decide whether we will be Winners or Losers at a very early age, because of some particular formative experience of success or failure, or perhaps because of what parents say about success or failure. For example, parents might repeatedly use a phrase such as *Do you want to grow up like your brother?* to a young boy. The older brother is on the streets and in trouble with the police. The parents see this as an awful warning. But for the kid brother the answer to the question might be YES! because he sees the brother as having a good time and always having money in his pocket. Such is the material from which scripts are constructed. But, we should emphasize, there is much of this kind of material, there are many scripts, and they may be reformed during the various phases of maturing for the individual. What we are trying to explain is the nature of the script and its origins. For proper detail you should refer back to Berne's work.

■ Scripts are Limiting

Berne sees scripts and games as not only being predictive but also as being limiting. Even Winner scripts are not a good thing because, for example, they may push the **script driven** person to try and win at all costs, even at the cost of their relationships or of their own lives.

An example of a Loser's script is one where a woman sees herself as a born victim, but one who must keep on suffering to prove that she is a victim. She is the one who marries the violent or abusive male because she can then play games such as KICK ME. In fact, Berne would say, this is the slogan on the back of her sweat-shirt. Of course, on the front she wears a brave face. The script line for the front is about being tough and about being able to keep going for the sake of the marriage. Somewhere in the past she became imbued with parental views about the importance of never giving up at any price. This was a Controlling Parent who allowed no space for autonomy, decision making, and simply learning when to give up on a bad deal. She gets what she 'wants' – plenty of kicking to confirm her script and her dominant game plan. But she doesn't deserve this. She needs to be allowed to break free. She needs to feel OK about giving up on the man. The psychotherapist would try to get her to recognize this, to free herself of that script. Of course, to do this he has to decode her communication, and has to communicate effectively with her.

KEY QUESTIONS

Scripts
Describe as honestly as you can the main features of your own life script.

Explain how a life script might impede the personal growth of an individual, or might have a negative effect on their relationships.

8   I'M OK – YOU'RE OK

This is a good position to be in. It means that one feels good about oneself and good about the other person. **The significance of being OK or NOT OK (see Fig. 5.3) is that it shapes and predicts a person's approach to interaction, and so of**

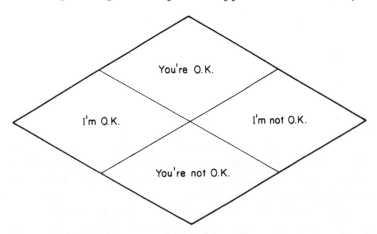

Fig 5.3 *The OK diamond – four states of being*

course to the communication which is the essence of that interaction.

Harris proposes that in fact every human starts off feeling NOT OK because of the birth trauma, and that the destructive nature of games can be traced back to this life position and a desire to work it out. In fact the baby human wants to get the OK person (parent) to be good to them because the baby feels NOT OK. Looked at from one point of view it becomes another way of explaining how communication starts. If the baby is going to get the grown-up to do something they have to get this across. And if they are going to know what the grown-up feels then they have to recognize and decode communication.

■ Life Positions

These TA **life positions** are as follows:

1 I'M NOT OK – YOU'RE OK
2 I'M NOT OK – YOU'RE NOT OK
3 I'M OK – YOU'RE NOT OK
4 I'M OK – YOU'RE OK

■ Positions and Scripts

Further, Harris says that position 1 of the first year of life is then either confirmed in years 2 and 3, or the child shifts to position 2 or position 3. But **to reach position 4 there has to be some conscious decision, and not everyone makes this shift.** In other words, many people go through life feeling that either they and/or others are NOT OK. This rather gloomy state of affairs must of course affect attitudes, relationships and the communication that is part of these. Such life positions are fundamental to the kind of script that a person writes for herself or himself. One half of the equation writes a script, the other half a **counterscript.** This would mean that for position 1 a person might write a script in which they punished themselves for feeling NOT OK. Or it might mean that they write a counterscript in which they try to emulate (and win the approval of) the OK person. They are always trying to win the approval of some grown-up who in later life might be the girlfriend or the boss.

■ Shifting Positions – Consequences

One important reason for shifting position might be to do with whether or not the child receives strokes from the parent. This idea of offering rewards and approval to others has elsewhere been described as a social skill. Put colloquially, being pleasant to other people improves their feelings for you, your feelings for yourself, and the quality of communication between you. Nowhere is this more true than in childhood. There is overwhelming clinical evidence that love and affection are far more important to the development of children than are physical comforts (within reason, of course). Jules Henry in *Culture against man* has described movingly and tragically how well-cared-for middle-class children nevertheless were disturbed and withdrawn for lack of physical and verbal affection. A child who does not receive messages about being OK and being loved, dominantly in terms of body contact, may decide to change its life position. It may shift to position 2. In which case a possible life script could involve self-destructive and disturbed behaviours, the sort which end up in institutions, because this individual feels bad about everyone including him or herself. Their time structuring is an extreme one identified as **withdrawal**. In effect, communication may break down or become incoherent. This person can't make meanings effectively because social interaction is too painful to bear. **So this area of TA helps explain why communications do not take place or why some people seem unable to interact according to the social conventions learnt and used by most of us.**

Similar conditions of upbringing may cause a shift to position 3. The child may lack stroking, it may have been positively brutalized. There is no doubt that for it, others are NOT OK. It has decided that others are to blame for its situation, but it also decides that *it* is not. The Adult in the developing mind reasons this out. So this child writes scripts in which this can also lead to destructive behaviours. At the least it predicates a tendency to paranoia. It may also lead to criminal and violent behaviours, easily justified when one believes that others are wrong anyway. Someone in this position could become very successful in material terms. Their feeling about being OK in themselves would lead to very positive communication traits, where they might talk with confidence and assurance. Their attitude that others are not OK might lead them to be pretty ruthless in business deals for example, so bringing material success, and further confirming a view of themselves as being OK. There might well be arrogance in their communication style. This kind of person might behave 'correctly' but would not give strokes to others.

It is a TA precept that, even with the possibility of achieving position 4 through self-knowledge (TA), still one must remember that the other positions are around. In particular the I'M NOT OK attitude is always there as an early experience. It can be dealt with, but cannot be simply wiped off a slate. Put rather simply it means that if one listens to the way that people talk, even some perfectly pleasant people, one might recognize anyone dropping into one of the two positions in which they are NOT OK.

■ Position and Communication

To recognize such a position in action is to understand why that person talks the way that they do, because one is able to infer something about self-image and self-esteem. **To recognize such a position in oneself is to achieve some self-knowledge, and potential for change.** There is an intimate relationship between the Self and acts of communication, between inward and outward aspects of a person. Change in one means a change in the other. In a sense it does not matter which of the two one changes first. Control of social interaction means control of communication. It is perfectly possible to learn at least some uses or patterns of communication which represent social skills. But the content is bound up with the form. So it would be our contention that in learning what to say, for example, in order to gain others' approval or to express approval towards them, one cannot help but learn the values and beliefs that motivate that communication. Put another way, we are saying that there is a limit to people's ability to say something without meaning it and without being caught out. All forms of words are used for the first time at some point. With practise their meaning becomes really felt.

TA theory starts with the self rather than the communication. But of course for recognition, change and control to mean anything in practice then the use of the two channels of communication must also change. The outward expression and the inner position have a dynamic relationship and are interdependent (see also the ideas behind Neurolinguistic Programming).

Scripts are about who we are and how we behave, and so is the study of interpersonal communication. It is a sense of common cause and common interests in different but related disciplines which is encouraging. It is encouraging because, if there is agreement about the object of study and even about conclusions which may be drawn from observation, then we may all be on the right track. Comparisons between Transactional Analysis and Communication Studies are the substance of our next section.

KEY QUESTIONS

How can we help others to feel OK?

How would you describe your own life position, in various situations?

9 TA AND IPC

We have already made a number of points about the overlap between TA and interpersonal communication in previous sections. So in reading what follows, don't forget those previous points. We may even repeat some of them, in order to emphasize the fact that, while the terminology may be different, the words themselves are often getting at the same meaning.

9.1 Signs and Transactions

The smallest unit of communication that carries a meaning is a sign. It is interesting to note that the idea of the transaction is extremely similar. True, it includes an exchange of signs – in effect two signs, at its most basic – but still it seeks to identify the building blocks of communication. It is also concerned with the meaning of those signs. The transaction is the object of study, like the sign in Communication. Analysis looks for the meanings of those transactions, just as the Communication student would look for the meanings of the signs.

9.2 Needs and Hungers

For Berne and those who continued his work, Hungers motivate all transactions and time structuring. In Communication Studies, Needs motivate all acts of communication (the production, exchange and decoding of signs). There is room for discussion about the merits of the descriptive lists of each. But again, they bear some comparison. In effect, Hungers look like Personal and Social Needs by another name. Once more we could say that the measure of agreement which this represents confirms the validity of both approaches. It reinforces one's belief in the reasons why communication does take place.

9.3 Self and Ego States

In Communication Studies, the Self is that essence of the person out of which we communicate, and which necessarily affects how we communicate. In TA it is the ego states out of which come the transactions, and which can be read back from these. Each discipline has different ways of describing the constituent parts of that Self, but both are interested in the same thing. Both agree that the Self is a complex notion composed of various elements. But both agree that one element has to do with how we rate ourselves (self-esteem). Both approaches accept the idea that beliefs and values are part of that Self, being formed in early years, and being crucial to the ways in which communication (or transactions) are carried on.

9.4 Self-Esteem and Scripts

In fact, self-esteem is bound up with the idea of scripts in particular because scripts include the idea of feeling OK or NOT OK about oneself. Self-esteem is concerned with how one rates oneself in various ways and according to various criteria. But in general, high self-esteem is likely to be expressed through confidence. A similar generalization may be made about having an OK position about oneself. This position also is likely to show itself through signs of confidence in communication. Here too the idea of **positive or negative self-image** is relevant. How one feels about oneself affects how one communicates.

9.5 Strategies and Games

If strategies are units of interaction designed to achieve specific ends, using communication in ways that have previously been found to be successful, then they have something in common with games. Many strategies may be used for benign purposes and not to manipulate, whereas games are all about seeking to gain advantage over another person. But still both have qualities of being time-structured, of having an overt purpose, of seeking to influence the attitudes and feelings of the other, and of having been developed through practice.

So the five examples above all support the idea that communication study and transactional analysis have much in common: that their very terminology overlaps in meaning and application.

10 TA SKILLS

TA skills are based on essential perceptual skills – recognizing what is going on with another person, and recognizing our own behaviour. One then has to do something about what has been perceived. We would also advise our readers to be cautious and humble in making judgements and in taking action. It is possible to obtain training in TA skills. This takes time and care. So in what follows we are trying only to describe a few skills and to suggest basic actions which may improve your dealings with others:

- Try to tune yourself to **be aware of the more obvious verbal and non-verbal utterances of others which signify one ego state or another.** Look out for the most obvious cues, such as the parental 'ought' and 'must' or child-like shouting or arm waving.
- Stay tuned to your own utterances and try to control your NVB and what you say, so that you **represent the ego state you want.** For example, if you think it is important to be Adult then stick to the relevant non-verbal control and reasoned statements which you think are right, and don't respond to someone else's Child by being childlike yourself.
- Having become aware of the ego state of another, **try to make an immediate decision about how you want to sound in response.** If someone else is giving off Parent signs, you don't have to respond as a Child or compete in trying to out-Parent them.
- Think about how others have been dealing with you and you with them – everyone does! But in particular, **think if you have been playing games.** If you have, consider why, and whether you couldn't get on better if you were more straightforward in what you say. If you **think that certain other people tend to play games with you,** perhaps to make you feel bad if you don't do what they want, then try to sort out what it is in you that lets you become Victim, and what sort of things they say to put you in a double bind. Ideally, one notices a game as someone is playing it on you, but you have to become quite skilled to actually pick this up as it is happening.
- When you have sorted the Hook and the Mark, then decide what you are going to do about it. **The skill is to break up someone's game without causing a row,** if you can avoid it. With hardened game players this may be unavoidable, though all you have to say is something like, 'I can see you are trying to get me to do X and I'm not prepared to go along with it.' But you

may also recognize that friends are playing games because they want to make themselves feel OK by making you feel NOT OK. Becauase they are friends, you might want to use some basic assertiveness skills, for example, 'I don't want to do X, but why don't we do Y tomorrow?'

- Finally, we think it is worth trying to **practise the skill of analysing your own life script**, which may include your games. Nobody really wants to be the victim of a bad script. You need to recognize habitual ways in which you deal with situations and with others, to recognize how you feel about your life and about the future. For example, do you put things off a lot? Do you tend to assume that you can't cope with situations? Do you assume that things will go wrong, and avoid actions because of this? Then it may be that you have cast yourself in the general life role of Victim. It may be that you often act out of the Adapted Child ego state.

- Then you can decide whether or not you want to practise further skills in changing and controlling how you deal with others and deal with situations. You try consciously to do things differently. You tell yourself that you will not make excuses, you will say 'yes' sometimes and not 'no' every time, you will politely refuse to do things that you don't really want to do.

The situations in which these TA skills may apply are of course as various as the wide number of encounters that we have in everyday life. However, it may be useful to recognize a few. For example, encounters in education, at any level, throw up the Parent–Child transaction. The problem is that this is often not appropriate, especially at higher levels, where the encouragement of intellectual skills means precisely that one would expect Adult encounters. In friendship groups it is not uncommon to find people who play games, in order to achieve and maintain power and status in the group. In the workplace, people's life scripts may emerge, as they talk about their jobs and their aspirations, and as the patterns of the ways in which they deal with situations and people at work emerge over months and years.

You may find it useful to look for examples of TA in action, out of these situations. You could also discuss with people you know and trust, TA concepts and the related communication behaviour of others and of yourself. The acquisition of knowledge and understanding is one kind of skill. The use of these, their application is another kind of skill.

REVIEW

You should have learnt the following things from this chapter.

1 Why it is useful to study TA as a student of Communication.

2 Ego states
These are described as Parent, Adult, Child, with different versions of Child and Parent.

These are characterized by certain uses of verbal and non-verbal communication.

These are one way of describing the personality, which must influence all communication.

3 Transactions
There are four types: complementary, crossed, angular, duplex.

They involve an exchange between various combinations of the ego states in any interaction between people.

Crossed transactions offer an excellent explanation of the causes of breakdown in communication between people.

Angular and duplex transactions help explain how we may communicate on two levels at once, and offer both covert and overt messages.

4 Hungers
There are three of these, described as sensation, recognition and structure hungers.

These hungers underlie all transactions and even the development of ego states in the child.

Hungers are the equivalent of needs in Communication Studies.

5 Time Structuring
Social interaction, and by implication communication, is organized in long and short blocks of time.

Short blocks are described as rituals, games, or work, among other things.

Long blocks are scripted.

Such structuring reinforces communication ideas such as that of the convention.

6 Games
Games are short blocks of interaction in which one person tries to manipulate the other, and gain some psychological advantage.

Games are designed to make the victim of the interaction feel stupid, inadequate and frustrated, but to make the manipulator feel good.

Games describe communication used in conflict, and when analysed may reveal the sources of the conflict.

Games may be referred to aspects of communication theory such as covert messages, or the issues of when communication is intentional or not.

7 Scripts

A script is a life plan formed in childhood and carried into adult life.

Scripts, like games, have payoffs for the user which explain why they are used.

Scripts are generally optimistic or pessimistic, are about Winners or Losers.

Games are chosen to fit scripts, and to confirm their plan.

Scripts influence the communication style adopted by the individual.

Scripts limit the autonomy of the individual and are best revealed and exorcized.

Scripts can be revealed by analysing the communication (transactions) of the people concerned.

8 I'm OK – You're OK

This describes an ideal life position for every person which can only be achieved through coming to terms with the NOT OK position which every child is thought to adopt.

There are three other positions: I'M NOT OK – YOU'RE OK; I'M NOT OK – YOU'RE NOT OK; I'M OK – YOU'RE NOT OK.

Receiving strokes is important if the child is to feel OK about others.

These positions shift as the individual matures: some positions cause the individual to become disturbed or criminal.

These positions create scripts and counterscripts.

All these life positions are to be recognized through the communication behaviour of the individuals concerned.

In that they are fundamentally about self-esteem so they must affect the uses of communication by that individual.

9 TA and IPC

There are a number of comparisons to be made between the terminologies of TA and Communications Studies. Examples of overlap are: signs and transactions; needs and hungers; the Self and ego states; self-esteem and scripts; strategies and games.

10 TA Skills

These skills include recognizing ego states in Self and in others, controlling responses, refusing to play games, recognizing life scripts.

CASE SITUATION I

A Complementary Transaction

Look at the model for a complementary transaction. See if you can answer the following questions from the story extract which goes with the model.

What ego states are displayed by the characters involved?
How are these displayed?
Write a passage which shows that age has nothing to do with the expression of ego states.

Mrs Martin plucked at her cheek anxiously and reviewed her kitchen with some apprehension, having just got home from work. She liked things to be in their place and they were not. She was a neat person, in profile and in dress, who characteristically pulled her skirts or her dress into line every 20 minutes. They had to know their place. Now she badgered some bread crumbs from the bread board and seized a tea cup from the draining board in order to give it a proper wash behind the ears. The freshly baked cake which she had spotted when she came in was an interloper that she did not know how to deal with.

'Hello, dear,' Her mother came into the kitchen. 'You're home nice and early. I've only just had a cup of tea, but I can soon make another one.'

'Hello.' And a kiss to anoint the forehead from a dutiful daughter. 'It's all right. Don't fuss. I can put the kettle on myself.'

'Whatever you say, dear.' Her mother seated herself placidly.

Mrs Martin placed the kettle precisely between the teapot and the coffee grinder. 'Mother, there was no need for you to make that cake. But thank you, of course.'

Ellie Williams studied her hands. 'I thought Danny might like it. I'm sorry if you rather I hadn't. He always says how much he likes my cakes.'

Mrs Martin folded her arms as she looked down at her seated parent. 'Now don't misunderstand me, mother. I'm very grateful for what you do. But you shouldn't try to do too much. You ought to get your afternoon rest.'

Her mother smiled placatingly. 'Oh, but I have had it. I feel fine. I just thought it would save you trouble. I know how hard you and David work.'

Mrs Martin patted her mother on the back encouragingly. 'I appreciate that. Now why don't you go and rest on the lounger. I'll bring you your tea in a minute.'

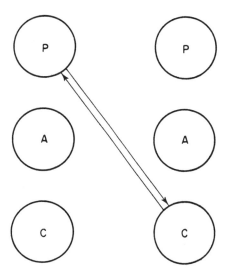

Fig 5.4 *A model for a complementary transaction (after Berne, 1972)*

CASE SITUATION II

A Cross Transaction

Look at the model for a crossed transaction. See if you can answer the following questions from the dialogue which goes with the model:

Which phrases show which different ego states?
At what point does the lecturer switch ego states, and which ego state does the lecturer switch to?
Try rewriting the end of the dialogue to show a positive outcome to the interaction.

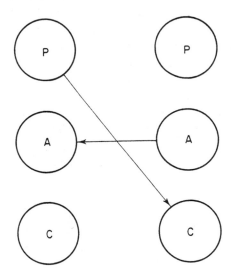

Fig 5.5 *A model for a crossed transaction (after Berne, 1972)*

Lecturer:	Morning, Lesley. I'm glad you've come. I've wanted you to tell why you're so far behind with your assignments.
Student:	Er – yes, I'm sorry about that. I was going to come and see you.
Lecturer:	Well – about time. You must get a grip on yourself. We can't have you wasting your time, can we?
Student:	It depends on what you mean by wasting time. I calculate that I have spent 37 hours reading and making notes for your last two assignments. And according to my record book those are the only two I owe you. Is that right?

Lecturer: Er – I think so – but – that's not the point. You ought to be able to keep up with the assignments if you're going to make it through the course.

Student: I see. Have you any reason to think that I won't make it?

Lecturer: Lesley, if I were you I would concentrate more on actually getting things done.

Student: I don't think that quite's fair. By all means let's look at the situation. I'd like to have some suggestions about how I should rearrange my schedule, bearing in mind that I am covering three other subjects as well.

Lecturer: Look – don't get smart with me, young lady! I get pretty fed up with you people coming to my office and moaning about how much you have to do. I should show you my work load sometime – and no one cares about that. My advice to you is to get on with it, or you'll be sorry.

CASE SITUATION III

Games – If You Really Loved Me (A Variation on 'Corner')

Read the dialogue that follows, showing a game. See if you can decode the game through answering the following questions:

Who is initiating the game?
What is the gimmick involved?
Where does the switch take place?
Can you tell anything about the scripts or life positions of the people involved?

This is about a young couple who have been going out together for some time. The man has just come round to see the girl at her apartment.

Helen lets Mick into her apartment in the early evening. He is in a cheerful mood and is carrying his sports bag. They make conversation and eat a light meal that she has prepared.

– That was great. Thanks. Don't forget that I'm doing the same for you tomorrow night.

– Nick! As if I would. But don't expect me before 7.30. I said that I would call in to see Mum and Dad on the way home.

– No problem. My masterpiece won't be ready until 8.30. But don't worry, I'll soften you up with wine as soon as you get there.

– Now, not too much of that, or I won't be able to drive back.

– I'll work on that as well.

– I bet you will . . . So, how did the game go?

– Terrific – didn't I say? It was pretty close actually. But so what – it means we're through to the next round. So Friday is our next big day, if Terry has recovered.

– Oh, Nick I was hoping we could catch that new movie on Friday.

Now, gentle reader, at this point we have to reveal that Helen knew very well that the next round of the local tennis tournament was to take place on Friday. But, truth to tell, she was feeling just a little bit jealous that her husband-to-be was off on his own playing tennis. Helen preferred togetherness, and felt that a tennis racket should not come between the two of them. Nick is now on the horns of a dilemma.

– Helen, I'd loved to see the movie. But it was always on the cards that we'd be playing on Friday. How about Saturday?

– Nick, you know I promised Mum and Dad that I'd take them to see Uncle Bill. It's pretty difficult for them to get out since Dad had his stroke.

– I know that. I guess I had forgotten about Saturday. But the movie is on next week, too. And I can't just walk out on Terry and the tournament.

– Hey, what about me! What about our relationship. Damn it, Nick – if you really cared . . .

Suggested Reading

Berne, E. (1964): *Games people play*. Harmondsworth: Penguin.
Berne, E. (1972): *What do you say after you've said hello?* London: Corgi.
Harris, T. (1970): *I'm OK, you're OK*. London: Pan.

F Group interaction – at any age

6

Communication in Groups

> In the future, in the present, the person trained in small-groups skills will be a valued employee in the public and private sector of our economy, for futurist scholars have stated that by the year 2000, half of the jobs in our country will be service-related. That astonishing prediction means that there will likely be a high priority for people trained in effective interpersonal and problem-solving communication skills. Need we say more?
>
> Carl L. Kell and Paul R. Corts: *Fundamentals of effective group communication*, 1980.

1 INTRODUCTION

1.1 What is a Group?

Like most words in daily use, the term 'group' has a wide range of meanings according to the context in which it is used. In general it refers to **a collection of people who interact in some way and share some common goals or interests.** Hence it can refer to a small group of say two to twenty people in face-to-face contact (which will be the focus of this chapter), but it can also refer to very large groups of people which might include thousands or millions; for example, any particular profession or employment category who have shared values and interests might be described as a group such as teachers or civil servants or students or hairdressers. Each of these terms will conjure up a set of stereotypes in you that would probably differ if you are in or out of that group. We categorize, and indeed stereotype, people according to their group memberships. Some of these groups may be accidental (e.g. age, gender), others may be achieved through our own efforts (e.g. social clubs, work organizations).

Kelvin (1969) sums up these different definitions of the term group like this:

> From a psychological standpoint it is probably sufficient to distinguish between only two kinds of basic groups: there are the face-to-face groups to which the individual belongs in a strictly physical sense, and there are the

stereotype reference groups to which he 'belongs', in the sense that he identifies himself with the norms and values of the stereotype. The common element in both cases is expectation. In essence a group consists of people, who know, or believe they know, what to expect from one another.

We can refine this notion of a group being defined by **mutual expectations** if we identify more precisely some of these expectations. In describing how groups communicate, we usually think in terms of **role differentiation** (different ways in which the members behave and ascribe status to each other), **patterns of leadership**, a **set of norms** and **rules of membership**.

In seeking to analyse how groups communicate there are three aspects which we need to concentrate on:

- How group members communicate and interact with each other: these are usually known as **group processes**.
- How groups are formed in order to achieve certain tasks or goals: this is usually known as a **task performance**.
- How groups are structured in various ways, which means that individuals occupy roles, have status and power and conform to a certain extent to **group norms**.

1.2 Group Tasks and Group Processes

We shall concentrate on two broad fundamental aspects of groups in this chapter:

■ *The tasks of groups*

This includes the goals, purposes and problem-solving aspects of groups. We choose to belong to groups or form groups in order to achieve stated goals for ourselves and for the group. In addition to the overtly stated aims there may also be 'a hidden agenda' for group activities. Under this heading we include what we have previously referred to as the 'content of the interaction', what the communication and group processes are about.

■ *Processes of groups*

This includes the nature of the interactions between group members and the relationships that develop. It is the social dimension of groups that leads to group cohesion, interdependence and issues of role relationships and leadership. Often in group communication a good deal of energy is spent simply on the 'group dynamics' to develop and maintain a set of individuals as one cohesive group.

1.3 Your Groups

What groups do you belong to?

You may like to pause and create a list of your group memberships. As we have suggested, some may seem to be accidental (e.g. family, age, gender, social class). Others may be more consciously sought (because they fulfil your perceived needs). Others may have been urged upon you (e.g. a committee, working party, task group) because a larger organization or a larger group of people wanted to achieve a particular purpose and mobilized a small group to work towards it.

So we choose some groups and have others assigned to us by birth. We also usually belong to a number of groups at the same time. Some communication behaviour carries from one group to another; other behaviours change because of notions of appropriateness. For example, someone might retain a cheerful, jokey persona from school peer group to Baptist youth group, but would change when it came to the chapel service. This change of communication style does of course change the dynamics of the group: roughly, who talks to who in what way, how and why. You may also see that these dynamics vary from the fairly unstructured patterns of chat at school, to the (probably) more organized activities of the youth group, to the very structured and ritualized patterns of communication and interaction in the religious service.

The groups we belong to and how we behave within them also relate to matters of culture or subculture. On the one hand it can be said that a youth group in any city will behave generally much like any other. They will want to meet somewhere, to talk about the same things. But then particular kinds of group behaviour depend on the exact subculture they choose to belong to – 'jitters', for example.

The conventions of behaviour within a given subculture shape the communication of the groups belonging to that culture. Social conventions often relate to factors such as age and gender. If you are female white British you will have a relatively free involvement in youth group activities. It is accepted that you can interact with males in such groups. But if you are an Asian female then this is frequently not so. Or again, if you are Afro-Caribbean in background then you may well recognize that your ethnicity affects how you behave within various groups.

Such cultural differences make the study of communication very interesting and help one understand all the better how concepts such as role or convention really do have meaning in our lives.

In the rest of this chapter we will look at a number of key concepts for groups, as well as some of the issues that they raise.

2 GOALS

We join and form groups because we believe that 'two (or more) heads are better than one' or 'many hands make light work'. These clichés sum up the common view that an effective group can call upon increased thought power, greater access to information and ideas, can distribute responsibility to accomplish aims, and can have a more coherent and committed approach to fulfilling any task. This idea is succinctly stated by Judy Gahagan (1975): *'a group of people is considerably more than the sum of its parts'*.

The explicit tasks of a small group might include:

- Research and fact finding, for example a research group might be asked to investigate the causes of an accident.
- The pooling of ideas and information, for example an environmental pressure group might wish to collate information on a particular ecological area.
- Recommending a particular course of action, for example a working party might be set up to suggest ways of improving productivity in a work place.

In addition to overtly stated aims of a group, there may also be '**a hidden agenda**' of other unstated aims. In the setting up of a task group to investigate productivity, an unstated aim may also be to create a reason for workers from different parts and levels of an organization to meet together simply to engender better relationships and mutual trust. Explicitly or implicitly, groups always have those two dimensions of task, the content of their work together; and relationship, the social processes of their interactions.

We form and join groups to accomplish tasks that could not be accomplished by individuals alone, and also to foster social relationships and a sense of belonging. We create our social identity through group memberships: a theme which was explored in earlier chapters of this book.

The psychological term which is used to describe the way in which individuals can achieve more by working with others is '**social facilitation**'. People have tended to assume that individuals achieve more and perform better when other people are present to observe them and also that individuals working as a group are more effective in performing a task than an individual working alone. There has been a good deal of social psychological research into these assumptions since the 1920s and this is well summarized by Donald Pennington (1986) in his book *Essential social psychology*. The research suggests that groups can solve problems faster than individuals, but in terms of person-hours this may not be more economic, and in '**brainstorming**' to generate novel ideas four separate individuals will generate a greater number and more original ideas than four people working together.

3 COHESION

One of the assumptions behind the idea of group working is that a group of separate individuals can harness their separate talents and unite them to achieve more than they could achieve separately. This is self-evident in that to achieve many large-scale work tasks we have to organize people into working teams with divisions of responsibility and labour. However, the notion of group cohesion goes further than merely identifying a team of performers such as was described in Chapter 4.

Davis (1969) identified 'group behaviour' as a function of three classes of variables:

- person variables, such as abilities, personality traits or motives;
- environmental variables that reflect the effects of the immediate location and larger organization, community, or social context in which group action takes place; and
- variables associated with the immediate task or goal that the group is pursuing.

Individual group members may have joined the group because they share a mutual interest in achieving a specific task. They may be prepared to adapt their individual ambitions in order to gain the benefit of group effort. Alternatively, an individual may have joined a particular group simply because he wishes to be with other members of that group, i.e. for purely social reasons. These three variables clearly interreact and influence the development and effective working of individuals within a group.

Work groups or leisure groups offer both specific activities and social reward – a sense of belonging and of friendship. People stay in jobs sometimes because they value greatly the social dimensions of their work group. Someone may join a drama group because they believe they would value the social exchange and sense of togetherness as much as making a play. The same thing applies to some people's need to join subcultural groups. A person will choose to join with a group that goes to Raves and enjoys certain kinds of music as much as for the social aspects as for the music itself. This commitment also enhances cohesion.

3.1 Stages of Group Formation

Groups consist of interacting individuals. These interactions become part of the social experience of the group and it is usual to describe stages through which a group becomes more cohesive and the individuals accept a way of working together. Tuckman (1965) suggests that there are four developmental stages:

- **Forming** – anxiety, dependence on a leader, members find out about the task, the rules and nature of the situation.
- **Rebellion** – conflict between individuals and subgroups, rebellion against the leader, resistance to rules and demands of the task.
- **Norming** – development of stable group structure, with social norms, conflicts resolved, cohesiveness developing.
- **Co-operation** – interpersonal problems are solved, the group turns to constructive solution of problems, energy is directed to the task, some degree of cohesiveness is achieved.

Not all groups will necessarily go through these four identifiable stages, but the issues mentioned here will usually be part of the experience of a group as it develops into a cohesive group of individuals.

For example, it is now common for a collection of individuals to join together to form a **pressure group**. At the start the founder members need to define their purposes and their strategies, and will need to designate specific roles such as Chairperson, Secretary, Public Relations Person and so on according to the task. However, when the group is formed, it is likely that some people may believe that the group is not putting the right stress on certain issues or not using the most appropriate tactics – indeed, not achieving what they joined to achieve. At that point some members may opt out but those left will probably have developed a greater trust and commitment. The views of the group will be confirmed and the social interactions will be more group-oriented. They will work with greater confidence and co-operate to achieve the now agreed aims of the pressure group.

You may like to think of groups you know or belong to. Have they gone through some or all of these stages?

Any group of people is necessarily in a dynamic situation, that is, the relationships and the processes of the group can never be static. Hence, the notion of group cohesiveness is not something that can be seen as the ultimate aim of a group. A group may seem to be working in a cohesive way, but then tensions may arise which may damage that group identity. **Cohesiveness is generally regarded as characteristic of the group in which the forces acting on the members to remain in the group are greater than the total forces acting on them to leave it**. A cohesive group reflects a high level of interpersonal attraction and a desire for mutual association. The shared experience of the group and the familiarity with each other can lead to effective working relationships and pleasurable personal experiences.

Kell and Corts (1980) used the metaphor 'immature–mature' to describe the life and growth of a group. They characterize a mature group as having the following qualities:

- There is a growth rather than a loss of selfhood in the group which can lead to a high sense of self-concept and competence for all group members.
- The mature group exists in an atmosphere of trust and friendship.
- The mature group shows a uniform concern, a positive regard for the least, the loudest and the best of its members. Ideas and other contributions are weighed according to their value and not according to who expressed them.
- The mature groups uses positive non-verbal communication to help each member to participate, to struggle with issues, personalities and with themselves. A system of mutual support develops and is demonstrated by the ease of non-verbal communication between the group members.
- The mature group strains; it adapts to points of disagreement. Groups can cope with disagreement, crisis and conflict.

- The mature group is marked by members who are ready and willing to relinquish any position in the group for the general benefit of the group.
- Finally, the mature group has a good time. Membership of a group can lead people to actually love the experience of being with group members.

3.2 Group Think

Any group that exhibits these characteristics of a mature group must surely be said to be a cohesive group. Such cohesiveness seems to be a desirable aim for any group to pursue. If the individual can find fulfilment in the group task then the group could be expected to work effectively. However, we need to be aware that such cohesiveness can lead group members to be totally concerned for maintaining the relationships of the group and in so doing downgrade or neglect the tasks for which the group came together. This notion has been characterized as '**group think**'. Janis (1972) has made a study of this phenomenon which can occur in a highly cohesive group which is striving for unanimity of opinion rather than a realistic appraisal of the situation they are in. Group think has been defined as '*a deterioration of mental efficiency, reality testing and moral judgement that results from in-group pressures*'.

Janis argues that a group can become so cohesive that it develops symptoms of group think, which he lists as:

- illusion of invulnerability
- collective rationalization
- belief in inherent morality of the group
- stereotypes of out-groups
- direct pressure on dissenters
- self-censorship
- illusion of unanimity
- self-appointed mind guard.

He and others refer to several significant political movements of decision-making such as Pearl Harbor, the escalation of the war in Vietnam and the Watergate Affair as evidence of group think operating amongst a close circle of politicians and their advisers.

The effect of this group think was a kind of smugness, even stupidity, in which the presidential team ignored uncomfortable information in its discussions and made bad decisions. Pearl Harbor 'couldn't happen', Vietnam could be conquered, no one would find out about Watergate – or so they brought themselves to believe.

For a group member, group think means that he or she loses the ability to think independently or to criticize other members of the group or what the group is proposing. Certain sects such as the Moonies actually encourage group think in order to subdue possible criticism and to reinforce the validity and very existence of the group.

This phenomenon also ties in with ideologies. Those who adhere to a particular ideological value system may also want to believe that such values are inherently right and all others are wrong. Religious and political groups have lapsed into this position throughout history, from Calvinists who believed that only their followers could go to heaven, to versions of Communism with an equally bigoted view of their own rightness. In a personal sense it is of course comforting to the Self to believe that one belongs to the only 'right' ideological position. It makes the person feel OK, and may be used to justify all kinds of behaviour towards others.

KEY QUESTIONS

Group Cohesion

Describe the main features which give identity to a group of football fans and to a group of soldiers.

What in your opinion gives cohesion to a family?

4   ROLES

We have used this term in several different sections of this book. The word is used with different emphases in different contexts which often reflects whether it is a label being used from a sociological or a psychological perspective. In this book we are trying to use the insights from both sociological and psychological studies to analyse communication processes. **Fundamentally, role refers to a notion of public behaviour (rules, norms, expectations) that the person believes is appropriate for the situation and his or her position in it.**

In any group context, it is inevitable that individuals adopt roles *vis-à-vis* the other people present. In Goffman's terms we 'perform' to manage the impressions other people receive from us and to define the situation as we see it. People are assigned **status** in any particular group according to the role they play. For example, in family groups we tend to have very clear role designations as daughter, son, mother, father. These roles are certainly being redefined and changed in specific family contexts and in broader social contexts, but nevertheless the labels do suggest notions of relationships and status. In work groups, once again we can see clearly assigned roles and relationships which they reflect.

Shaw (1981) suggested there are three different aspects to this overall concept of role: the expected role, the perceived role and the enacted role. The **perceived role** is the behaviour which the person believes he or she should enact; the **enacted role** is the actual behaviour which the person engages in; and the **expected role** is the behaviours thought appropriate by others in the group. If these three are in harmony there will be little if any conflict between the role player and other members of the group. However, if there is any difference between any two or all three it may often result in group conflict: if perceived and/or enacted roles differ greatly from member expectations the person occupying the role may either be put under pressure to conform, asked to vacate the position or unusually attempt to change the expectations of other members of the group. We adopt roles as a normal part of our public behaviour. The social or group expectation of a particular role will be interpreted by the individual according to his or her self-concept and his or her reading of the social situation and the expectations of others. Hence, each individual performs a role in accordance with his or her personal attitudes, values, beliefs, perceptions and experience (see Fig. 6.1. Role playing).

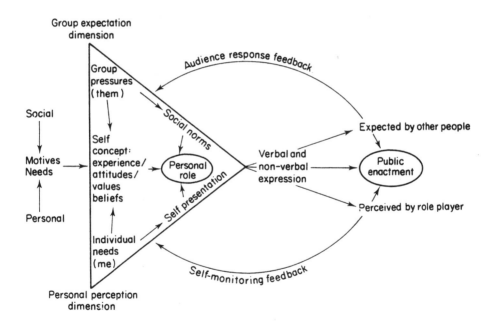

Fig 6.1 *A model for role playing – the interface of me and them*

KEY QUESTIONS

Group Roles
Describe the various roles taken on by members of your family in all aspects of their lives.

How does a sense of role affect the way that people communicate?

5 ANALYSIS OF GROUP DYNAMICS

A number of ways have been developed to analyse the contributions to group dynamics and the roles which people play in regard to the task of the group and the social processes of the group. These methods can, for example, deal with the amount of communication that is going on in a group, with the qualities of that communication, with its frequency, with the directions in which communication seems to travel between group members.

There are three principal ways of recording these analyses:

5.1 Participation in a Group

You can record levels of participation by drawing a circle to represent each member of the group and placing a mark in the circle for each time the person speaks (see Fig. 6.2). For example, in a group of five people labelled A to E we

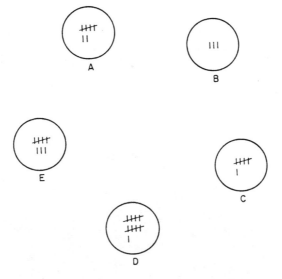

Fig. 6.2 *Participation in the group process – scoring the number of times that each group member speaks*

could record the participation of each person. This sort of analysis can indicate who is speaking most in the group. It obviously is an unsophisticated recording device, since there is no way of recording people's listening involvement or people's non-verbal interactions with other group members.

5.2 Interaction in a Group

To record the interaction between people in a group we can use the same circles as in Fig. 6.2, but indicate the particular verbal contributions between specific people and to the group in general. This sort of diagram is often called a sociogram.

Figure 6.3 is an example of how a record of a group meeting might appear. In Fig. 6.3 we can see that person A spoke generally to the group twice, spoke to person B twice and spoke to person E twice; person B on the other hand spoke generally to the group four times, spoke twice to person A, once to person C, once to person D and once to person E. The patterns of speaking and interaction between each of the people can thus be recorded.

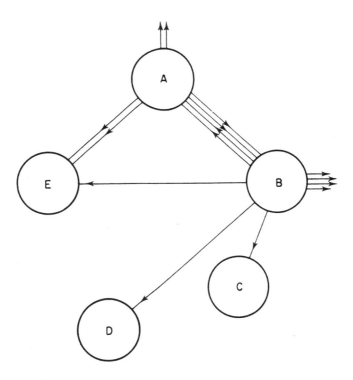

Fig 6.3 *Participation in the group process – representing lines of communication as group members interact*

If one wished to use such a record to indicate group communications, it would be useful to have each group member describe their own experiences of the group interactions as part of the debriefing since once again this sort of recording offers no information about people's non-verbal communication or their listening or their intrapersonal thoughts concerning themselves and the group. This can only be revealed as far as people are able and willing to discuss their own perceptions.

5.3 Interaction Process Analysis (IPA)

Bales (1950) developed a coding system for analysing group processes which he called '*interaction process analysis*' or IPA. Interaction process analysis is based on the assumption that all behaviours, both verbal and non-verbal, occurring in small groups can be described within four main headings: positive and negative socio-emotional behaviour and information giving and information seeking concerned with the task of the group. Once again, we can see that the dimensions of the task and content of the group as opposed to the social relationship dimensions of the group are fundamental to this analysis. Figure 6.4 reproduces Bale's interaction process analysis chart which can be adapted as a grid for recording group communication processes.

An example of such an adaptation can be found in Fig. 6.5 (analysis sheet for observing communication). If you are planning to use a grid such as this, and you can, of course, draw up your own particular headings, you need to brief the observers carefully so that they are as consistent as possible in recording both verbal and non-verbal communication from each of the group members.

In our experience of using these sorts of interaction analysis grids, we find that it is very important in the debriefing period to have each member of the group compare their own perceptions of their performance and other people's performances with that of the outside observers.

We suggest you might like to use this recording technique for a small group, either in your college or school class, or amongst a group of friends. You can set up a simple decision-making task for this purpose. An example might be to have each member of the group choose a well-known person from history and then for the group to decide which of those people chosen has made the greatest contribution to human happiness.

A number of books on communication processes indicate various networks of communication amongst groups of five people. If you wish to follow this up you can find these networks in, for example, James Davis's *Group performance* (1969) or Dimbleby and Burton's *More than words* (1992). Networks of controlling communication in groups usually lead to certain members of the group gaining positions of dominance. Dominance of course may not be the same as group leadership, to which we now wish to turn.

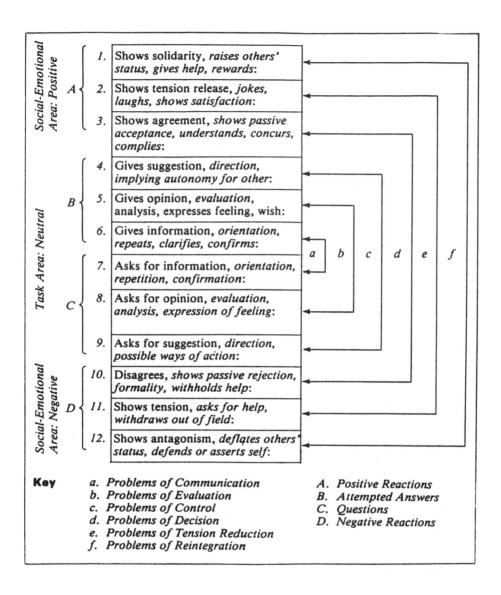

Fig 6.4 *Bales' system of categories for describing and observing group processes and communication (Bales, 1950)*

Types of Group Communication		People				
		A	B	C	D	E
	Tasks					
1	Giving information					
2	Questioning/seeking information					
3	Organizing ideas					
4	Clarifying ideas					
5	Summarizing					
6	Evaluating					
7	Deciding					
	Relationships					
8	Encouraging					
9	Harmonising					
10	Sharing/gate keeping					
11	Listening					
12	Relieving tension/compromising					
	Individual needs					
13	Blocking					
14	Seeking attention					
15	Dominating					
16	Not involving					

Fig 6.5 *A score sheet for recording the types of and quality of contributions in group interaction*

6   LEADERSHIP

Issues of leadership, and particularly what makes an effective leader, have long been the concern of social psychologists and other students of human behaviour. **In previous generations the favourite theory was that leadership was a function of personality.** However, most students of leadership would now see this as an extremely limited view.

A more modern view of leadership sees it as a function of several variables. These do include the leader's personality and behaviour, but also cover the composition and function of the group, the social context, the structure of the group, the nature of the task, and whether the leader can be described as effective or ineffective in mobilizing the group and completing the initial objectives.

Tedeschi and Lindskold (1976) suggest that three components of leadership are now identified as the most significant:

- **Social influence** – this refers to how far a person can direct and control other people's behaviour, attitudes and opinions and persuade group members to conform to assigned roles and group norms. This notion stresses that an effective leader must be able to conform to assigned roles and group norms. This notion stresses that an effective leader must be able to form satisfactory relationships with group members and influence the social, group dynamics.
- **Behaviour** – this refers to the leader's ability to clarify group objectives, make decisions and suggest ways of achieving objectives. This suggests that an effective leader must have an informed understanding of the tasks which the group are seeking to complete. The leader must be seen to be able to match those tasks in his or her own behaviour.
- **Authority** – this can be a result of the leader being assigned a role of authority, for example by being nominated or elected, or it can reflect other people's perceptions of his or her authority in being able to achieve the group's goals and manage the situation.

Hence, rather than stressing the individual personality, modern views of leadership stress the ability of a person to perceive the task that is set and to handle personal and social relationships.

Myers and Myers (1985) suggest that it is possible to look at four approaches to leadership, each of which indicates how leadership might be improved and how people might be trained in leadership skills:

- **Trait approach** – this comes from the historical personality view of leadership. This is now considered to be limited because there is no agreement on what characteristics are exclusively and consistently the property of leaders, and it is also difficult to measure personality traits; many characteristics which leaders seem to possess are also possessed by non-leaders,
- **Situational approach** – these theories contended that a person rises to the occasion of leadership. If you are trained to be ready for a situation and you wait for that situation to arise then you can become the leader when it happens. This theory is too specific to be widely applied.
- **Functional approach** – this view stresses that different members of a group may perform some functions necessary to keep the group working towards some goal and working together smoothly. In these terms, emphasis on one leader misses the point since different people could fulfil the functions of, for example, the task and the social process.

- **Contingency approach** – Fiedler (1973) developed the idea that leadership is a combination of (1) the kind of situation and (2) the style of the person performing leadership functions. In this view, leadership depends on finding the proper match between a leader's style of interacting with subordinates and the degree to which the situation gives control and influence to the leader. For example, a situation in which respect and trust and power are high or low and the task is highly structured or quite unstructured is especially good for the task-oriented leader.

6.1 Leadership Styles

Research has also been carried out on leadership styles. These are usually classified under three headings: **authoritarian, democratic** or *laissez-faire*. These styles were used in a class experiment by Lewin *et al.* (1939) to demonstrate how leadership style affects group performance. Ten- and eleven-year-old boys working in groups where they had to carve models from bars of soap were exposed to these three leadership styles. Authoritarian leaders made all the decisions for the group, did not participate in group activities, assigned boys to tasks without saying why and made changes without consultation. Democratic leaders made decisions only after consultation with the group, were friendly to group members, participated in group activities, gave reasons for praise and criticism and offered help when required. *Laissez-faire* leaders played a passive role, did not attempt to direct or co-ordinate the group and made neither positive nor negative evaluations of the group.

The democratic style of leadership was found to produce highest morale in the group and greatest friendliness and co-operation; however, groups with this style of leadership produced fewer models than those under authoritarian leadership, though the models were of higher quality. The boys also kept working in the absence of the leader. The authoritarian style resulted in more models being made, but misbehaviour occurred when the leader was absent. Poorest performance was under the *laissez-faire* style of leadership. Here fewest models were produced and misbehaviour occurred all the time. However, the boys were friendly towards the leader. After the boys had experienced each type of leadership style they were found to prefer the democratic approach most. In summary, group performance in terms of quality of models made and group cohesiveness was highest with the democratic style of leadership.

A further style of leadership could be described as **'collective' style**. In this case no one person would be designated as the leader of the group and each member of the group would be assigned equal status and power, and actions and decisions would be a matter of consensus within the group. In practice, within such a group different leaders might well emerge according to different tasks and situations.

There are no conclusive answers to these issues of leadership. Perhaps some sort of conclusion might be drawn in stressing that all groups have both the task dimension and the social dimension. An effective leader within a group will be able both to contribute towards the completion of the task and maintain the social relationships of the group. In order to do this a leader requires considerable communication skills in order to manage other people and in order to achieve group goals. Theoretically, a person who has effective communication and social skills – ability to express and to read verbal and non-verbal messages, to perceive other people's needs and to maintain open social relationships is likely to be an effective leader. He or she will be able to persuade other people and gain other people's trust and loyalty.

In this discussion of leadership, inconclusive though it is, it is possible to say that an effective leader of a group is not the person who dominates and imposes his or her will on the group but is rather a facilitator for the group task and is sensitive to the social dynamics of the group.

One also needs to recognize that notions of leadership have a cultural dimension. Subcultural groups such as Hell's Angels have a positive attitude towards an authoritarian style which is more extreme than that of the main culture within which they exist. Equally, cultures other than those of the Western nations also have differing views about leadership.

KEY QUESTIONS

Leadership
Describe the leadership qualities which you admire in other people.

Explain why different kinds of leadership may be appropriate in different situations.

7 NORMS

The concept of 'norm' is often used both in describing people's behaviour in small groups and in large-scale socio-cultural groups. In its widest sense a **norm can be said to be a standard against which the appropriateness of a behaviour is to be judged.** Within a group there may be overtly stated rules and expectations for behaviour, but there will also develop unwritten standards. Davis (1969) suggests that norms vary in a number of respects. Some norms (perhaps most) apply to overt behaviour, while others seem to guide subjective states when the individual is faced with uncertainty. Some norms are formal, in that they are written or otherwise conspicuously and intentionally adopted by a group (rules or operating procedures). On the other hand, many norms are informal in their origin; they arise from the interaction of the group members over time. Working norms emerging in this way may even occasionally be in conflict with the formal group norms which ostensibly govern behaviour in some particular case. Formal norms are not necessarily equally evident to all group members; but in most small groups that have existed for a time, there is little likelihood that norm violations occur frequently without the awareness of most of the members.

With regard to what we described earlier as reference groups, norms can be quite clearly observed. For example, a particular profession may have clearly stated codes of conduct for its members. A particular group may signal its adoption of norms through clearly visible clothes or other symbols. These could range from turbans for the Sikh male to the CND badge to the uniform of a member of the police force. A pressure group may consist of members who display quite different behavioural norms, but whose views on a particular issue are following a set pattern, for example members of an organization like Greenpeace may adopt very different norms in their general social behaviour but will share the same opinions about treatment of endangered species and the need for conservation in general.

The concept of norm presupposes that some individuals will deviate from the norms of the group to which they belong. Obviously, each of us is a member of a number of groups and these may have different norms. At some time in our lives these may lead to conflicts which we shall have to resolve. If we feel particularly attracted to one group to which we belong then we are likely to be prepared to conform to the norms of that group. If we want to be identified as clearly part of a particular reference group then again we are prepared to conform to the norms of that group. Our self-esteem may be closely tied to the social identity which comes from particular group memberships. Someone who wants to be identified with a local group of heavy metal fans will adapt their appearance and behaviour (including communication) to be accepted by that group.

It is one of the assumptions of this book that individual processes of perception and experience are dynamic, and that group processes are also dynamic. Hence, we would not expect that an individual member of a group or the group itself can remain in a static norm state. It may be that a member of a group is content to follow the norms of that group for a certain period, but then something will occur in his or her life that leads to a desire for deviation from this norm. As we said in an earlier section, excessive conformity to group norms can lead to a sterile state of '*group think*'. In concluding these remarks on norms, we wish to stress that they are not imposed on groups from the outside. They develop as a result of the interactions between the individual members of the group, and hence themselves change and develop with the group. Research has shown that if there is one deviating person in a group then he or she may be isolated and excluded; however, if two people deviate in a small group then they may well be able to move the whole group across to their new norm.

KEY QUESTIONS

Group Norms
Describe what you believe are the norms for an ethnic group and a youth group which you know about.

Explain how being in a group can change the norms of behaviour (and values) shown by someone as compared with their behaviour as an individual.

8   CONFLICT

In the past few sections, we have been discussing groups as if they take on a life of their own through cohesiveness and norms of behaviour and belief. It is impossible to conceive, however, of an active group of individuals maintaining a position of 100 per cent cohesiveness and conformity for a long period. Inevitably there are going to be challenges to the norms of the group and conflicts between individuals. These conflicts may arise from several sources. One of these may be simply the personal differences of needs and aims of the members of the group. These personal needs may well change over a period of time. Another source of conflict may be as a result of the roles which people are playing. A role which is expected within one group may conflict with a role that the same person is expected to play in another group. Such role conflict may reach the point where the person has to change his or her role position.

Obviously an individual is playing a range of roles in his or her life, indeed in any one day. As the context and group expectations change, so the role player's behaviour will change; but of course he or she remains the same person. If one is taken over completely in a role without maintaining some personal consistency then other people become anxious about 'who's the real person?' or about honesty and reliability. We interpret roles according to our own beliefs as well as other people's expectations (see Fig. 6.1, Role playing, above).

Playing different roles can create personal tensions and conflicts, for example, if at work you are expected to play a subordinate role, but at home you need to play a leading role, then the latter may become excessively dominating to compensate for frustrations at work. Or, if you are 'the boss' at work you may want to play the boss at home when you are expected to be part of an egalitarian family group. You may be able to think of other 'role conflicts' that can arise from shifts in context and expectations.

Within groups, people are assigned different status levels. Once again these will change over time and the process of change may be a cause of conflict.

8.1 Managing Conflict

In order to maintain the group, individuals often avoid conflict situations. In writing about conflict, many social psychologists and practical communicators suggest that conflict should not be ignored but should be faced and resolved. Blake *et al.* (1964) suggest that **we can manage conflicts in three ways:**

- **Avoidance** – we often avoid conflict or potential conflict in the hope that if we ignore it it will go away. Sometimes we seek simply to smooth over problems and do not face up to the sources of the difficulty. In such cases the conflict will often reappear in some other form and is not likely simply to disappear because we wish it would.
- **Defusion** – this strategy is used when a person involved in a conflict decides to hold until tempers have cooled off. Alternatively we might seek agreement on minor points and avoid the bigger problem that lies beneath them. Sometimes these defusion strategies can work; sometimes they are only a form of avoidance.
- **Confrontation** – in confronting a problem we can seek one of three outcomes. First, we can reach a win–lose situation. This may come about because 'the boss' imposes his or her ruling on a situation. Often this sort of problem is resolved by one side dictating the terms and the other side inevitably losing. Another strategy is the lose–lose strategy. In this case people involved in conflict may simply decide that neither of them will have their way and hence the conflict will end. Sometimes both people can decide to have part of what they want and give part of what they want. This may be a sort of compromise. However, a compromise can be more positively sought and lead to the third strategy which is a win–win strategy. This is generally described as the most desirable way of confronting a conflict. In this view people treat conflict as an issue to be solved, not a fight to be won and take the view that nobody has to lose completely. Time is spent defining the specified and unspecified sources of the conflict and working at alternative solutions which will satisfy both parties. It was suggested that this could be a form of compromise. However, this suggests that both parties do in fact lose in finding a solution. The more positive view of the win–win strategy is to see a new solution being developed by the parties to the conflict which actually leads to a new consensus which resolves the problem. Neither party wins or loses, but each contributes to the resolution of the conflict.

In the group context, the main source of conflict is behaviour that is individually oriented as opposed to behaviour that takes note of the needs of other group members and of the tasks and social processes of the group. In previous sections of this chapter we have stressed the task and group relationship dimensions of groups. This is illustrated in Figs 6.4 (Bale's interaction process analysis) and 6.5 (analysis sheet for observing communication). These group dynamics can be developed by a mutual acceptance of group norms and differentiated roles, and by a desire to put group cohesiveness before separate individual's needs.

However, in a group of people there are inevitably overt and covert tensions between the demands of the task, the group's maintenance needs and the individual's needs and motives. It is possible to summarize these tensions and conflicts that have been explored in this chapter as in Fig. 6.6 – task, group and individual demands.

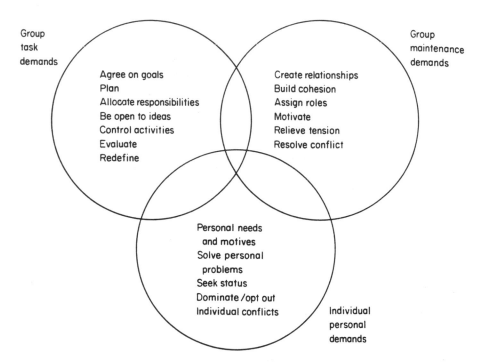

Fig. 6.6 *A chart to describe task, group and individual demands*

Nolan (1987) stresses that for effective group meetings it is not possible to have one person (even if he or she has the status of leader) who manipulates the rest of the people. Such manipulation is likely to lead to overt or covert conflict. Nolan expresses this idea forcibly:

> even if one party should 'win', the loser will not take it lying down: he or she will fight back, subvert, refuse to co-operate or undermine in one way or another. The win–lose contest becomes lose–lose as the loser sets up a return match on his or her own ground which that person is sure to win. If we are to have successful meetings, we must get away from the idea that 'meetings are manipulation'.

9 PROBLEM SOLVING

It will be no surprise to those of you who have read this far in this chapter, to be told that problems may need to be solved in either the task dimension or the social dimension. In the previous section on conflict, we are primarily discussing conflicts in the social dimension. In this section we are concentrating more on problems and their resolution in the task dimension. **It is useful to draw a distinction between open problems which require a creative imaginative approach and closed problems which require a more analytical and factually based approach.** In broad general terms, a group is probably more able to deal with open problems, since it can call on the imaginative resources of a large number of people, than it is to deal with closed problems. However, having said that, a group of people who have specialist knowledge may be very helpful in providing information to resolve a closed problem. In this case, however, it is likely at the end of the day that one person is going to have to take the decision about which particular solution they want to follow.

Whatever the problems are, for a group to be effective in tackling the problem there needs to be an openness to ideas and a willingness to listen to all the members of the group. If the group is constricted into notions of specified roles for group members, clearly designated status for group members, or constricting norms of what is suitable behaviour and thinking processes then a group is not going to be an effective vehicle for problem solving. Once again, we refer you to the notion of group think which tellingly illustrates the way in which a group of people can be confined within their own universe and unable to step outside their thinking and feeling processes to see that they are deluding themselves and are remote from the real world outside the group. Perhaps the conclusion to be drawn here is that a closed group with an unchanging membership is likely to become somewhat sterile in its thinking processes.

10 COMMUNICATION IN GROUPS: SOME CONCLUDING REMARKS

10.1 Individuals

It is a truism to say that a group consists of two or more individuals. However, it is important to remember this. Each member of the group has his or her own needs and motivations. Their relationships and performances in front of other people will be influenced by their self-concept and their attitudes, values, beliefs and past experiences. They will have developed their own communication styles which will include particular verbal and non-verbal strategies for expressing themselves and for interpreting other people's communication. Each member will inevitably be performing in front of other people: each person is seeking to manage the impression they give off and to define the situation. The personalities and characters of each individual will need to adjust to those of other members of the group if the group is to work as a group.

10.2 Interpersonal Factors

For a group to come into effective existence, there needs to be a sharing of each member of the group. This sharing will depend on the perceptions that each person has of every other person in the group. It will also reflect the expectations they have of each other and of the group as an entity. Each person will be adopting certain roles *vis-à-vis* the other persons in the group. Notions of appropriate behaviour and mutually accepted performances are important. In order for a group to become a mature group, degrees of trust and familiarity need to be developed between the individual members on a one-to-one, interpersonal basis.

The quality of verbal and non-verbal interactions will determine the strength of the group. In general, we are taught to think of communicating with each other as speaking to each other. However, in a group, each member is going to spend more time listening to other people than speaking. Being sensitive to other people's feelings and emotions, most of which will be conveyed non-verbally, is a crucial element in group communication. This non-verbal interaction will be largely responsible for creating the climate of the group which determines how open and supportive it is. The development of this climate will be one of the determinants of the group norms. These are developed from within the group and are likely to reflect the needs of the individuals within that group.

10.3 Differences between Interpersonal and Group Communication

Finally, in this chapter we wish to stress that there is a basic difference between individual and group communication. In a one-to-one situation we are presenting our Self according to our self-concept and our perception of the other person(s) and the social context. When we are part of a group, however, the dynamics of the group, its tasks and social relationships mean that we are more conscious of playing a role and of being concerned with the *group*. The group, when it's working cohesively, develops a life of its own of which the individual members are merely a part – we subordinate our individual needs and motives for the sake of the group.

The focus of this chapter has been on small groups, but at the start of the chapter we also referred to membership of large reference stereotype groups which influence our self-perceptions and behaviour. As a teacher, for example, one is constrained by notions of professional responsibility and conduct that might include a tendency to take control in a situation, to care for pupils, and to speak and behave in a way that provides a socially acceptable model of behaviour.

Another dimension of group behaviour to note is 'crowd behaviour'. If an individual feels totally submerged in a group so that the usual personal responsibilities, norms and inhibitions of behaviour disappear then some individuals feel free to behave in ways that are out of character. The power that comes from group membership enables people to achieve more than they could alone; but group membership can also be used as a mask to cover individual responsibility and to give licence to perform what individually would be unthinkable. Such group-dominated behaviour is at its most extreme in what Goffman (1976) called '*total institutions*', such as the Army or a religious order, where a person is denuded of individuality. This notion of **deindividuation** is used to explain why people in crowds will commit acts of violence and not feel individually responsible for what has been done. Eiser (1986) reports the work of Reicher (1984) which suggests that people shift their attitudes when in a group because there is a shift in their social identity. Their sense of who they are and what they should or should not do becomes bound up with the group. In 'normal' life our group memberships influence our self-concept, our roles and our personal attitudes, but they do not rob us of our individuality. The strength of a group grows out of the strength of the individuals in it and their social interactions.

11 GROUP SKILLS

Once more we can say that there are two broad areas of skill in group participation: one set is to do with recognizing what is going on, the other is doing something about what we have recognized.

Clearly, the kind of group that we are involved with influences what we may mean by being skilled. If one is with a group of friends then it isn't appropriate to exercise leadership skills in the same way that one might at work. If one is in the middle of a team game it isn't appropriate to stop and evaluate the worth of the captain's request for you to take some particular action – now! On the other hand it is surprising how many skills are broadly appropriate across a range of groups. It is as important to contribute to harmony and cohesion in a family group as it is to a peer group.

Group skills ride on the back of other interpersonal skills, not least of which is being able to listen properly and constructively to others. These skills are distinctive in that one is talking about behaviour (verbal and non-verbal) which contributes positively to the well-being and the working of the group as a whole. Group skills also overlap with what one may recognize as skills in problem solving or decision making. Items 1 to 9 of the Bales categories (Fig. 6.4) offer one kind of summary of skilled behaviour. The following list is a variant on this and includes an indication of communicative behaviours.

1. To offer information and ideas
   How would it be if we did X?
2. To develop ideas and information (recognize worth of other's ideas)
   That's good. And we could do X (leaning forward into group).
3. To evaluate ideas and information
   So how would that work in practice? What would happen if . . . ?
4. To ask for others' contributions or evaluation
   So what do you think about X (direct gaze held on respondent).
5. To summarize ideas and opinions
   So what we seem to be saying is X. Is that right?
6. To suggest courses of action
   Then why don't we do X? (looking round the group).
7. To praise and recognize others' contributions
   That's a really good idea! (smile and direct gaze).
8. To offer supportive action
   All right – well, I'll put the leaflets through the door.
9. To offer humour
   (making a joke about a problem, using laughter).

In terms of leading or managing groups in a formal sense it is usual to recognize adaptability and a wide range of skills in leaders. Effective leaders of small groups are not usually directive in their communication so much as good at bringing things together and at moving things on. So skills 5 and 6 are particularly ones to be valued in a group leader. Contributions are directed towards leaders.

Positive, constructive communication in groups can be seen in a wide range of situations. To be skilled as a group member one simply has to think about what one is saying and how one is saying it. Ask yourself, am I saying something which will help the group, which will please other people, which will help sort something out? These skills could cover working with others at some task in a job, or organizing a birthday treat for a member of your family without them knowing about it, or just talking with friends at a party. You can look at what this chapter tells you about negative or self-oriented behaviour to see how this underlines the existence of skills. We feel better for working positively with others, we often benefit in practical as well as in emotional ways.

REVIEW

You should have learnt the following things from this chapter.

1 What is a group?
- A collection of people who interact in some way and share some common goals or interests.
- We belong to small groups (2–20 people) and to large (possible millions of people) reference stereotype groups.
- We belong to groups through accident (e.g. gender, age) or through achievement (e.g. committee or employment).
- We can analyse processes of groups in terms of *tasks* – overt and covert goals of the group – and in terms of *maintenance of relationships*.

In groups we find mutual expectations, role differentiation, patterns of leadership, sets of norms, rules of membership.

2 Goals
We belong to a variety of groups with a variety of aims.
   The concept of 'social facilitation' suggests that individuals achieve more and perform better when other people are present to observe them.

3 Cohesion
Cohesive group behaviour is a function of three variables:
- personal abilities, characteristics and motives
- environmental factors of the context of the group
- task to be achieved.

3.1 Stages of Group Formation: To achieve group cohesion the following stages are often necessary:

- forming the group identity
- rebelling within the group
- developing norms of group behaviour
- co-operating to solve the problems and to fulfil the agreed goals.

3.2 Group think: A small group can become so cohesive that it becomes separate from the outside world and confined within its own limits of thought and behaviour.

4 Roles
Roles refers to a notion of public behaviour (rules, norms, expectations) that the person believes is appropriate for the situation and his or her position in it.
   People achieve status through the roles they play.
   It is useful to divide 'role' into three aspects: the perceived role of the individual; the expected role as perceived and expressed by the group; and the enacted role which is the actual behaviour displayed by the individual.

5 Analysis of Group Dynamics
We can observe and describe group communication processes through:

* participation of group members
* interaction of group members
* interaction process analysis:
    positive (group-oriented) social emotional contributions
    negative (self-oriented) social emotional contributions
    task contributions.

6 Leadership
Leadership is now perceived as a function of several variables: personality and behaviour; composition and function of the group; social context; structure of the group; nature of the task; whether the leader can be described as effective or ineffective in mobilizing the group and completing the initial objectives.

6.1 Leadership Styles: It is possible to see four major styles of leadership: authoritarian, democratic, *laissez-faire*, collective.
   Leadership skills can be summarized as:

* **Openness** – ability to receive and respond to group members' ideas.
* **Information** – apparent knowledge base for group problem solving.
* **Persuasion** – ability to influence others.

7 Norms
A norm is a standard against which the appropriateness of behaviour is to be judged.
   A group develops its own norms of thought and behaviour, but these are not static – they develop as the group develops.

8 Conflict
Conflicts arise from the personal differences of individuals and from different role expectations. They also arise from demands of the task, the group maintenance and the personal needs of members.

8.1 Managing Conflict: We can manage conflict in three ways: avoidance, defusion, or confrontation.

9 Problem Solving
Problems exist in both the task dimension and social relationship dimension of groups.
   Groups are effective in solving problems where they are open to ideas and willing to harness the contribution of all members.

10 Conclusions
A group develops as a result of the interaction between individuals and their own needs and motives and the desire to form a group. For a group to function effectively its members need to agree on mutual roles and norms of behaviour. Each member of the group needs to contribute verbally and non-verbally to develop a mutually supportive

climate. In group communication, individual members subordinate their own needs to those of the group, but to submerge individual needs totally to those of the group can lead to extreme results.

11 Group Skills
These skills include, giving and evaluation information within the group, giving and evaluating ideas, suggesting actions, recognizing the worth of others and of their contributions.

CASE SITUATION

Read the extract below, about group behaviour in a meeting, and try to answer the following questions:

What is revealed about conflict in groups?
What is revealed about leadership?

If you were talking to this group of people about their behaviour, what advice would you give them to improve their co-operation and communication?

Who Runs This Project?

The last time that they had a meeting Joe had noticed that Pauline appeared to be totally bored for most of the time. She spoke only twice, mostly just shuffled her papers, avoided eye contact and drew elaborate doodles around her agenda. Every letter on the left hand margin became an illuminated manuscript.

He hoped that today she would get involved. Competition for contracts was tough. So the project needed her. Anyway, Joe knew that she had a lot to contribute because he had watched her really pull things together on the Waterstones project. She had transformed the graphic design of the leaflets. He glanced around the table as people shuffled their papers, waiting for something to happen.

Maybe she was disappointed because again it was Jane who was asked to be project leader. Everyone knew that Pauline had more experience and artistic flair than Jane. But then Pauline was a bit arrogant, she didn't really listen to other people. She seemed to even despise her colleagues, though he didn't care. But he could see why Calvin wouldn't have her as leader. People needed encouragement. There was Bob who was desperately trying to get a job out of London and who seemed really to have lost interest. Lindsey had only just joined the company and seemed too worried about not making a mistake, though she had good experience. There was Marc who was new and very green, but promising. Joe himself was very comfortable with his own niche.

Jane looked round the group trying to attract attention. 'OK, let's start,' she said. 'Last time we agreed on broad approaches to this promotion. The exhibition is the centrepiece for creating a positive image. Considering our client's interests we're going for an ecology theme. So – Bob, you were going to come back today with ideas about how we can develop the theme, bearing in mind we have a month to deliver. What have you got?' She focused on him directly.

Bob looked at the ceiling and twiddled his pencil. 'Yeah – well, I haven't actually got much on paper yet'. . . 'Typical!' muttered Pauline, looking down, but knowing they could all hear . . . Bob glared at her. 'But I have given it some thought and I reckon we could go on the back of the Greenpeace logo, so long as we don't make it too obvious. You know, endangered species and all that. We're already into a safe image in the brochure mockup. Pollution free. In fact we could borrow some material and blow it up for the exhibition. Lindsey has taken some photos and tried composites to show how everything blends in with the surroundings.' He turned to Lindsey with a flick of an eyebrow. She nodded.

'Yeah, well I did take some. But they were really for the brochure and the display ads. I'm not really sure how they would look blown up.'

'Is anyone round this table sure about anything!' Pauline's Yorkshire accent fell with a bang into the discussion. 'I don't feel we have a proper co-ordination policy here. Nobody has made clear what the budget is. So we don't know how far we can go with colour. We haven't discussed video. Can we get video? Do you actually know the real budget, Jane? Or are you in the dark as well? Video would make all the difference, and we still have time to put it together. Let's get on with it.'

'Wait a minute!' Jane pushed herself forward and looked round at the rest of the group, but avoiding Pauline. 'Let's hold back a minute. We haven't decided that at all.' She glared at Pauline. 'We're not ready.'

'And never will be at this rate,' snapped Pauline, leaning across Joe and looking razor blades. 'We've actually met twice now and got nowhere. Completely wasted our time.' She was largely right, thought Joe. 'If Bob couldn't bring in something more than a vague idea then he should have said so. I suppose he will expect Lindsey to rescue him again.' The room snapped with atmosphere, everyone was wide awake and sitting up.

'Now wait a minute, Pauline. We're not going to get anywhere if we just attack one another'. . .

Suggested Reading

Adair, J. (1986): *Effective teambuilding*. London: Pan.

Gudykunst, W. B. (ed.) (1986): *Intergroup communication*. London: Edward Arnold.

Kell, C. L. and Corts, P. R. (1980): *Fundamentals of effective group communication*. New York: Macmillan.

Shaw, M. (1981): *Group dynamics, 3rd edn*. New York: McGraw-Hill.

See also the resources list at the end of the book.

La comunicación es un proceso mediante el cual distintas culturas usan signos para dar significado al mundo que nos rodea así como a nuestros pensamientos.

| সাই ততাদাদিতুদ দদাদাদাদ ততা

তুদ দদাৰা তদ ততাদাদাতাদা ও ততাদুদাদাদ তদ দততদ দদা

দাততদাদ তুদ সাই দততুদতাদাদ তদ দদা দদততদা

দাততদতু দদাৰ।দ. দদাৰাদাদ তুৰা দত দাৰাততা

Communication is a process through which signs are used within cultures in order to give meanings to the world around us and to the world inside our heads.

G Communication, culture, process and signification

Communication Theory – Bringing it all Together

> I have never doubted the truth of signs, Adso; they are the only things man has with which to orient himself in the world. What I did not understand was the relation among signs.
>
> Umberto Eco: *The Name of the Rose*, 1980

1 INTRODUCTION

In this chapter we will review the previous six chapters in terms of three main strands in communication theory. These are: the **process approach; semiotic analysis; cultural studies.**

As we make these explanations you will realize that much of what we have written is dominated by the process approach, but with a strong sense of semiotics and structural analysis of communication incorporated within this. We have made little reference to Cultural Studies as such, partly because it is tied up with semiotics anyway, and partly because we don't think it offers so much that is appropriate for the topics that we have dealt with. However, this implies no lack of sympathy for alternative approaches to Communication Studies. Indeed we think that the perspectives offered by Cultural Studies have a great deal to recommend them, with reference to the area of Media and Communication in particular. As we have suggested in our Introduction to this book, we don't accept artificial distinctions between one theoretical approach and another. We have pointed out in a number of sections that certain terms from different approaches or different academics actually mean much the same thing anyway. We are not going to repeat these points of comparison, but we are going to review what we have said overall, looking at each of the three strands described, in turn.

2 THE PROCESS APPROACH

This approach describes what is happening when we communicate, how we communicate, and what affects this communication. Because we are the sum of all our experiences, and because everything that happens around us may have some bearing on communication, it is possible for this all-embracing approach to include an enormous number of events and activities. One tries to make this mass of evidence more manageable by breaking it down into basic areas described in simple models for communication (such as context or direction of communication). Further description of process then elaborates on these basic terms. In effect one describes parts of the process, and activities in the process. This description is followed by interpretation of its significance. This is all about answering the SO WHAT question, about explaining why the description matters in terms of **explaining how and why communication takes place**.

The process approach sees communication as being **active** (something that is about doing). It is **dynamic** – activity which is continuous and always subject to change. It is **irreversible** – what is communicated cannot be taken away, but only added to the sum of our knowledge and experience. It is **continuous** – that is to say we will always communicate something in the presence of others (the meaning of silence), and we will even be communicating on our own (because we are always taking in and dealing with outside experience of some kind).

As a process, any communication activity must relate in some way to all previous experience of the communicators, and to the entire culture that surrounds them.

Chapter 1 – The Core of Process

Communication within and to the Self must be at the core of any model of the communication process. Although there are examples of solitary communication activities, when we are interacting with others we are still communicating within ourselves. We evaluate what is going on and decide how to react to the other person. In these terms, and in terms of constructing and making sense of messages, the **encoding and decoding** of the stream of symbols which make up communication is an essential part of process. This is the stage at which meanings are made and understood.

Intrapersonal communication is concerned with the collection and categorization of information that comes in through the senses. In a conventional process model these might be described as messages. And the flood of messages is continuous, having to be dealt with from our first moment of consciousness and even when we are asleep.

Within schemata, we build rules for and assumptions about communication with others. These are dealt with intrapersonally, and are also described as conventions of behaviour. They will influence the process of communication between people. These conventions appear within roles that we adopt and define that role behaviour. They are also incorporated within strategies, where we habitually adopt certain patterns of communication which we have found will get us what we want.

One sees the impetus to the whole communication process as part of the intrapersonal area. This is to say, our needs and the purposes that we build from these needs, start within ourselves.

And finally, we are also dealing with the whole Self, the beginning and end of the communication process. This Self is active, it evolves, it changes, it adapts. As such, it represents these same qualities in the whole process, which includes others and the external environment.

Chapter 2 – Process Links the Intrapersonal and the Interpersonal

Perception of others enables communication to take place between people. It relates the Self to Others in the communication process.

This aspect of process encompasses recognition, understanding and evaluation of the outside world, and of people in particular.

It is a continuous monitoring of others, of the progress and conduct of interaction. It requires reassessment of one's communication style, of the success of one's communication, and so may lead to changes in these. In this sense it is also very much about the dynamic quality of process – the continuous interplay between Self and Others which also requires continuous shifts in how communication is used.

Perception links back to intrapersonal communication in that evaluation takes place within the Self. This evaluation is carried out with reference to internalized categories (perceptual sets). This part of the process operates with reference to external signs and to internalized information set within frameworks that govern understanding and affect how communication is carried on.

Chapter 3 – Process as Interplay between People

Social interaction focuses on acts of communication that take place within a social and physical context. So this part of process deals with at least some elements that are tangible – the sounds of speech, the room in which conversation takes place, the social event which brings people together.

If the process approach takes a holistic view of communication, then interaction does indeed have something to do with the whole environment, all our relationships, and our past, as well as the communication as it happens.

The interactive process is about the use and control of systems of signs in order to convey meaning and to negotiate different kinds of relationship.

One is concerned with verbal and non-verbal signs, with how and why they are exchanged. Social skills are about controlling the flow of signs so that their meanings are acceptable and even beneficial to those involved. This part of process is about those factors and terms that exist between Sender and Receiver in basic models. It would refer to message content and treatment, as well as to signs and meanings.

Above all it is about **communication as action**; communication as behaviour which influences the behaviour of others and produces changes. However one imagines a process, it is true that what is happening part way through or at the end of a process is different from what was happening when it started. **Process and communication are about activity and change.**

Chapter 4 – Process and the Interface with Others

Self presentation is of course a part of social interaction.

It is an attempt to control the Self as perceived by others.

It is an attempt to control and shape the process of communication.

It is an attempt to influence the outcome of any interaction.

It is an attempt to define a situation so that we can control it, and other people's perception of it.

Presentation is active, it contributes to the activity which defines the idea of process. It is an **active representation of the Self to the outside world.**

Presentation is dynamic because it shifts according to needs, to the audience, and to a given situation. We show ourselves in different ways according to other factors such as the role that we have assumed, and according to social conventions and the expectations of others.

Chapter 5 – An Alternative Description of Process

TA also includes the idea of action between people, of a dynamic interplay between them, and of the changing style of communication which people adopt.

Terms used to describe elements in TA are comparable to terms used to describe elements of the communications process – hungers are much like needs which initiate the process; transactions are much like the exchange of messages.

The idea of continuous process is implicit in descriptions of transactions.

The idea that process is about continuity over a period of time may be related to scripts. It can be said that a script helps define how the individual will carry on their communication over a period of time. **A script will influence the style and use of communication.**

The idea that process is active and may be structured in certain ways according to certain conventions is to be seen in games. **The rules of the game are its conventions.** They help organize the pattern of interaction.

Chapter 6 – Elaboration of the Process

In this case, much of what has already been said also applies here. Group inter-action is more complex because there are a number of people involved. There is a special kind of dynamic in a situation which requires co-operation between people, the recognition of different needs. Concepts such as that of role become especially important.

The direction and pattern of the process is elaborated because one can no longer, as with two people, talk about *exchange* or about a *circular relationship*.

Some terms are simply shifted to apply to the group where we had previ-ously applied them to individuals – purpose and need. Equally one cannot for-get that individual needs still exist within the group. So the process of communication within groups and between groups and others is built on what we already know about process in terms of intrapersonal and interpersonal communication. The means of communication remain the same, of course.

What is distinctive in group process are those elements that distinguish any small group for what it is – an identity, norms, members' roles, varying fre-quency of communication, motivation by goal, stages of bonding and patterns of decision making.

3   THE SEMIOTIC APPROACH

This approach is much concerned with the signs that we use in communicating and with the meanings generated by these signs. It is also concerned with struc-tures and patterns in communication and within interaction. Semiotics, which has its roots in language study, offers terms through which to identify specific parts of communication in any form, and through which to explain ways in which meaning is constructed.

The notions of codes, both primary and secondary, and of syntagms (or structures within a code) provide a means of analysing any example of com-munication.

Semiotics should be cross-referred to Structuralism and Cultural Studies because the language and the interpretations offered by all three overlap to a considerable extent.

Chapter 1 – Internal Symbol Shifting

Semiotics would be concerned with the internal production of meaning from external signs recognized in communication activity. In effect, words and non-verbal signs have to be decoded internally. The decoding is the production of meaning. The meaning is about an understanding of the world and, in turn, affects the encoding of communication by the individual.

Semiotics proposes that the symbols themselves are organized in paradigms such as the alphabet. We must have knowledge of these structures within us before we can decode any form of communication.

Further kinds of categorization or structure would be the codes and syntagms. A code is a co-ordinated sets of signs, perhaps working at a primary level (the English language), perhaps at secondary level (the codes used in television news). Syntagms are structures within codes, such as a sentence which is an organized set of word signs.

The idea of structure and organization also implies that there are rules that govern the pattern of the structure. These rules are called conventions. They help make sense of signs by organizing them into a pattern. Through these patterns meanings emerge. For example, a photograph is merely a collections of colours of more or less intensity unless we 'know' what the parts of the picture signify, unless we can 'see' how the parts relate to one another to make a whole. The signs, the structures, their meanings, are all learnt. Once learnt, they can be used. For instance, we learn the 'rule' that a large object (which also has to be recognized!) that obscures a smaller object in a photograph is 'in front' of it. We learn to see a two-dimensional image as a three-dimensional representation.

So these signs, structures and their meanings exist within ourselves, and are recognized and understood through intrapersonal communication. It is important to remember that meanings are indeed created within our minds and are not the same thing as the signs themselves, whether these signs are words or gestures or pictures.

Chapter 2 – Recognition of External Symbols

In semiotic terms, perception of others is about recognizing the signs of communication for what they are, and then making sense of them.

Once we have identified as words the sounds that someone makes, or the hand movements that they make as gestures, then we may attempt to attach meanings to these. Points made with reference to Chapter 1 must also apply here. We do not of course decode every single sign individually and laboriously when looking for meaning. Rather, we look at collections of signs, at a complete statement, at a set of body movements, and then make sense of the signs collectively, using the categories and rules that we have learnt. Signs may signify many different things. In isolation they are relatively ambiguous. When we read the word sign BOW we do not know whether is is an action or an object unless it is placed within the linguistic context of a whole sentence or paragraph. So **perception is also about making choices of possible signifieds in order to decide on what the actual signification is in a particular case.**

Semiology is interest in social rather than individual meanings. So a sentence which ran – *bow to your superior knowledge* – would be analysed in terms of the symbolic significance of 'bowing down', rather than just as a statement made by one individual to another. We should make it clear that a communication student might well make both kinds of analysis. Semiotics does not own the idea of making analysis of social meanings from signs and symbols, it merely places an emphasis on such an approach.

Finally, semiotics offers terms which help describe the different qualities and functions of signs. It has been sufficiently described elsewhere (Fiske, 1982) that communication signs may be described as symbols or indices or icons.

Chapter 3 – Symbolic Interaction

Communication and social interaction may be seen as an exchange of signs between people. If all communication is made up from signs, then we can only exchange information, ideas, meanings through signs. We are joined through signs. All relationships are conducted in terms of symbols. We can never deal in the original experience, the actual idea, but only in the signs which stand in place of the experience or the idea. To this extent it is a second-hand world that we live in.

The various forms of communication which we deal in may be described as codes. That is to say, English language or computer users' language are examples of primary and secondary codes respectively. So are visual forms such as the language of photographs or the language of comics.

We have already referred to structure in our comments on Chapter 1. Social interaction may be seen as structured in terms of codes and of the segments of these labelled syntagms in the language of semiotics. More importantly, **interaction is bound by conventions.** These rules operate on a primary level, where for instance the rules of grammar help make sense of verbal signs. But there are also conventions binding secondary codes, and the use of communication in, for example, various social situations. If we agree that we would use a certain kind of language in, say, a religious ceremony, then we are saying that we would select certain signs appropriate to this occasion. We would expect by convention to use these. We would understand their meaning through conventions.

Chapter 4 – Sign Selection

Self presentation is about the conscious selection of signs for effect. We use the power of symbolic representation to make a statement to other people about our Self, our status, our relationships.

The close examination of signs and their meanings is especially relevant to an analysis of self presentation precisely because it helps uncover the performance and its purpose.

Semiology is also concerned with the power of signs and symbols. From one point of view, self presentation is an attempt to exert power. In a small way it may be about trying to make someone else see you in a certain light, probably a favourable one. **We try to use the power of signs of dress or of certain uses of language to define others' views of us.** In certain cases, one can argue that presentation is specifically about power. This is most obvious at ceremonial occasions when communication rituals invoke strong symbols of power. Military parades are an example. The uniforms of the troops represent the power of those who can require them to be worn, as well as standing for the group identity and norms of the troops themselves. Then again, the dress and gestures of those who review such a parade also represent their power. The clothes, the decorations, the salutes are all signs of communication which have been invested with particular meaning through repetitive use.

Chapter 5 - Signification by Another Name

In many ways it might seem that Transaction Analysis is least easily related to the study of signs. TA comes out of a very humanistic approach to communication in which the condition of the individual is central. There is nothing much here about the production of social meanings.

Yet **the attempt to analyse transactions precisely has the same intention in principle as the idea of identifying and analysing signs.** As we have pointed out in the relevant chapter, Berne's description of a transaction is much like a description of an exchange of two signs.

Transaction Analysis is also concerned with the meaning of the transactions, as semiotic analysis is concerned with the meaning of signs. Where they differ is in the kinds of meaning identified. TA seeks meanings about the Self and the effect of these on relationships with others. Semiology generally looks for meanings in a larger social sphere, especially those that are concerned with how ideology is defined and maintained in people's consciousness. Communication Studies is concerned with the whole range of meanings that may be communicated through signs: meanings which are about the person and their social relations and their beliefs.

Chapter 6 - More Complex Social Interaction

Communication in groups is, as we have said, another kind of social interaction. As such, points made with reference to Chapters 1 and 2 remain relevant. On a practical level, the sign systems of communication remain the same.

Semioticians' belief in the social production of meaning (as opposed to the creation of meaning by individuals) has relevance in this case. The argument would be that meanings are created and agreed collectively in a society – or through groups within that society. Certainly there is clear evidence for this when one looks at subcultural groups where one can see various kinds of argot, slang, or even patois developing alongside the main language code. Apart from the obvious reasons such as creating a distinct identity, it is argued that these new signs and their meanings are created by these social groups precisely to resist the meanings (specifically the values) of the main culture. Sometimes existing word signs are actually turned on their heads by these social groups – conveniently proving that meanings do not belong to signs by some natural law. One current example is the use of the word BAD. Its meaning, its connotations of disapproval, are pretty clear in its general use. But in some black and pop subcultures it is a well recognized term of approval, and has been such for at least 15 years.

In the same way the signs of identity adopted by various social groups (types of language or dress) are also to be analysed in terms of values. The signs stand for beliefs. They stand for a view of that group's place in society, and implicitly comment on dominant values. The original punk movement (to be summarized briefly as being about violence and opposition in its style of language, dress and music) clearly made such a comment. In this case semiotic analysis has led to recognition of ideology, and an opposition to the dominant ideology. You should also note that these comments could just as well have been made in the context of Cultural Studies, supporting our remark that these two strands overlap to a large extent. What we would argue of course is that we are within the domain of communication. What one is looking at is the communication used by a particular group. **Whether one is talking about signs within a code of dress or a code of language it is the communication which comprises the meanings and which makes (implicit) statements about group values and about ideology.**

4   THE CULTURAL STUDIES APPROACH

This approach contains much in common with semiotics, and you may refer back to use and meaning of terms in the section. Cultural Studies is concerned with signs and meanings, but with particular relation to social groupings within society. In terms of social groupings it is also interested in divisions between them and in the naturalization of these divisions through the force of ideology working in the social system. We would say that **if ideology operates, if these divisions are to be recognized, if they are naturalized – then these three things happen because of the way that communication is used.** For example, there are now a number of studies which demonstrate that spoken and written language does much to define the place of women in our society. This place, which has to an extent been marked by lack of economic and political power, is naturalized by the language which is used about women and by women. The dominant ideology takes it for granted that women's position in various types of social and power relationship is quite 'normal'. This normality is similarly defined by communication (see, for example, Spender's book, *Manmade language*, 1980).

In these respects, it seems that Cultural Studies has most affinity with our chapter on groups, though we will point to some relevance in other cases. The interest is not in dyadic interaction nor even much in small groups, but rather in the communication and behaviour of large identifiable groups such as sub-cultures (Bikers), or large sets of people (Classes).

Communication is seen dominantly as an instrument of identity, or power, and even of repression. We believe that these perspectives are valuable and plausible within certain terms of reference. But again, we would wish to focus on patterns and uses of communication, and would wish to incorporate this approach within a wider one which can also deal with the individual and with relationships. This is an endorsement of a holistic approach, which takes a number of perspectives on such groups. Such an approach seems more plausi-ble and valuable than an exclusive one. This is because, for example, people within any of these generalized groups do not behave exclusively within the patterns identified in cultural studies. Members of a group of Bikers, in their day-to-day living, have relationships and use communication in ways that have nothing to do with class or ideology, and that are certainly not examples of 'resistance through rituals'. Similarly, it is not true that women always experi-ence language as an instrument of repression. There is a variety of situations and uses of communication in everyday experience, which in our view requires an inclusive approach, if we are to understand why and how communication happens. So, as we go on to sketch in the main points of relevance in a Cultural Studies approach, you should be clear that, nevertheless, we take a pluralistic view. This means that **we think that there are a variety of ways of making sense of communication.**

Chapter 1 – A View of the World

In this case, the beliefs, values and ideology that are part of the schemata that we have described are relevant because they include this view of what are 'nat-ural' relationships. For example, the idea of class means something to us because there are categories by class in our heads. We have also learnt that upper class somehow means something 'better' than lower class. These descrip-tions do not stand up to examination. But nevertheless such beliefs are held, at least until someone asks you to deal with them and see how meaningful they really are. Beliefs about class may be associated with ideas about economic power – an acceptance that there are social divisions based on who has most or least wealth, and that this is a natural part of the *status quo*. In Communica-tion Studies we would be interested in how these beliefs are communicated and incorporated within the Self. In this way it may be seen that power lies not in ideas but in the communication that spreads those ideas.

In terms of intrapersonal communication, we are dealing with **a view of the world which is received from without but constructed and endorsed within ourselves.**

Chapter 2 – False Views or True Views?

Perception takes place with reference to internalized categories. So perception of others might, in this third approach, be framed by an unconscious acceptance of ideology. The **evaluation that takes place, it could be argued, will be inclined to confirm a view of the world which endorses social divisions and power relationships.** To take a very particular example, a stereotypical person in business will be male, middle-aged and dressed in a dark suit. This stereotype, which we carry in our heads, will include ideas about this male's social status and ability to wield economic power. Even in a television sitcom depicting such a stereotype, still there would be an assumption that this status and power is natural and OK.

By implication, **effective perception is that which questions our own categories,** especially where they include assumptions about how one group of people should fit within society. The careful perceiver would not immediately accept some socially agreed signification of signs used, but might consider what else could be signified as an alternative. To take a simple example, one might be dealing with someone who offers paralinguistic signs of a strong regional accent and hesitation in speech patterns, as well as peppering their speech with verbal signifiers described as slang, dialect and swearing. These signs might be taken wrongly to signify that this person's place in the class structure, their intelligence and their communication skills are all inferior in some way. But an alternative signification would be that they came from a certain area and lacked confidence in articulation. Depending on who they were dealing with, it might be that their style of address was perfectly effective. And it might also be the case that, if one listened to the content of their speech, it showed them to be sensible and reasonable.

Chapter 3 – An Exchange of Views

As we have said, the Cultural Studies approach is not readily applicable to social interaction as such. However, it could be argue that **there is relevance in terms of analysing conversations whose content and language represent the social divisions and the process of naturalization already referred to.** For example, there have been studies made of the language used at interviews where the interviewee is from an ethnic minority. Analysis of the conversation provides evidence that the exchange represents false assumptions and cultural divisions. One is led back to some of the concerns of Cultural Studies, even though we are not really looking at the kind of situation that is usually addressed through this approach. It could also be easily argued that such analysis of language was and is carried on outside Cultural Studies anyway.

One particular notion that may have some use here is the idea of TEXT. The borrowing of the term from its place in literary criticism does at least endorse the principle of analysing other forms of communication. A conversation may be taken to be a text. **The significance of the conversation would be seen in the meanings taken from the whole,** from the sum of its parts. This is entirely analogous to the process approach in Communication Studies, in which meaning is also taken to be the sum of the parts. These parts may still be examined carefully and separately. Remarks made in a conversation may not seem too significant on their own, but might represent kinds of cultural assumption if taken together. For instance a conversation larded with phrases such as – one does like to keep up appearances – *I found a super little man to do the garden – those dreadful people on the estate – Henry is such a gentleman* – collectively represent assumptions about status and about cultural divisions. They would help maintain and promote those divisions.

Having said this, it is also true that many interesting examples of the textual approach are to be found in study of the Media – assuming that, for example, a television programme is a text to be analysed. This text should also be understood within the discourse of television. This difficult word discourse would, briefly, be taken to refer to the whole output of television and to the assumptions about social relations and divisions implicit in all those programmes. So the one programme as text would need to be understood not only in its entirety, but also with reference to the discourse of which it is a part.

It should be clear from this that there are difficulties in applying the Cultural Studies approach to examination of interpersonal communication. It is best dealt with in broad terms – of remembering to approach interaction as a whole text, and of an awareness that there may be meanings to be found that concern social relations and divisions.

Chapter 4 – Making a Statement

Presentation of Self and its associated terms also come out of a humanist and a process tradition. We have pointed out in the semiotics section that one can make something of the notion of signs and meanings; that the form of self-presentation can be examined in its detail in order to see what it signifies as a whole. But where we have taken as crucial the statements that are being made about the Self, **the Cultural Studies approach would be looking for statements about social position, social attitudes, and, probably, about conflict with the dominant culture.** Certainly once more these meanings would be seen as significant if they said something about social divisions. Our position is that such readings may or may not be possible, but they do not have to be assumed. A problem is that the methodology of Cultural Studies is attractive when it goes for objectivity and picking up covert messages, but the selection of material for study and the conclusions about the overall meaning are not always so objective, or rather they exclude alternative explanations. Working-class history will be examined more readily than the history of the (so-called) upper classes. The behaviour and beliefs of ethnic minorities within our main culture receive more attention than, say, those of the Welsh or of old people.

So once more we have a situation where we would wish to reflect on the meanings and significance of self presentation with regard to the individual as well as to that person as a member of a group. For example, football supporters have been the subject of a number of studies in which, in effect, their self presentation, their communication style and performance, have been explained in terms of divisions and tensions within our society. Clearly the rituals at a football match do have meaning, as does the dress. But it also needs to be remembered that those same supporters present themselves in other ways at other times, for other reasons. The wider study of communication seeks to embrace those other occasions, and to explain what is going on and why.

Chapter 5 – Tenuous Connections

We have already said that Transactional Analysis may be seen to have a few comparisons with a semiotic approach. These analogies cannot be taken too far, and the main thrust of Cultural Studies is even further away from the spirit of TA. However, whilst it is true that Cultural Studies is interested in the signs of a cultural group rather than in the individual person within that group, still one could make a point about the idea of scripts in TA theory. As a preliminary, one needs to grasp the idea of *Ideological State Apparatus* (ISA), which in Cultural Studies is taken to refer to those institutions which endorse, reproduce, and pass on the dominant ideology (or main value system and world view) of our society. If one was to take the situation of a young black person who felt NOT OK about themselves, it could be that part of that feeling stems from what they perceive as their position within the culture – that might be an inferior and repressed position. It might also be the case that this feeling could be traced back partly to bad experiences with the law or at school (both examples of ISAs). So in this case, understanding of cultural values and experiences can be linked with an understanding of the person in TA.

Chapter 6 – Group's Views of the World

The extent to which Cultural Studies relates to the study of communication is best defined in terms of signs and meanings, and of the conflict of group values between our society in general and specific groups within that society. Once more, strictly speaking, the Cultural Studies approach is not really concerned with the process of communication within the group or with individuals of that group. What it is more concerned with is what the communication of the group signifies for the group identity, for its relationship with the rest of society, and for the ways in which that social position is made natural and acceptable. So the interest here is in decoding the communication of a subcultural or large social group in terms of what this says about the group's view of itself and of its place in society as a whole. There would also be interest in the power or lack of power held by that group within the economic and political structure.

Much of what has been said under the heading of semiotics also applies here. So we would also repeat the point that in Communication Studies, while we are interested in the signs of cultural place and division, we are also interested in individuals and in interpersonal relationships within these groups. In this case we are also talking about communication whose signification has nothing to do with notions of social division and repression.

For example, if one was to examine the position of a large set of people identified as female office cleaners, then it is possible to make an analysis of their occupation, their dress, and of communication directed at them. From this one might draw conclusions about their depressed economic position within society, and about the lack of regard in which they are held as women and as cleaners. In principle one could even consider a group of cleaners in a particular building as a kind of text for analysis. This is perfectly proper, and forms of communication are relevant here. They would tell us something about how the women see themselves and about how they are seen. But we would also say that this specific group has other dimensions – group roles, friendships, group norms and goals – which may also be examined through their communication, and which will tell us something about the group and its members. These dimensions would be represented through their communication.

5 CONCLUSION

We have tried to separate these three strands in Communication Studies and to explain briefly what their particular qualities are. We have tried to explain where, as separate approaches, they might place emphasis on communication. But we should also return to the notion that these strands are not distinct. One keeps coming back to the main study of forms of communication, how they are generated, how they are used, and how they underpin our very existence as individuals and as members of a society. The act and fact of communication must be the focus of our study. And communication in all its forms is demonstrably a structure of signs which gives sense to all aspects of our lives and of our relationships. People, groups, cultures, whole societies are what their communication says they are. They are what their communication makes them. Those groups, cultures, and societies are based on and operate through communication. This communication is always part of some process in which meaning is conceived, expressed, passed on and understood. So we must say that process, signs, culture, all come together within COMMUNICATION.

Suggested Reading

There is no material directly relevant to the substance of this chapter. However, we will recommend three books as having indirect relevance and a fairly wide scope. *See what I mean* embraces the process approach and visual communication. *Introduction to communication studies* covers a semiotic and structuralist approach. *Key concepts in communication* is a work of reference which has full and useful entries for terms relating to semiotics and Cultural Studies.

Fiske, J. (1990): *Introduction to communication studies, 2nd edn*. London: Methuen.
Morgan, J. and Welton, P. (1992): *See what I mean, 2nd edn*. London: Edward Arnold.
O'Sullivan, T. *et al*. (1994): *Key concepts in communication and cultural studies, 2 edn*. London: Methuen.

Glossary of Communication Terms

This list provides a brief definition of the meaning and use of some important terms within Communication Studies. We also suggest that you consult the index of this book for terms defined in the text.

For further references and information see *Key concepts in communication studies* by T. O'Sullivan, J. Hartley, D. Saunders and J. Fiske; *A dictionary of communication and media studies,* by J. Watson and A. Hill; and *The dictionary of personality and social psychology,* edited by R. Harré and R. Lamb.

Attitude: in terms of interpersonal communication this refers to our mental orientation towards another person. Basically, attitude is measured in terms of the degrees of hostility or friendliness that we feel towards that other person. Attitudes are founded on beliefs that we hold as a result of previous experience.

Attribution: refers to the mental process through which we assign characteristics to another person. These characteristics may also be called their ATTRIBUTES. These will include aspects of personality, emotion, attitude. ATTRIBUTION THEORY attempts to explain how we carry on this mental process. (See also *perception* and *judgement* in the main text.)

Beliefs: are convictions that we hold, dominantly about social reality and social relationships. They are concepts which contribute to the Self, and which act as reference points when perceiving other people and when carrying on social interaction. Beliefs define how we think things are and think they should be.

Code (Encode and Decode): refers to a system of signs bound by cultural conventions. There are many types of communication code, e.g. verbal, non-verbal and graphic, through which we generate and share meanings. **Encode** refers to our putting information into signs for other people. **Decode** refers to our interpreting signs from other people.

Cognition: is the mental process through which we recognize external stimuli (signs) and then assign them to categories to try and make sense of them. The term refers to both the ways that we take in information and to the ways that we organize that information in our minds.

Cognitive Dissonance: describes anxiety that arises from a sense of inconsistency between one belief that we hold and another, between what we believe and what we think we should believe. It may also arise as a result of our doing something which we then realize is inconsistent with our beliefs. An advertiser may arouse a sense of this dissonance when they suggest that a caring parent will use their product. If one of the audience does not use this product then they may feel that they are not caring – hence the anxiety.

Communication: means many things to many people. Essentially it is about the creation and exchange of meanings through signs. Communication between people is a process in which the signs of verbal and non-verbal language are used in an attempt to make known that which otherwise only exists in the minds of the communicators. What is made known may be many things – experiences, ideas, feelings. How well these things are made known depends on the signs selected for use, how well they are used, and how far the communicators share agreement about what the signs mean anyway. There are many other ideas about what defines communication, including those which propose that communication must be intentional. Distinction has been made between process, semiotic, and cultural approaches to studying and defining communication. This book has proposed that such distinctions are largely unnecessary.

Competence: refers to the psychological and the behavioural abilities that enable one to fulfil certain functions. (*Performance* is the actual goal-directed behaviour resulting from this competence.) **Communicative competence** refers to our ability to use appropriate means of verbal, non-verbal communication (as well as communication technology) to achieve goals through interaction with others. **Social competence** refers to our ability to use social skills to manage social interaction through appropriate verbal and non-verbal behaviour. **Linguistic competence** refers to our ability to use written and spoken language in an appropriate range of registers to express ourselves and to share meanings with other people.

Conventions: are a system of culture-based rules and practices defining how signs are used within codes, and how behaviour takes place within social interactions.

Cultural Studies: is the study of cultural behaviours, of the interaction of cultures, of the meanings produced by specific cultures. It focuses on the relationship between the ideas that inform a culture and the practices through which these ideas are revealed. Cultural Studies often concerns itself with the characteristics of subcultures and with the relationship of these to the main culture. To this extent it is also concerned with cultural or social divisions and with the ways that these are both represented and naturalized.

Culture: is a collection of beliefs, values and behaviours distinctive to a large group of people, which is expressed through their various forms of communication. It is the means by which societies make sense of and reflect upon their common experience. It also refers to the social practices in which societies engage as part of their way of life.

Deindividuation: refers to the lessening of social, moral and societal constraints upon individual behaviour; to a belief that one may cease to be responsible for one's own behaviour, and can allow group identity and norms to take over this responsibility.

Discourse: is a term used in linguistics to refer to verbal utterances and texts that are longer than a sentence. The term is also used elsewhere by extension to identify other longer types of discourse – e.g. television discourse may be described as the characteristic modes of verbal and visual representations in broadcast television.

Discourse Analysis: looks at the production and structures of such discourses. It would investigate the structure of paragraphs and texts, as in a monologue or in an interaction between two or more people. It seeks to explain how one utterance follows in a rational rule-governed way, to create a meaningful sequence and structure to communication.

Ego State: is one of the concepts attached to the theory of TRANSACTIONAL ANALYSIS. It describes a particular kind of Self which will affect attitudes towards the other person, as well as the characteristics of their communication behaviour. The three primary states are those of Adult, Parent and Child.

Empathy: being able imaginatively to enter into another person's feelings and experiences, without filtering these through one's own beliefs, values and experiences. When we empathize we imagine how it would make sense to behave as the other person is behaving.

Games: is another concept attached to TRANSACTIONAL ANALYSIS. They are recognizable episodes of social interaction in which one person will attempt to gain psychological advantage over another.

Group: a collection of people who interact in some way and who share common goals or interests. One speaks of *small groups* (people who interact face-to-face); *reference groups* (stereotypes with which individuals identify or are identified); and *statistical groups* (defined as simply having one or more characteristics in common).

Halo Effect: is that PERCEPTUAL BARRIER which results from allowing one feature of the other person to dominate our attention, with the effect of excluding or diminishing the importance of other features.

Icon: in semiotic terms an icon is a sign which looks like the thing it is meant to stand for. Pictures of people are iconic: names of people are not.

Ideology: is another term about which whole books have been written. Fundamentally, it stand for that coherent set of values and beliefs which is dominant in a culture and which is particularly held by those social groups who have power. To this extent an ideology is often seen to be repressive of alternative views of society. It must be represented through communication, and is usually there by implication. Ideology is also necessarily concerned with social and power relationships and with the means through which these are made apparent.

Idiolect: is a personal repertoire and capacity for language use (e.g. vocabulary, syntactic structures, register, accent) resulting from our own knowledge and experience.

Index: an index is a sign which refers indirectly to the thing it stands for. If we hear a knock on our door, this indexical sign refers indirectly to the presence of someone outside the door.

Interaction: is the exchange and negotiation of meaning between two or more participants located within given social contexts. It may consist of behavioural events which occur merely because people happen to be in the presence of others. Or it may be more focused through mutual engagement of the people concerned (see also *transaction*).

Interpersonal communication: is any form of communication both verbal and non-verbal between two or more people face to face.

Language: refers to the whole body of words (vocabulary) and ways of combining them (grammar) that are used by a nation, people or race.

Leakage: refers to the notion that non-verbal behaviour or unconscious physiological feedback may give away how we really feel. This may contradict our more consciously controlled verbal communication. In practice it is not possible to separate verbal and non-verbal channels since they interact in our self-presentation, intentionally or unintentionally.

Meaning: what is signified by the messages conveyed through the signs that we give off and that we perceive. We assign meanings to all human behaviours through agreed cultural conventions.

Neurolinguistic Programming (NLP): describes the notion that each person has internalized a particular pattern of language use and physiological/neurological behaviours according to a personal programming of perceptions, experiences, knowledge and imaginings.

Non-verbal Behaviour: people cannot behave in the presence of others. The effect is that we are giving off messages through means other than speech all the time. These messages may be intentionally encoded and represented, in which case one can talk of **Non-verbal Communication**. But they may be unintentionally given off, though still decoded by other people. In this case one is dealing with non-verbal behaviour.

Non-Verbal Communication: see *non-verbal behaviour.*

Paradigm: is a set of items (very possibly signs), that clearly belong to one category. The alphabet is a paradigm of letters from which words are constructed. Similarly, non-verbal signs from a coherent category, and are a paradigm. When the signs operate together according to CONVENTIONS or rules, then one has a CODE. Paradigms may be culture specific – that is to say only that culture recognizes that a particular set of items 'goes together'. Often paradigms coexist. A pack of playing cards includes the paradigms of cards, of number, of suites, of kings and queens.

Perception: is that part of the interpersonal process of communication through which we make judgements on the other person in terms of their attributes. In respect of interpersonal communication, it includes both sensory recognition of verbal and non-verbal behaviours, and also interpretation of these.

Perceptual Set: is much the same as a schema: that is a related set of notions or of information held in the memory, which form a category of ideas or of experience.

Performance: refers to the idea that each of us performs in various roles when presenting ourselves to others and when interacting with others (see also *competence*).

Personality: a set of traits which it is believed are characteristic of the individual, and which describe their distinctive qualities. There are alternative views of personality as being relatively fixed, with a core, or as being mobile, changing its characteristics according to need and situation.

Phatic Communication: is communication which often serves to confirm social relationships. It is often represented through small non-verbal signs of recognition and of bonding between people and within groups.

Prejudice: is about prejudgements. People who have pre-formed attitudes and values which they immediately call up when perceiving the behaviour of another person may be said to be prejudiced. It is often supposed that these predispositions are negative. But this need not be the case. One may be prejudiced for as much as against.

Presentation: see *self presentation*.

Redundancy: is about the degree of predictability in a message which aids accurate decoding and which may strengthen social relationships. So what is redundant are those elements of encoding that are not strictly essential to conveying meaning, but which seek to reinforce the message or foster a relationship which will help with the sharing of meaning.

Register: is that stylistic variation of language use which may change according to situation and context. It also includes choice of vocabulary, use of syntax and paralinguistic features.

Ritual: refers to repetitive and highly convention-bound behaviours which have become a matter of habit. Our communication behaviours are full of rituals in certain situations. Meetings of Guides or of Freemasons will have ritual communication, especially at the end of the meeting. But even informal social interaction may become ritualized – what members of the family say and do at breakfast time.

Role: is a socially defined pattern of behaviour which reflects specific expectations, conventions and norms. It will inform the regulation of interaction and of relationships. It includes a notion of public behaviour which the communicator believes is appropriate to the situation and to his or her position within this.

Role Conflict: is experienced by people who feel that the behaviour patterns of a role that they are expected to play conflict with the patterns of either a role which they would prefer to play or with the patterns of a role which seems just as appropriate.

Saliency: refers to the relative dominance or importance of, for example, certain features of another person's behaviour as this is perceived. Certain behaviour may have saliency because it fits in with expectations or because it fits in with some previous experience of the perceiver in which such behaviour was important.

Schemata: (see *perceptual sets*) are ways of organizing our knowledge and experience, including the categorizing and grouping of items of information. We call on these schemata to check new information and to make evaluations of people.

Self-concept/Self-image: is defined as an internalized view that we have of ourselves. One important element of this SELF-ESTEEM. The Self also includes the ideas of the self as seen by others, the ideal self, and the self as we believe we are seen.

Self-disclosure: refers to a revealing of Self to others. Self-disclosure includes coming to know oneself more honestly and the idea of building relationships with others, because disclosure also means offering trust to the other person by telling them something about oneself.

Self-esteem: is about how we rate ourselves. We have degrees of self-esteem, rating ourselves more or less positively. We may rate ourselves in terms of elements such as social attractiveness or skills.

Self presentation: is public behaviour that we use to present ourselves to other people in order to match an ideal self-image, or enact what is perceived to be an appropriate role, or to influence others' view of us, or to define the situation in our own terms, or to influence the progress of the interaction – or any combination of these.

Semiotics: refers to the study of signs, of sign systems, and of their meanings.

Sign (Signification): a sign is a sign because we agree that it is. Any small piece of behaviour, whether it be a sound that we call a word, or a movement that we call a gesture, only becomes a sign because we have learned through a socializing process that it is indeed meaningful. The particular meaning, or SIGNIFICATION, of a sign is also socially agreed. Learning to talk is the same as learning to recognize one code of signs, to acquire the agreed meanings of those sound signs. Signs have no meanings in themselves.

Social Cognition: is that process through which a person acquires, assimilates and organizes knowledge of events and of social reality. Through this process we come to 'know' the world and to use this knowledge to interpret our perceptions.

Social Facilitation: refers to the idea that individuals can achieve more by working with or in the presence of other people than they can on their own.

Socialization: describes those processes by which a person becomes a participating member of society, through learning how to live (and interact successfully) in that society. The term includes the idea of assimilation of socio-cultural values, attitudes, conventions and norms of behaviour. It is not necessarily a passive personal process, but can include negotiation and rejection of a socially constructed consensus.

Social Reality: is constructed in the mind. Communication helps us to share the social reality that we have constructed in our heads, and to agree on what this includes. This reality includes beliefs about our roles, our relationships, about the structure of society, as well as the values which underpin all these things. This reality is for us as individuals the truth of what society is like, what rules it lives by, what it believes in.

Social Skills: are sets of goal-directed interrelated social communication behaviours which can be learned and which are in the control of the individual. These skills include the ability to control and monitor the information that we give off to others, and to interpret information that others give off to us through verbal and non-verbal behaviours.

Stereotype: is a generalized and simplified social classification of individuals or groups which represents incomplete assumptions and judgements about these people. Such categories are often seen in a negative light, as being fixed, prejudiced and closed to modification through future knowledge and experience.

Strategy: is co-ordinated communicative behaviour designed to achieve specific purposes and goals in social interaction.

Strokes: in terms of social interaction and social skills one is said to be **giving strokes** when one gives some signal of reward and recognition to the other person. Praising someone in verbal terms, together with a friendly glance and a pat on the back would be a commonplace example of giving strokes.

Symbol: a symbol is a sign that bears no literal relationship to what it refers to. It stands for something else because there is a social agreement that it should do so (see also *icon, index*). The word 'giraffe' is symbolic. It does not literally represent a giraffe in any way. But a picture of a giraffe would be iconic because it does literally represent the animal.

Symbolic Interaction: refers to the fact that interaction between people takes place through symbols. Also the communication behaviours involved may be culturally symbolic. If a male opens a door for a female and says 'After you', that person is firstly using word symbols to control behaviour, but is secondly symbolizing a culturally determined view of the relationship between men and women. Here, we are back to the nature of communication itself. This interaction through symbols is a way of negotiating meanings between people.

Syntagm: is a combination of signs from within a paradigm which, through the operation of conventions has come to have meaning as a unit. A sentence is composed of letter and word signs. It is seen to be a unit on its own. It obeys the rules (conventions) of syntax and grammar. The meanings of syntagms are understood only through their relationship to one another. In a piece of writing the meaning of one sentence can only be fully understood by looking at the other sentence.

Transaction: in terms of Transactional Analysis this is the smallest unit of interaction that can be identified as taking place between two people. So a glance given and received could be considered to be a transaction. In more general terms, a transaction may be defined as interaction where two or more people mutually and simultaneously take one another into account. In the transaction these people will work out their role relationships and conduct their interaction by a set of rules. Such interaction is focused and goal directed.

Reading List

Adair, J. (1986): *Effective teambuilding.* London: Pan.

Aitchison, J. (1976): *The articulate manual: an introduction to psycholinguistics.* London: Hutchinson.

Altmann, I. (1972): *The reciprocity of interpersonal exchange.* 80th Meeting of the American Psychological Association.

Anderson, S. and Williams, D. (1985): Cognitive/affective reactions in the improvement of self esteem. *Journal of Personality and Social Psychology* 48, 1086–1097.

d'Ardenne, P. and Mahtani, A. (1992): *Transcultural counselling in action.* London: Sage.

Argyle, M. (1973): *Social interaction.* London: Tavistock.

Argyle, M. (ed.) (1973): *Social encounters.* Harmondsworth: Pelican.

Argyle, M. (1983): *The psychology of interpersonal communication*, 4th edn. Harmondsworth: Penguin.

Argyle, M. (1988): *Bodily communication*, 2nd edn. London: Methuen.

Argyle, M. (1992): *The psychology of everyday life.* London: Routledge.

Argyle, M. and Dean, J. (1965): Eye contact, distance and affiliation. *Sociometry* 28, 289–304.

Argyle, M. and Henderson, M. (1985): *The anatomy of relationships and the rules and skills needed to manage them successfully.* Harmondsworth: Pelican.

Argyle, M. and Trower, P. (1979): *Person to person.* London: Harper & Row.

Arnold, M. (1932): *Culture and anarchy.* Cambridge: Cambridge University Press.

Asch, S. (1946): Forming impressions of personality. *Journal of Abnormal and Social Psychology* 41, 258–290.

Atkinson, J. M. (1984): *Our masters' voices: the language and body language of politics.* London: Methuen.

Atkinson, J. M. and Heritage, J. (1987): *Structures of social action: studies in conversation analysis.* Cambridge: Cambridge University Press.

Axtell, R. (1991): *Gestures: the do's and taboos of body language around the world.* New York: John Wiley.

Bales, R. F. (1950): *Interaction process analysis.* Cambridge, MA: Addison-Wesley.

Bandler, R. and Grinder, J. (1979): *Frogs into princes: neurolinguistic programming.* Moab, Utah: Real People Press.

Bannister, D. and Agnew, J. (1977) The child's construing of self. In Landield, A. (ed.), *Nebraska Symposium on Motivation*, 1976. Lincoln: University of Nebraska Press.

Barker, L. (1984): *Communication.* New Jersey: Prentice-Hall.

Baxter, L. A. (1986): Gender differences in the heterosexual relationship rules embedded in break-up accounts. *Journal of Social and Personal Relationship* 3, 289–306.

Beattie, G. (1983): *Talk: an analysis of speech and non-verbal communication in conversation.* Milton Keynes: Open University Press.

Bem, D. (1967): Self perception. *Psychological Review* 74, 183–200.

Berger, C. (1974): *The acquaintance process revisited.* Paper for the Internation Communication Association (referred to in Patton and Griffin).

Berne, E. (1961): *Transactional analysis in psychotherapy.* London: Souvenir Press.

Berne, E. (1964): *Games people play.* Harmondsworth: Penguin.

Berne, E. (1969): *Layman's guide to psychiatry and psychoanalysis.* London: Souvenir Press.

Berne, E. (1972): *What do you say after you've said hello?* London: Corgi.

Birdwhistell, R. L. (1968): Kinesics. *International Encyclopedia of Social Sciences* **8**, 381–299.

Blake, S. M., Moulton, J. and Shepard, A. (1964): *Managing intergroup conflict in industry.* Houston: Gulf.

Bolton, R. (1986): *People skills – how to assert yourself, listen to others, and resolve conflicts.* Sydney: Prentice-Hall.

Borisoff, D. and Merrill, L. (1991): *Listening in everyday life.* Maryland: University of America Press.

Brigham, J. C. (1971): Ethnic stereotypes. *Psychological Bulletin* **26**, 15–38.

Butterworth, C. and MacDonald, M. (1985): *Teaching social education and communication.* London: Hutchinson.

Carnegie, D. (1938): *How to win friends and influence people.* Tadworth: World's Work.

Clifford, E. and Clifford, M. (1967): Self concepts before and after survival training. *British Journal of Clinical Psychology* **6**, 241–248.

Coates, J. (1991): *Women, men and language: a sociolinguistic account of sex differences in language.* London: Longman.

Cooley, C. (1902): *Human nature and social order.* New York: Charles Scribner & Sons.

Coopersmith, S. (1967): *The antecedents of self esteem.* Los Angeles: Freeman & Co.

Corner, J. and Hawthorn, J. (1990): *Communication studies: an introductory reader,* 2nd edn. London: Edward Arnold.

Davis, J. H. (1969): *Group performance.* Reading, MA: Addison-Wesley.

Deaux, K. and Wrightsman, L. S. I. (1984): *Social psychology in the eighties.* London: Brooks/Cole.

Dickson, A. (1988): *A woman in your own right – assertiveness and you.* London: Quartet.

Dimbleby, R. and Burton, G. (1992): *More than words: an introduction to communication studies,* 2nd edn. London: Routledge.

Duck, S. W. (1986): *Human relationships: an introduction to social psychology.* London: Sage.

Duck, S. (ed.) (1993): *Relating to others.* Oxford: Oxford University Press.

Duck, S. (ed.) (1994): *Dynamics of relationships.* London: Sage.

Duck, S. W. and Perlman, D. (eds) (1985): *Understanding personal relationships: an interdisciplinary approach.* London: Sage.

Duncan, S. (1972): Some signals and rules for taking speaking turns in conversation. *Journal of Personality and Social Psychology* **23**, 283–292.

Eiser, J. R. (1986): *Social psychology.* Cambridge: Cambridge University Press.

Ekman, P. (1982): *Emotion in the human face.* Cambridge: Cambridge University Press.

Ellis, A. and Beattie, G. (1986): *The psychology of language and communication.* London: Weidenfeld & Nicolson.

Eriksen, E. (1972): *Childhood and society.* Harmondsworth: Pelican.

Fast, J. (1970): *Body language.* London: Pan.

Festinger, L. (1954): A theory of social comparison processes. *Human Relations* **7**, 117–140.

Festinger, L. (1957): *A theory of cognitive dissonance*. Evanston, IL: Row, Peterson.

Fiedler, F. (1973): The trouble with leadership training. *Psychology Today*, February 1973, 23–29.

Fiske, J. (1990): *Introduction to communication studies*, 2nd edn. London: Methuen.

Gahagan, J. (1975): *Interpersonal and group behaviour*. London: Methuen.

Gahagan, J. (1984): *Social interaction and its management*. London: Methuen.

Gergen, K. and Gergen, M. (1986): *Social psychology*. New York: Springer Verlag.

Glass, L. (1992): *He says, she says – closing the communication gap between the sexes*. London: Piatkus.

Goffman, E. (1959): *The presentation of self in everyday life*. Harmondsworth: Penguin.

Goffman, E. (1961): *Encounters: two studies in the sociology of interaction*. Indianapolis: Bobbs Merrill.

Goffman, E. (1963): *Behaviour in public places: notes on the social organisation of gatherings*. New York: Free Press.

Goffman, E. (1963): *Stigma: notes on the management of spoiled identity*. Harmondsworth: Penguin.

Goffman, E. (1968): *Interaction ritual: essays on face to face behaviour*. Harmondsworth: Penguin.

Goffman, E. (1971): *Relations in public: microstudies of the public order*. Harmondsworth: Allen Lane.

Goffman, E. (1976): *Asylums*. Harmondsworth: Penguin.

Goffman, E. (1979): *Gender advertisements*. London: Macmillan.

Goffman, E. (1981): *Forms of talk*. London: Macmillan.

Gross, R. D. (1992): *Psychology: the science of mind and behaviour*. London: Hodder & Stoughton.

Gudykunst, W. B. (ed.) (1986): *Intergroup communication*. London: Edward Arnold.

Hall, E. T. (1969): *The hidden dimension*. New York: Anchor Books.

Hall, E. T. (1973): *The silent language*. New York: Anchor Books.

Hamilton, D. (1976): Cognitive biases in the perception of social groups. In Carrol, J. and Payne, J. (eds): *Cognitive and social behaviour*. New Jersey: Erlbaum.

Hargie, O. (eds) (1986): *A handbook of communication skills*. Beckenham: Croom Helm.

Hargie, O., Saunders, C. and Dickson, D. (1994) *Social skills in interpersonal communication*. London: Routledge.

Harré, R. and Lamb, R. (eds) (1986): *The dictionary of personality and social psychology*. Oxford: Blackwell.

Harris, T. (1970): *I'm OK, you're OK*. London: Pan.

Hartley, P. (1993): *Interpersonal communication*. London: Routledge.

Harvey, C., Banks, W. C. and Zimbardo, P. G. (1973): Interpersonal dynamics in a simulated prison. *International Journal of Criminology and Penology* 1, 69–79.

Hayes, N. (1984): *A first course in psychology*. Walton on Thames: Nelson and Sons.

Hayes, N. and Orrell, S. (1993): *Psychology: an introduction*, 2nd edn. Harlow: Longman.

Heider, F. (1958): *The psychology of interpersonal relations*. New York: Wiley.

Hewson, J. and Turner, C. (1992): *Transactional analysis in management*. Blagdon: The Staff College.

Hickson, M. L. III and Stacks, D. W. (1993): *NVC: Non-verbal communication – studies and applications*. Oxford: Brown & Benchmark.

Hill, C. and Stull, D. E. (1987): In Derlega, V. and Berg, J. (eds), *Self disclosure: theory, research and therapy*. New York: Plenum Press.

Hodges, B. (1974): The effects of volume on relative weighting in impression formation. *Journal of Personality and Social Psychology* 30, 278–381.

Honey, P. (1988): *Face to face*, London: Gower.

Howitt, D., Billig, M., Cramer, D. *et al.* (1989): *Social psychology*. Oxford: Oxford University Press.

Janis, I. L. (1972): *Victims of groupthink*, 2nd edn. Boston: Houghton-Mifflin.

Jenks, C. (1993): *Culture*. London: Routledge.

Kell, C. L. and Corts, P. R. (1980): *Fundamentals of effective group communication*. New York: Macmillan.

Kelley, H. (1967): Attribution theory in social psychology. *Nebraska Symposium on Motivation* 15, 192–238.

Kelley, H. (1969): In Levine, D. (ed.), *Attribution theory in social psychology*. Lincoln: University of Nebraska Press.

Kelley, H. (1971): Attribution: Perceiving the causes of behaviour. In Jones, E. *et al.* (eds), *Attribution*. New Jersey: General Learning Press.

Kelvin, P. (1969): *The bases of social behaviour*. London: Holt, Rinehart & Winston.

Langer, E. and Dweck, C. (1973): *Personal politics: the psychology of making it*. New Jersey: Prentice-Hall.

Lewin, K., Lippett, R. and White, P. K. (1939): Patterns of aggressive behaviour. *Journal of Social Psychology* 10, 271–299.

Livingstone, S. (1987): *Accounting for relationships; explanation, representation and knowledge*. London: Methuen.

Luft, J. (1969): *Of human interaction*. Palo Alto, California: National Press Books.

McArthur, L. (1972): The how and what of why: causal attributions. *Journal of Personality and Social Psychology* 22, 171–193.

McGuire, W. and Padawer-Singer, A. (1976): Trait salience in the spontaneous self concept. *Journal of Personality and Social Psychology* 33, 743–754.

McGuire, W., McGuire C., Child, P. and Fujioka, T. (1978): Salience of ethnicity in the spontaneous self concept. *Journal of Personality and Social Psychology* 36, 511–520.

March, J. and Simon, H. (1958): *Organisations*. New York: John Wiley.

Markham, U. (1993): *How to deal with difficult people*. London: Thorsons.

Markus, H. (1977): Self schemata and processing information about the self. *Journal of Personality and Social Psychology* 35, 63–78.

Marsh, P. (ed.) (1988): *Eye to eye: how people interact*. London: Sidgwick & Jackson.

Maslow, A. (1984): *Motivation and personality*. New York: Harper & Row.

Mead, G. H. (1934): *Mind, Self and Society*. Chicago: University of Chicago Press.

Mehrabian, A. (1971): *Silent messages*. New York: Wadsworth.

Miller, C. and Swift, K. (1979): *Words and women*. Harmondsworth: Penguin.

Montgomery, M. (1986): *An introduction to language and society*. London: Methuen.

Morgan, J. and Welton, P. (1986): *See what I mean*. London: Edward Arnold.

Morris, D. (1977): *Manwatching: a field guide to human behaviour*. St Albans: Triad Panther.

Myers, G. and Myers, M. (1992): *The dynamics of human communication*, 6th edn. New York: McGraw-Hill.

Nierenberg, G. L. and Calero, H. H. (1973): *How to read a person like a book*. London: Heinrich Hanau.

Nisbett, R. and Ross, L. (1980): *Human interference: strategies and shortcomings.* Englewood Cliffs, New Jersey: Prentice-Hall.

Nolan, V. (1987): *Communication.* London: Sphere.

Nolan, V. (1987): *Problem solving.* London: Sphere.

Nolan, V. (1987): *Teamwork.* London: Sphere.

Noller, R. (1980): Gaze in married couples. *Journal of Non verbal Behaviour* **5**, 115–129.

O'Connor, J. and Seymour, J. (1990): *Introducing neurolinguistic programming.* London: Aquarian.

O'Connor, J. and Seymour, J. (1994): *Training with NLP: skills for managers, trainers and communicators.* London: Thorsons.

O'Sullivan, T., Hartley, J., Saunders, D., Montgomery, M. and Fiske, J. (1994): *Key concepts in communication and cultural studies*, 2nd edn. London: Methuen.

Park, R. E. (1950): *Race and culture.* Glencoe, Illinois: The Free Press.

Patton, R. and Griffin, K. (1981): *Interpersonal communication in action.* New York: Harper & Row.

Pease, A. (1992): Body Language. Sheldon Press.

Pease, A. with Garner, A. (1989): *Talk language: how to use conversation for profit and pleasure.* London: Simon & Schuster.

Pennington, D. (1986): *Essential social psychology.* London: Edward Arnold.

Radley, A. R. (1974): The effect of role enactment on construct alternatives. *British Journal of Medical Psychology.*

Reicher, S. D. (1984): The St Paul's riot. *European Journal of Social Psychology* **14**, 1–21.

Rogers, C. R. (1990): *On becoming a person: a therapist's view of psychotherapy.* London: Constable.

Rosenberg, M. (1965): *Society and the adolescent self image.* Princeton: Princeton University Press.

Rosenberg, R. and Jones, S. (1972): A method for representing and investigating an implicit theory of personality. *Journal of Personality and Social Psychology* **20**, 372–386.

Ross, L. (1977): The intuitive psychologist and his shortcomings: distortions in the attribution process. In *Advances in experimental psychology*, Vol. 10, New York: Academic Press.

Schachter, S. (1964): The interaction of cognitive and physiological determinants of emotional state. In Berkowitz, L. (ed.), *Advances in experimental social psychology.* New York: Academic Press.

Schultz, R. (1976): The effects of control and predictability on the psychological well-being of the institutionalised aged. *Journal of Personality and Social Psychology* **33**, 563–573.

Schultz, W. (1958): *Firo: a three dimensional theory of interpersonal behaviour.* New York: Holt, Rinehart & Winston.

Schultz, W. (1966): *The interpersonal underworld.* Palo Alto, California: Science and Behaviour Books.

Schwartz, J. and Schaver, P. (1984): *A prototype approach to emotional structure.* A paper given at the American Psychological Association Convention (referred to in Gergen and Gergen).

Scollon, R. and Scollon, S. W. (1995): *Intercultural communication: a discourse approach.* Oxford: Blackwell.

Sentis, K. and Markus, L. (1979): *Self schemas and recognition memory.* Unpublished paper (referred to in Gergen and Gergen).

Shaw, M. (1981): *Group dynamics*, 3rd edn. New York: McGraw-Hill.

Shotter, J. (1984): *Social accountability and self-hood.* Oxford: Blackwell.

Spender, D. (1981): *Manmade language.* London: Routledge & Kegan Paul.

Stubbs, M. (1989): *Discourse analysis: the sociolinguistic analysis of natural language.* Oxford: Blackwell.

Tajfel, H. (1969): Cognitive aspects of prejudice. *Journal of Social Issues* **25**, 79–97.

Tajfel, H. and Fraser, C. (eds) (1986): *Introducing social psychology.* Harmondsworth: Pelican.

Tannen, D. (1991): *You just don't understand: women and men in conversation.* London: Virago.

Tannen, D. (1992): *That's not what I meant: how conversational style makes or breaks your relations with others.* London: Virago.

Tedeschi, J. T. and Lindskold, S. (1976): *Social psychology: interdependence, interaction and influence.* New York: J. Wiley.

Toomey, Stella Ting (1991): *Cross-cultural interpersonal communication.* London: Sage.

Triandis, H. (1985): Some major dimensions of cultural variation in client populations. In Pederson, P. (ed.), *Handbook of cross cultural counselling and therapy.* Westport: Greenwood Press.

Trudgill, P. (1983): *Sociolinguistics.* Harmondsworth: Penguin.

Tuckman, B. W. (1965): Developmental sequence in small groups. *Psychological Bulletin* **63**, 384–399.

Turk, C. (1985): *Effective speaking: communicating in speech.* London: Spon.

Turner, C. (1983): *Developing interpersonal skills.* Blagdon: Coombe Lodge.

Turner, J. C. (1982): Social comparison, similarity and in group favouritism. In Tajfel, H. (ed.), *Differences between social groups.* London: Academic Press.

Videbeck, R. (1960): Self conception and the reactions of others. In Argyle, M. (ed.), *Social encounters.* Harmondsworth: Penguin.

Watson, J. and Hill, A. (1994): *A dictionary of communication and media studies*, 3rd edn. London: Edward Arnold.

Weiner, B. (1985): Spontaneous casual thinking. *Psychological Bulletin* **97**, 74–84.

Wilkinson, J. and Canter, S. (1982): *Social skills training manual.* London: Wiley.

Williams, R. (1983): *Culture and society.* Columbia: Columbia University Press.

Wyer, R. and Srull, S. (1980): The processing of social stimulus information. In Hastie, R. (ed.), *Social perception.* Hillsdale, New Jersey: Erlbaum.

Zimbardo – see Harvey, Banks and Zimbardo.

Index

Refer also to the Glossary on pages 250–8 for a brief note on many of the words listed here.